DAMASCUS
DIARIES

DAMASCUS DIARIES

PETER CLARK

G

GILGAMESH
PUBLISHING LTD

Damascus Diaries

Published by Gilgamesh Publishing in 2015
Email: info@gilgamesh-publishing.co.uk
www.gilgamesh-publishing.co.uk

ISBN 978-1-908531-35-3

CIP Data: A catalogue for this book is
available from the British Library

CONTENTS

to
Ayoub Ghurairi
Vanda Harmaneh
Motaz Hadaya

FOREWORD

Syria is a fascinating country, little known in Britain. For many centuries it has been a key player, together with Egypt and Iraq, in the politics of the entire Middle East. In recent generations Syria has carried the flag of Arab nationalism, notably in leading Arab resistance to Israel. Syrians are rightly proud of the historical importance of their country and they are also proud of their long-standing links with Europe.

Syrian society is both intricate and extremely complex. Very few foreigners gain much understanding of it but Peter Clark is an exception. His fluent Arabic and wide experience of the Middle East were a great help but he also had the invaluable ability to gain a real understanding of Syrian society without losing his objectivity and sense of proportion.

These qualities made him an outstanding representative of the British Council who made an enormous range of contacts during his five years in Syria. This diary is a record of how he set about getting to know the Syrians in their daily lives and how he built up British cultural links with their country. It required patience, understanding and commitment which were amply rewarded by the respect and affection in which he was held. His achievements were all the greater because the Syrians were, throughout his time in Damascus, in the grip of a ruthless police state whose multiple secret police forces were deeply suspicious of all contact between Syrians and Western embassies.

The attempt to overthrow the present regime that began with demonstrations in March 2011 has lifted the veil on the internal stresses that, for at least a generation, had been suppressed by the threat of force. The result has been a disastrous breakdown in Syrian society and, literally, millions of victims. It is, therefore, especially fitting that the royalties from this book will go to help today's refugees.

Sir Andrew Green KCMG

INTRODUCTION

Apart from a few years in the 1970s I have kept a page-a-day diary since 1960. I usually write it up in the morning, recording events, encounters and conversations of the previous day. Making the entry is as essential a daily ritual as brushing my teeth. I rarely read entries once I have written them. So looking back at diaries I kept for the five years I was based in Damascus I have felt like a literary Rip Van Winkle. It has been as if I was looking at the life of someone else.

These published diaries have been edited. I have sometimes improved grammar, spelling and punctuation. I have also clarified parts. In order to protect the guilty I have suppressed some names and disguised others. But otherwise nothing substantial has been altered. I have not wanted to hide the fact that Peter Clark was sometimes smug, wrong-headed and vain. What follows is what was scribbled at the time.

I fell in love with the country on my first visit in 1962. I lived in two neighbouring countries, Jordan and Lebanon, between 1968 and 1970 and often travelled to Syria then. In later years, less frequently, I returned. I was thrilled to be Director of the British Council for five years from 1992. There was no disenchantment.

After I left in 1997 I returned several times escorting British and American tour groups. The last was in April 2011 when the present crisis was in its early days. Since then the country has imploded, with unspeakable savageries being committed, the displacement of millions of people and a total disruption to the warm and friendly

Syria that I have described. There is no clear resolution to the current catastrophe. Syrians need relief, and Syria will need to be reconstructed. I have decided that all royalties for this book should go to the Said Foundation who have been doing outstanding work for Syrians in crisis.

I am grateful for the friendship of hundreds of Syrians, as should be clear from these pages. I would also like to thank Penny Young for her comments on an earlier draft. Above all I wish to thank Theresa Clark for her love and companionship in Damascus, and for her useful observations on the text.

Peter Clark

1992

In the autumn of 1991 the United Kingdom and Syria renewed diplomatic relations after a break of five years.

At that time Peter was Cultural Attaché and Director of British Council operations in the United Arab Emirates. He was living in Abu Dhabi with his wife, Theresa, and son, Nathaniel, aged eight. Another son, Gabriel, aged ten, was at a boarding school in southern England. Peter's son from his first marriage, Paul, was 19, a student in Brighton. Kate, Theresa's daughter from her first marriage, was 23, a lawyer in London.

Peter had been in the Emirates for three years and was due for a move in 1992. The British Council wanted him to go on promotion to Saudi Arabia, but Peter resisted. Saudi Arabia was, like the Emirates, a bizarre creation, modern and moneyed. The relationship with Britain was commercial and Peter wanted to work in a real country with its own history and deep-rooted culture. There was the possibility of a posting to Kiev, opening a British Council office in the newly independent former Soviet Republic of Ukraine. Such a posting would have been outside his area of interest and expertise, but he reflected that parts of the Ukraine – and in particular the Crimea – had been part of the Ottoman Empire.

On the day the resumption of diplomatic relations was announced, Peter phoned his British Council masters in London and volunteered to reopen the British Council in Syria. He had known and loved Syria since the early 1960s. In early 1992 the hope became first a probability and then a certainty. There was no queue of applicants for the job. The new British Ambassador in Damascus, Andrew Green, was reported as saying that there was no point in an Embassy being there without a British Council.

In June 1992 Peter made a reconnaissance trip to Damascus.

Sunday, 7 June 1992

I am met at the airport by Ian Blackley, the angular Counsellor in the British Embassy, whom I knew in Lebanon in 1973. He takes me to the Sheraton Hotel and we have tea and run through all sorts of things. I ask about education for our son, Nathaniel. Ian has a son the same age. There are hardly any British children at the American school, the only international school. It has playing grounds but no swimming pool. The Principal is leaving and his Deputy has one toe missing. There is a good American teacher.

Ian leaves and I walk into the city, just over a mile away. The river Barada is cleaner than it has been on previous visits. The city seems less polluted than it was ten years ago. I skirt the hotels I used to know, savour the architecture of the area called Victoria and walk through Souk Hamidiya.

Between 1970 and 1971 Peter was based in Shemlan in Lebanon, studying Arabic. In May 1971 he went by himself to Syria, to improve his spoken Arabic. He drove around the countryside north of Damascus giving people a lift and talking to them. He took one passenger to the small town of Yabrud, 70 kilometres north of the capital. Peter accepted an invitation to stay the night. The following morning his hosts asked if he would take their niece, Bouchra, aged 17, to Damascus. Bouchra was a very attractive and bright girl. Peter agreed, and took her to her parents' flat in King Faisal Street, north-east of the old city. This was the beginning of a beautiful friendship. In 1972 she married Ahmed, who had a small business in the souk. Over the next two decades whenever he came to Damascus Peter would always call on and sometimes stay with Ahmed, Bouchra and their family.

I find Ahmed's shop selling underwear near Bab al-Barid. He is not there and I am scribbling a note for him when his smiling son, Ala, short for Ala al-Din, turns up. The family has moved to the flat near Bab Touma that I knew when I first met Bouchra. Ala takes me through the winding streets and alleyways to King Faisal Street and I am overjoyed to meet Bouchra and Ahmed again. They now have five children. The oldest, Husam, is in the army, doing his military service. Ala is at school, as is the second son. There are two little girls, Mayas and Lilas. Bouchra's mother died last year. I cannot stay but take a taxi back to the hotel.

Monday, 8 June

Ian and I make a number of official calls. First we call on Anwar Fadil, Deputy Director of the Cultural Department at the Ministry of Foreign Affairs. He comes from near Tartus and has served in Embassies in Tokyo, Rio and Brussels. We talk of religion. "When a young person reaches maturity," he says, "he should decide for himself." Next we see Dr Ali al-Qayim, Deputy Minister of Culture. We talk of Syrian painters and writers at length. Then to Dr Omar Karmo, Deputy Minister of Higher Education, who studied sewage engineering in Ireland and doubles as a Professor at the University.

I go back to the hotel and see several people who are interested in working for the British Council. The most impressive is a young Damascene, Motaz Hadaya. I also meet Helen Bachour, a British widow who has lived in Damascus for 23 years. She tells me that her son, as an only son, is not liable for military service.

An Embassy driver takes me to the Ambassador's Residence for the Queen's Birthday Party. It is the custom, I am told, for Ministers to vie with each other in sending huge bouquets for the occasion. I meet heaps of people including the Honorary Consul for Aleppo, Tony Akhras. I walk back to the hotel, bubbling with excited anticipation. The place seems more relaxed than I expected.

Tuesday, 9 June

Ian takes me to call on the Rector of the University of Damascus, Dr Riad Shuwaiki. His office is in a building that used to be the French Governor-General's office during Mandate times. Nearby is an attractive Ottoman building, part of the university. It was the military hospital at the end of the First World War, the scene of desolation in T E Lawrence's *Seven Pillars of Wisdom* and in the film, *Lawrence of Arabia*.

I have a spare couple of hours and call on a Mr Bakdash who owns some flats. I would like to see what is available. He owns a *confiserie* and we are delayed there. His assistant has gone off to pay an electricity bill, and he cannot leave the shop untended.

I then call at the Damascus Community School and meet the unimpressive American Principal. Roman remains have been found in the school grounds that are overlooked by the Air Ministry.

Wednesday, 10 June

At ten, Ian takes me to call on the Head of the English Department at the University of Damascus, a graduate of the University of St Andrews.

After a final coffee with Ian I wander off by myself to look up old haunts. I check myself into the Palmyra Hotel where I stayed in December 1962 on my first visit to this city. No longer is there a stove on the landing that used to soak the whole place with a pervasive gentle smell of paraffin. The small room I am given has a television set and a smaller en suite shower room and lavatory: it stinks. But there is a pair of sandals under the bed: that has not changed. The rate is US$22 a night, in contrast to US$210 at the Sheraton Hotel. I walk out to the east of the city. A hammam I used to go to is now a tourist office. Thawra Street has sliced the old quarter of Souk Saruja in two. I wander down to Souk Buzuriya and buy 100 grams of *sahlep*, the powder from the roots of orchid that, mixed with milk and with the addition of pistachio nuts and cinnamon, makes a welcoming winter drink. Then by Dar Anbar, a 19th-century Jewish house that became the elite secondary school and Bab Touma where I have a glass of tea and read for an hour. Finally I walk around the southern side of the city, just loving Damascus and rejoicing that it will be our home for a few years.

Thursday, 11 June

I break it to the people working in the hotel that I stayed here 30 years ago. They seem suitably impressed. Most of them had not been born then.

I buy a large bouquet and walk over to Bab Touma, taking a couple of small presents for Bouchra's little girls. I am early and the whole family turn up – Bouchra's rather than Ahmed's. Bouchra's brother, Marwan, is 42. He has two children with him, Shakir, aged 13, and Muhammad, aged four. The second brother, Ghassan, has brought his wife, Muna. The youngest brother, Bashar, has a job delivering heating fuel to houses. His wife, Suzanne, breastfeeds her infant at least three times in an hour. Tit on demand.

The food is a banquet, lovely dishes, followed by fruit, ice cream, tea and coffee. We chat away, exchanging idiot jokes. Elephant jokes do not translate well into Arabic. Ghassan says the biggest liars in the world are Arabs. I say, "You are an Arab. And if you say Arabs are liars, then your statement is false." He says, "There are 50 Arabs who are honest." Roars of laughter. A neighbour drops in to greet us and we develop the fantasy that he is a merchant of lies.

Friday, 12 June

I go for a final stroll around Damascus, wandering around the south-west of the old city. I see the mosque of Sinan Pasha, named not after the great Ottoman architect but after a 16th-century Governor. I buy a volume of short stories by Abdul Salam al-Ujaili and a novel by Hanna Mina. The bookshop has a book on the Jews of Damascus and works by George Zaidan, the Lebanese Christian who, a century ago, wrote about the Muslim heroes of the Arab world. His works are banned in some Arab countries, including the UAE.

Peter and his family left Abu Dhabi in the summer, and made calls on his headquarters in London. And others.

Monday, 24 August

I call on the Syrian Chargé, Rustum al-Zubi. We start off in English and switch to Arabic. I am actually happier talking Arabic to Arabs about official matters. He tells me that the Syrian government sends 300 to 400 Syrians to study in Britain each year. That must be the equivalent of about £5 million in invisible exports, amounting to the value of 10 per cent of total British exports to Syria.

Tuesday, 25 August

I call on Sir James Craig who was British Ambassador in Damascus in the 1970s. We spend an hour and a quarter together. I warm to him immensely. He says he is too lazy to keep his Arabic going and – I am reassured to hear – needs Syrians to explain jokes on the television to him. He loves Damascus – the finest city in the Middle East. He talks of drinks – *husrum* and *sus* – and of Syrian hospitality. We talk about Syrian Ministers and literature.

Monday, 31 August

I fly via Paris to Damascus and am met by Rick, the Commercial

Attaché. Two of my three suitcases fail to turn up. One of them is crammed full of documents, including papers of varying degrees of confidentiality. It has Andrew Green's confidential report on Syria and the valedictory report of the most recent British Ambassador to Lebanon. There are also my instructions, the breakdown of my budget, and heaps of briefing notes. The case is unmarked and unlocked. I have a quick nightmare fantasy of them being published, causing embarrassment and personal humiliation. I cannot operate without these papers. I report the loss of the bags and am driven to the Meridien Hotel. I finish reading *Despatches from Damascus*, written by a British official, Gilbert McKereth, who was here in the 1930s, and start reading the novel by Hanna Mina.

Peter was going to start as Cultural Attaché and to work inside the Embassy building, as a member of the Embassy staff. His budget was independent of the Embassy and the Foreign Office, and his Line Manager was based at the British Council headquarters in London. The Ambassador, Andrew Green, and his wife, Jane, were still on leave and had kindly offered Peter and his family the use of the Ambassadorial Residence at Mezze, three or four miles west of the main city.

Tuesday, 1 September

I am given a lift into the Embassy and enter the two rooms allocated to me. I work out my immediate needs. I have multiple copies of the British Council London telephone directory and instructions on how to analyse my activity. I pile things up on shelves and place papers for visitors to see. I shall need an Education Adviser soon. Indeed I shall receive my first visitor tomorrow morning. Someone wants information about learning English in Dublin! I am able to operate according to the rules but am still hamstrung by my lost baggage. I cannot remember what my budget is or what my instructions are.

Wednesday, 2 September

There is no news of my missing bags.

But I make some progress. I phone Vanda Harmaneh and ask her to come and work tomorrow. I met her and her husband, Nabil Batal, in June. I will appoint her Personal Assistant but tell her she has to be ready to do anything from sweeping the floor to representing the British Council. I have a phone call from Ayoub Ghurairi and might employ him as Accountant/Office Manager.

Thursday, 3 September

My bags have not arrived.

Vanda turns up. I tell her I want to recruit her and start by telling her her salary and work from there. She is a nice, bright lass, a Christian Jordanian from Madaba, mid-thirties, with two children. We go off to buy some stationery and furniture. We call at the shop of Sami Krikorian, a graduate of Engineering from the University of Lausanne, but with excellent English. We have no transport. It is hot and sweaty. Taxis are all busy with the International Fair. The temperature is about 40 centigrade – Abu Dhabi heat.

I have lunch with Ian and his wife – correct and formal as ever. They love Syria and we talk of Old Damascus, of the Druze singer and possible Second World War spy, Esmahan, and of former British missions.

I return to the Residence and wander along to the military cemetery which, as Sir James Craig said, is the best garden in Damascus. There are rows upon rows of graves – Indian, British, African. Neat and wellmaintained. Hundreds of graves. I wander along a track at the back of the cemetery. Here is a bit of rural Syria in the suburbs of the city – unmade roads, chickens and children all over the place: a charming spot.

Friday, 4 September

Damascus comes to life today. I have been unable to plunge into Damascene life. The Blackleys and others at the Embassy have been kindness itself but theirs is the perspective towards Syria of expatriates, happy outsiders.

I walk up to Muhajirin. From Mezze I walk along long new roads, with blocks of flats overlooking the city. Past ancient madrasas and mosques. I am then in the heart of a busy souk. Trellises overhang the narrow road. All sorts of fruit, vegetables and meat are on sale. No foreigners. There is an authenticity missing in downtown Damascus. I then descend to Souk Hamidiya.

I need some Syrian cash. I should have thought of this before. As anticipated, a man sidles up to me and offers to change money. I agree, asking the rate. Forty-six to the dollar. Fine, for that is the current rate and I am wanting to change US$100. I accompany him up some stairs to a tiny craft shop. There I share a breakfast and sip tea with some others while he goes off to get the required 4,600 Syrian pounds. He hands them to me in dribs and drabs. At first he is reluctant to take my hundred-dollar bill. It is dated 1985, and there was apparently some big scandal of dollar bills forged in Iran a few years ago.

I walk to Bouchra and Ahmed's flat in Bab Touma.

"Would you like to go to the Arab Games?" Husam asks.

"Yes," I say, after only a moment's hesitation.

Husam and I walk to the Abbasiya stadium. He tries to get us into a smart enclosure, but fails. I am happy to go into the terraces. There is a crowd of 30,000, and, fairly promptly, at five o' clock, the participating teams parade, ready to take part in competitive athletics. There is no Iraqi team. Only Lebanon, Syria and Egypt have women participants, but a little girl precedes the Saudi team. Oman has a small team and there is only one Libyan. Some of the participants wave to the crowd. There are cheers for most teams but boos for the Saudi and the UAE teams. Behind us is an electronic screen on to which slogans are flashed. Then speeches, and a helicopter flies over the stadium dropping parachutists with flags of all the Arab nations. *Su-ri-ya*, chant the crowds.

Saturday, 5 September
Another day off for the weekend.

In the late afternoon I walk to Bab Touma and sit, eating watermelon and gossiping with Ahmed and Bouchra. Then at seven, Ahmed, Bouchra, the two little girls and I go out. We take one bus that crashes into a car, abandon it and then another to Haraste, on the old road to Aleppo. The bus is crowded, dusty, dirty and slow. We get off at a vegetable market and walk to the first-floor flat of a cousin of Ahmed, Muwaffaq al-Nuwailati, a musician. His office is smoky, crowded and untidy, and we move into the salon. Muwaffaq plays the oud and sings. A son beats time on a *daff*, a drum. Two old ladies, neighbours, drop in. Then another neighbour who was a contractor in Dhammam for 20 years. The Nuwailatis have Iranian relations and Muwaffaq and his family have Iranian passports. Two attractive girls in their twenties come in. One is persuaded to dance to the music and is tremendous. Bouchra's younger daughter is also a lovely dancer, moving gracefully and naturally to Muwaffaq's music. The other girl joins in and I am invited to take part in a *dabka*. But in a moment of unaccustomed spontaneity I break into a dance by myself. I urge Muwaffaq to play faster and faster. I hear clapping and appreciative applause and, after five minutes, slow down and pause, covered with sweat.

Sunday, 6 September
I am exhausted all day.

Ayoub Ghurairi calls and I arrange to recruit him from 11 October. I give Vanda heaps of work, and receive a stream of visitors. Some want to work for the British Council, or to learn English. Others call to wish us good luck.

There is news of one of my missing bags – the grey one. I go with an Embassy driver to the airport. They want to see my passport, but that is with the Ministry of Foreign Affairs, with my application for a residence permit. But a smile, courtesy and patience steer me through and to my delight I am restored to, not one, but both missing bags. What a relief! I have had all sorts of nightmares about the bags, with the documents, being lost in Tenerife.

I am totally drained – partly relief at seeing the bags again; partly excited delight at being here. There are a million things to do and to sort out. But slowly, slowly.

Monday, 7 September
After work I go and call on Ahmed's shop. I sit in his shop while he does steady business, selling underwear. The price of a stall in the souk here can be four million Syrian pounds – the equivalent of four cars. Old men pass by. A young bearded man asks for a *shariati*.

"What is that?" I ask Ahmed.

"A pair of canonically acceptable long socks," I am told.

"Do your sons help out?"

Ahmed deplores the younger generation and his idle sons.

Tuesday, 8 September
I write to British Council London. I have been asked to propose an analysis of my activity for the financial year that starts in April next year. I write to say such an exercise is totally meaningless.

Peter is joined by his son, Nat, who is to go the Damascus Community School for one year.

Wednesday, 9 September
I take Nat to his new school and then we drive up Jabal Kasiyun, the mountain overlooking the city. We have a coffee and look down

on Damascus, partly concealed by a cloud. I chat to a couple at the next table. The man, a taxi-driver, asks me, "Are you from Homs?"

Later we go to Bab Touma, with presents for Ahmed and Bouchra's children. I marvel at this friendship. I feel as if I am part of her family. We have all become 20 years older. One generation has died off. New children have come along. There is a tranquillity in the relationship of middle-aged friends. We drink some *husrum* (which makes me feel sick) and all go out to Haraste. Ahmed thinks we are due there for dinner. We are not. So we go on to Douma. Ahmed tells me he bought a house in Douma in the late 1970s for 70,000 Syrian pounds and sold it seven years later for 900,000. With that money he bought the flat in Bab Touma that had belonged to Bouchra's family. At Douma we meet Bouchra's brothers, Marwan and Ghassan. Marwan tells me he saw me the other day in the city centre with a woman. I realise that it was Vanda; we were buying stationery for the office. But there are no secrets in Damascus!

Thursday, 10 September
In the evening I leave Nat in the Residence and drive to Bouchra and Ahmed's house. We go on to Haraste to our friend, Muwaffaq. More music, more dancing. Bouchra persuades a reluctant Ahmed to dance. Then she does a solo belly dance with a piece of black cloth wrapped around her broad waist.

Friday, 11 September
I am taken to see some flats. One of the people taking me is Munajid Imad al-Din. In London I was told he was someone to look out for. I cannot remember whether he is a total rogue to be avoided at all costs, or a man to be worth cultivating. (He may of course be both.)

Saturday, 12 September
Bouchra comes to the Residence with some friends. One particular

friend is Hunaina Farhat with whom she was at school. Hunaina is Christian, a lawyer from Homs, and was widowed ten days ago. Her husband died of cancer, but Hunaina does not seem to be overcome with grief. She brings along her three children. Her son, Bashar, who drove them here, is about 17 and studies law at the University of Damascus. A daughter, Reem, is 15 and writes poetry and short stories. Both speak very good English. And a little girl, Bouchra, is named after my friend.

Monday, 14 September

Theresa and all her baggage arrive and I drive home, getting hopelessly lost near Bab Touma.I have rented a car for three weeks. It is remarkably cheap, working out – with comprehensive insurance – at US$20 a day.

Tuesday, 15 September

I have not been invited to the weekly "prayer meeting", held by Ian Blackley as Chargé, and suggest to Ian that it might be mutually useful if I attend. He suggests we wait for the Ambassador to return before deciding. I quietly fume at the exclusion but am determined to be cool and affable to everyone.

After dinner I take Theresa to Bab Touma and we call on Bouchra and Ahmed. Ahmed is planning to go to the United States for a while. Bouchra actually speaks very good English – with confidence and a fine accent.

Thursday, 17 September

Theresa looks at flats and bounces into the office with news of one that should be ideal. The landlord, Saifi Hamwi, is a former Ambassador to Pakistan, a nice, gentle, elderly public servant.

We have dinner with the Defence Attaché, Jeremy Dumas, and his wife, Liz. He was Defence Attaché in Beirut before coming here.

Apparently his father had been Defence Attaché in Beirut 30 years ago: the Lebanese found the idea of the post being hereditary perfectly acceptable.

Saturday, 19 September

We negotiate terms for the new flat, which is next to a newsagent's. They have a copy of *Paris-Match* and an Arabic paper called *Baghdad*, presumably the journal of a Damascus-based opposition to Saddam Hussein. We then walk to some shops to buy furniture. I am carried away with ecstatic enjoyment of the architecture – lovely little bits of plasterwork or woodwork decoration on balconies – palimpsests in stone. Some buildings have an aspect of faded glory, structures diverted to other purposes. We buy cookers, fridges and all sorts of things.

Sunday, 20 September

Theresa goes to coffee with Pamela Blackley and other Embassy wives. They are a slightly depressed lot – not manic or desperate, but whingeing is the order of the day. Theresa feels like an old pro, unaffected by the gloom. There are no amenities, people say. A shopping trip to Chtaura in Lebanon is seen as a lifeline.

Tuesday, 22 September

I attend the opening of the Arab Book Fair. I browse. There are very few British books. Lots of religious books. Most publishers are from Syria, Lebanon and Egypt. The opening ceremony is performed by the Minister of Culture, Dr Najah al-Attar, a lady in a scarlet suit. She spends a lot of time at each stall.

Wednesday, 23 September

I have a series of visitors, some planned, some not. A woman from Sidon has been financing her nephew to study medicine at the

University of Nottingham. Her family deals in construction in the Gulf. Because of the Kuwait war and its aftermath, funds have run out. Can we help?

An Englishman studying Arabic here wonders if there are any British teachers he could stay with. I tell him he should go to a small shopkeeper and ask where he could take a room. If he wants to learn Arabic, he should avoid British people. Besides we do not have any teachers yet.

I am being marginalised by the Embassy. I have not been invited to the weekly "prayer meeting" – which the head of the British Council always attends. There is always a useful exchange of information at these meetings.

Thursday, 24 September
I have a call from Adam Ereli of the American Embassy, a wiry young man. We talk about their activities – looking after young American scholars learning Arabic, and a Fulbright Professor interested in Arabic literature translated into English. The Americans seem to do things so much better than we do. There is a seamless link between public service and scholarship. And the scholarship covers everything from literature to politics.

I call on the Minister of Culture, Dr Najah al-Attar. She has a PhD in Arabic studies from the University of Edinburgh. We start in English but talk for half an hour in Arabic about ideas I have – she is very supportive. She has been Minister of Culture for nearly 20 years but is not a member of the Ba'th Party.

Najah al-Attar was from a Damascus family. After her PhD she worked in the Ministry of Culture as a translator and a journalist. During the 1973 war with Israel she wrote stirring articles for the press and these caught the attention of the President, Hafez al-Assad. He made her Minister of Culture. It was an interesting appointment, because her brother, Isam, has been a leading Muslim Brother. When Isam's wife was assassinated Najah al-Attar showed family loyalty by wearing black at cabinet meetings. She was – with Assad's chum from student days, the Minister of Defence, Mustafa Tlas – Assad's longest serving Minister. Najah al-Attar had become a close friend of Anisa, the wife of the President. Her husband was Majid al-Azmeh, who had been the Director of the Military Medical Services, with the rank of General.

I call on the Minister of Health, Dr Muhammad Shatti. We talk in English. He has eight pictures of President Assad in his office. He was in Britain in July and my call is a follow-up to that visit, with the ulterior objective of spending some of my budget before the end of the financial year in March. He has the idea of sending a team of surgeons to Harefield in December and to build up an open-heart surgery unit in Damascus under the auspices of Sir Magdi Yacoub.

We have dinner with Adam Ereli and his Russian wife, Marina. The other guest is William Granara, head of the Foreign Service Institution in Tunisia, where US diplomats learn Arabic. He is a translator and we both enthuse about Arabic and literary translation.

Saturday, 26 September

We decide to get out of Damascus and drive up the Barada valley towards Lebanon. We reach Zabadani. There is no longer a regular train service but the track is still there. I remember, from visits in the 1970s and 1980s, two charming little villages, Bloudan and Zabadani, with little old Ottoman buildings in the hills. They are now popular resorts with masses of modern buildings. We eat and walk through the village, past villas with roofed open verandas but no walls. They resemble drawing rooms – chairs and sofas around a table and with pods of some plant laid out to dry.

Sunday, 27 September

The Security Officer at the Embassy, Jack, is a surly old bastard. He is reluctantly cooperative and I have to work hard on him. He has a notice in his room: "Speak only English in this room. If you want to speak any other language go to another room."

We buy some furniture for the flat we are to move into. I learn two new Arabic words: *munajjid*, a restorer of furniture, and *'abu*, the lower ground floor. The latter, in the written form is *qabw*, which I have come across in the novels of Hanna Mina. The dictionary translates it as "vault" but this was never clear to me. It is now: the advantage of living in the country of a writer one is studying.

I get a phone call at home to say I have appointments in the next two days with the heads of the three provincial universities of the country – at Homs, Lattakia and Aleppo.

Monday, 28 September

I am early for my appointment with Dr Abdul Majid Sheikh Husain, Rector of the Ba'th University, Homs. He is a graduate of the University of Bristol, a charming Anglophone. He was appointed Rector in 1979, when the university was founded and has been closely involved with the design and construction. "We are planning for the year 2100," he says. He shows me the Faculty of Engineering with an extensive range of steps leading to the entrance. "Students like sitting on the steps," he tells me, recalling Bristol. He takes me to a converted school, now the Faculty of Letters, and introduces me to several bright graduates of British universities, now on the staff, teaching English. One of them is Cornelia Khaled who wrote a PhD on the sexual politics of the Victorian novel. The Rector, Cornelia and a couple of the English staff – including one who has written a book on John Fowles – take me off to lunch at the Dik al-Jinn Restaurant overlooking the Orontes. The restaurant is named after a medieval drunken Shi'ite poet, Abdul Salam ibn Raghban, who used to come home carousing in the early hours, crowing like a demented cockerel – thereby acquiring the nickname, Dik al-Jinn ("cock of the djinn"). We discuss one line of his poetry where he writes about mixing wine with water. It is puzzling, says the Rector. Araq, the Syrian spirit that is like pernod or ouzo and is diluted with water, had not been invented then, and Syrians never dilute their wine. The Rector knew James Craig, who used to ask Syrians if they knew the word for a man with six fingers on one hand. Few did and he would say, *afnash*, triumphantly. How many languages, I wonder, have one word for that?

I leave at four and drive west towards Tartus. I drive near Krak des Chevaliers and get agreeably lost in the surrounding villages. They could be Greece, Southern Italy or Cyprus. Then down to the coast and on to Lattakia for the night.

Tuesday, 29 September
I call on the Rector of Tishreen University, Dr Khalid Hallaj, who speaks careful English. An engineer, he studied at the University of Dresden in East Germany.

Instead of going round the university I am given a tour of the city by a university official, Georges. I expected it to be an upmarket Hodeida, but it is rather a downmarket Naples, a palimpsest of eastern Mediterranean architectural history: the neglected shell of a Byzantine church, a Roman triumphal arch, a museum that is a former Ottoman khan – caravanserai – with stables that are solid and cool, the casino, a relic of the French Mandate. Georges is a cousin of the novelist Hanna Mina. Both migrated to Lattakia from the sanjak of Alexandretta – Iskenderun – that was ceded to Turkey in 1939. Many others moved into Lattakia and Aleppo after the Turkish annexation.

I drive during the afternoon to Aleppo and check in at the Hotel Baron and meet Koko Mazloumian, whose father and uncle founded the hotel before the First World War. He is in his eighties and virtually blind. We are joined by some travelling Germans. Koko speaks some German, having been at a German kindergarten run by Protestant sisters in Aleppo during the First World War. In protest against the German alliance with the Turks, he used quietly to sing *Deutschland, Deutschland unter alles* instead of *über alles*. Koko also remembers Baron Max von Oppenheim, the pioneer of the archaeology of northern Syria in the first quarter of the century. "I remember him when he was a sprightly 91-year-old. He used to pinch girls' bottoms. He spoke perfect French." Koko's wife, Sally, has been living here since 1948. She hopes a British Council will reopen in Aleppo. "It closed in 1956. We used to have a lecture every fortnight. People like Sir Ronald Storrs."

Wednesday, 30 September
The bill at the Baron is amazingly cheap: about £4 for bed and breakfast – tea, cheese, olives, bread and marmalade.

At ten I call on the University on the north-west slopes of the city. The Rector is away and I meet his deputy, Nazmi Qadi, the brother of a former Governor of Aleppo whom the Muslim Brethren tried to assassinate near the railway line. The university was founded in 1956 and now has 60,000 students, one third of whom are women. I meet Ghias Barakat of the English Language Advisory Service, a slick graduate of Texas.

Thursday, 1 October
We have moved into our new flat, leaving the Residence for the Ambassador, due back in a day or two.

Friday, 2 October
Vanda and her husband Nabil have invited us to Nabil's village to meet his family. Deir Attiyeh is 60 kilometres north of the city on the Aleppo road. It is the home town of the Minister of Higher Education, Dr Saliha Sanqar. We meet Nabil on the outskirts of the

village and follow him to the farm, *karm*. The whole family are present, including Nabil's grandparents who must be in their late eighties. Everyone seems to be busy, preparing food and pressing grapes to become raisins. Many of the family are well educated – dentistry students, teachers; one is a colonel in the army, who has studied in the Soviet Union, but also has a degree in English from the University of Damascus. The day is a family gathering, a *shtah*, though in the next village, al-Nabk, they call it *stah*. Before the food, prepared by Granny, there is some singing to the accompaniment of improvised instruments – sticks beating a rhythm on petrol cans. The main dish is boiled lamb with burghul and rice, with yoghurt added.

We leave and drive on to Tartus.

Saturday, 3 October

We take a small boat from Tartus to the island of Arwad. What a sense of the past the place has. We walk around the densely packed town. A surprisingly large number of people have fairish hair and bluish eyes. Crusader influence? Arwad was the last Crusader outpost to fall.

Sunday, 4 October

The Ambassador is back. It will be interesting to see whether I am invited to attend the weekly meetings. I miss them. I am not reading any local papers or listening to news broadcasts so I feel out of touch with news. In Tunis I was briefed at the weekly meetings of the gradual collapse of the Bourguiba regime. In Abu Dhabi I was fully brought in on the build-up to the Kuwait war. I also believe I can make a useful contribution. I am the best Arabist among the British in the building, and my network of contacts is likely to be better than anyone else's.

I am reading a novel by Hanna Mina about a Lebanese journalist based in London and his Bulgarian girlfriend. They are in mountains near Sofia and about to make love. It is told in the first person and the novel wanders off about the journalist's life and personality. He is from a Christian family from Izmir who migrated to Adana and then to Beirut. I am intrigued by the Christian Turks who have become Greater Syrian Arabs.

Monday, 5 October

At drinks at the Ambassador's Residence I meet Burhan Qassab-Hassan, a retired Syrian colonel, and the Palestinian representative, Mahir al-Hamdi. Mahir was one of the people who took over the Jordan Intercontinental Hotel in 1970. He has retired from terrorism and is now a writer of short stories and a diplomat. His wife, Nahid, is from Damascus and prefers to talk in English.

I go by myself to a party in the Kurdish area of Rukneddin, in honour of a cousin of Bouchra's. The party is in full swing when I arrive, with lots of people singing, clapping hands, dancing.

"We've not seen you for a long time," says Bouchra.

"Each week we are meeting more and more people."

"Don't forget us."

"Impossible. My first friends here are the most important."

Wednesday, 7 October

I am invited to attend the Ambassador's weekly staff meeting. Senior people, including me, sit around a table. Junior people, including Jack, the Security Officer, sit on more comfortable armchairs behind us. We sit like prefects in the presence of the Headmaster. Ian, who is no longer Chargé, sits bolt upright, like the Head Boy. None of us writes, makes notes or even has his – for we are all men – hands on the table. The Ambassador tours the horizon and talks of his call on the Foreign Secretary, Douglas Hurd, who will possibly visit Damascus next year.

Saturday, 10 October

Nat and I walk to the Saruja area, north of the old city. The traders in one street sell only fish, some of which comes from the Euphrates. A butcher's stall has sheep intestines that are yards long. The whole area has an odour of sweet, stale meat and urine. In another street people sell live chickens, rabbits and ducks – whether for eating or as pets I am not sure. The next street has caged birds, including ordinary sparrows. I ask about tortoises and we buy one for 100 Syrian pounds. The animal is placed in a black trash bag in a cardboard box and Nat carries it proudly home.

Monday, 12 October

The Ambassador asks me to represent him at the opening of Bahrain Cultural Week. I go along to this at the Assad Library and meet some writers and journalists. A little later Burhan Qassab-Hassan takes me to a *ta'ziya*, a condolence call, on the family of Adnan Baghtaji, a former Minister of Education, who was – I am told – a drunkard and a translator.

Tuesday, 13 October

I have a call from Warqa Barmada, who is charge of an English for Academic Purposes Unit at the University of Damascus. She is from a wealthy background. Her father was imprisoned in the 1940s by the French at Ain Warqa in Lebanon when she was born – hence her name. The family came from Aleppo and had lands at Harim in the north and around Antioch.

Wednesday, 14 October

Ian Blackley calls and we go to Isam al-Lahham's carpet shop. Ian loves carpets and gives us advice. He has strong views but is well informed. He fondles them, turns them over lovingly, runs his fingernails over the texture and gazes at them for minutes on end. It is fascinating to watch him.

Thursday, 15 October

I go off in an Embassy car and call on General Mahmud Zughaiby, the Director of Army Medical Services. He is an Alawite, was trained in Britain and is very pro-British.

Newspapers arrive from London, and I read that John Hanson has been appointed Director General of the British Council. I am sure I should have been informed by telex or cable. Perhaps my headquarters do not know that the British Council has reopened in Syria.

Saturday, 17 October

Ian takes us to the carpet shop again and we stay there for an hour and more. We buy a Mashhad carpet for 100,000 Syrian pounds. Ian has coveted it but it is either too large or too small for his needs, but he describes it as "honourable". Are we being extravagant? Probably. But to have the house fitted with carpets would be costly. This carpet gives distinction. The value will not depreciate, so we will not lose. We are unable to look at any other carpet while we are in the shop. We go on to buy other household items, including a precision screwdriver, in what Ian calls the precision screwdriver souk.

Sunday, 18 October

Our new Accountant/Office Manager, Ayoub, is a solemn Palestinian, born in Safed, who came to Damascus as an infant refugee in 1948. We invite him to lunch. He accepts only on condition that no alcohol is served. I tell him that we prefer his company to alcohol this time. I reflect that in future he can decide whether our company is preferable to the presence of alcohol. So we have a Pepsi on the patio.

In the evening we call on Bouchra and Ahmed. Ahmed is off to the United States on Tuesday. He does not know how long for. He has been struggling at English and will be in New York for a week and then go on to Tulsa. Husam will look after the shop while he is away.

Monday, 19 October
I have a weekly meeting with the Ambassador and tell him of the people I have been meeting. He asks me "to do a note on them". I see that I am likely to build up a far broader network of acquaintances than anybody else in the Embassy. The people they meet are roughly from three groups: officials; people who are pro-British because of business or family connections; the haute bourgeoisie. Through education, culture and English classes I shall reach out to a far greater number.

In 1986 Peter had a book published about Marmaduke Pickthall (1875-1936), a novelist who became a Muslim and translated the Holy Koran. Pickthall also wrote a novel, Saïd the Fisherman, *published in 1903, that was reprinted alongside Peter's book. The novel is about a Palestinian fisherman who travels to Damascus in 1860.*

Friday, 23 October
I have been glancing through *Saïd the Fisherman* and note Pickthall's description of Damascus – beautiful, smells, lots of dogs, offal, a mixture of the romantic and the realistic. If you substitute car fumes for dogs, not a lot has changed.

In the evening I go to the airport to collect Gabriel, on his half-term break. He seems happy and confident. I bring him back in the dark. The lights of the houses on Jebel Kasiyun are, he says, "like a Christmas cake as seen by a mouse."

Saturday, 24 October

We drive with the boys to Aleppo and check in at the Hotel Baron and have a drink with Sally and Koko Mazloumian. Koko talks about "bloody Turks", seeing them as Mongol invaders who destroyed Armenian Cilicia, or Silesia, as he seems to pronounce it.

Sunday, 25 October

After a visit to the university I walk back to the Baron via the railway station, just as a train draws in. The station is clean and well maintained, a smart building dating from 1911. There are four trains a day to and from Damascus, taking a stress-free six hours. On the platform is a large well-polished bell with "Bagdad" on it.

Monday, 26 October

At my meeting with the Ambassador I talk of my visit to Aleppo, and tell him of the university's request for me to bring a chemist out. "Take care," he says. "He might be manufacturing something unpleasant."

Later I call on the Spanish Cultural Attaché, a lovely Catalonian called Montserrat. She came here seven years ago to study Arabic and has been in her present post for two years. She is doing a doctorate on Arabic science – astrolabes in particular – and will be going to a less stressful posting in Rabat where she will finish it. We talk in French, occasionally lapsing into Arabic.

Tuesday, 27 October

I go to the Faculty of Letters at the University to hear Sulaiman Ahmed give an excellent lecture on Tennyson's poem, "St Simeon Stylites". This commemorates the centenary of Tennyson's death and the 16th centenary of St Simeon Stylites's birth. Tennyson wrote his poem at a time of emotional crisis, just after the death of Arthur Hallam. I have tea with Sulaiman afterwards, meeting Christa Salamandra, an American who is doing a PhD at Oxford on food culture.

Sulaiman Ahmed was an Alawite from near Tartus. He had worked simultaneously on two degrees after leaving school, English and Law. He went on to do a PhD at the University of Liverpool and was an acknowledged Hardy scholar. He edited Two Men on a Tower *for the Oxford University Press in a new edition of Hardy's works, the only editor not British, Commonwealth or American.*

Wednesday, 28 October

I spend time working out who are the UK graduates now teaching at the University of Damascus. I trace 71 names altogether.

I go to the American Cultural Centre and attend the second good lecture in two days. Allen Hibbard, a Fulbright Professor in American Literature, talks on Paul Bowles. It occurs to me that Pickthall succeeded where Bowles aspired.

Thursday, 29 October

I go to the Azm Palace where a French visitor is directing a production in Arabic of *Romeo and Juliet*. All the actors are Syrian and the action is around a pool in the courtyard. Every advantage is taken of the site. A shrub at the side becomes Friar Laurence's cell. Juliet is Amal Arafa, a lovely actress. Capulet is played by Taisir Idris, who plays, I suspect, stereotyped comic roles. Mercutio is a black man, Yasir Abdul Latif, who moves with beautiful balletic agility. I steal away through the alleyways home to a slumbering household.

Friday, 30 October

We go to Nat's school where there is a Halloween fancy-dress party. Two children are dressed as grocery packets – one a tube of toothpaste in a carton, the other as a fruit drink.

We drive out to Maloula. The place that enchanted me 30 years ago is a town full of breeze-block buildings. We have lunch at the new hotel built above the town, getting there just in time, for hordes of people come and attack the buffet like locusts. Food is piled high on plates. "Might it not be easier," observes Theresa, "if they moved their chairs to the buffet tables?"

Monday, 2 November
I have a call from a translator who would like me to work with him, translating Salman Rushdie's *Satanic Verses* into Arabic. I tell him I would not touch it with a bargepole. Good luck, I tell him, but remember that the Italian and Japanese translators have been assassinated.

Tuesday, 3 November
I give a talk to the British Women in Damascus about the work of the British Council. I turn things around and say I am looking for native speakers of English whom I can train as teachers in a teaching operation. About 30 are present.

Wednesday, 4 November
I go to the weekly "Prefects' Meeting" at the Embassy to be told that it is already over. I was not told that it was brought forward.

We go to a dinner at the Ambassador's Residence in our honour. There are plenty of interesting guests. Jacques Hakim is a lawyer whose father's memoirs I have. This father was a Minister in Faisal's brief reign between 1918 and 1920. Cynthia al-Wadi is a pianist from Cardiff. Her husband, Solhi, Iraqi in origin, is Director of the Music Institute. He was a student at Victoria College, Alexandria. Ni'met al-Jaza'iri is of Algerian origin. Her forebears accompanied the Algerian leader, Abdul Qadir, who was exiled here by the French in the 1850s. Her brother went recently to Algeria and had a warm welcome.

Thursday, 5 November
I send a copy of *Thesiger's Return*[1] to Malise Ruthven and wonder

whether it might be an idea to have a similar exhibition based on photographs taken by Freya Stark of Syria in the 1920s and 1930s.

Peter went to a British Council conference in Cairo, presided over by Edmund Marsden who explained how overseas Directors would in future work closely to Regional Directors. There will be a tighter control over overseas activity.

Tuesday, 10 November

Jim, from British Council headquarters, quizzes me on my work, asking me daft questions, like "What percentage of women are beneficiaries of your exchanges programme?" I tell him that when 50 per cent of British Council staff sent overseas from London are women then I will try to match that.

Friday, 13 November

I receive a copy of Salma Khadra Jayyusi's anthology of Palestinian literature in translation[2]. It is beautifully produced and over 700 pages long. I have two translations in it. I glow with pride.

Part of Peter's brief in coming to Damascus was to visit Lebanon where British Council operations had been suspended during the Civil War. The office continued to tick over with a Lebanese lady, Hassana Jabr Salam, in charge. He paid his first visit to Beirut – since 1973 – in mid-November.

1 Peter Clark, *Thesiger's Return*, Motivate Publishing, Dubai, 1992, tells the story of Wilfred Thesiger's return to the United Arab Emirates in 1990 to attend the opening of an exhibition of photographs he took of the Emirates between 1946 and 1950. The exhibition was organised by the British Council.

2 Salma Khadra Jayyusi (ed), *Anthology of Modern Palestinian Literature*, Columbia University Press, New York, 1992.

Sunday, 15 November

As we approach the Lebanese border there are signs of a run-down frontier economy. Nothing is settled beyond making a fast buck. The Damascus Embassy driver sees me through to the Lebanese side. There I am met by Joseph, a Beirut Embassy driver, plus an Embassy bodyguard. We get into one Land Rover with another to escort us. Signposts are down and there are nothing to indicate where we are. There is much reconstruction but, as we climb up into the hills after the turning to Baalbek, houses remain damaged and the big hotel at Sofar is gutted. The road is no wider than it was 20 years ago. When we reach Beirut I am totally lost and am surprised to be suddenly by the sea.

The Embassy is in the hills above Antelias. Checkpoints and guards are everywhere. I meet the British Embassy staff and discuss security. They all love it here. Things could be volatile and you have to travel constantly with a guard and a driver. But the food is good.

I have dinner with the Ambassador, Maeve Fort, at her Residence. She cooks a lasagne in the microwave and we talk Lebanon. Syrians are disliked as oppressive imperialists though their presence may be necessary.

Monday, 16 November

I call on Farid Tabib in the Embassy. Known as "Freddie", he used to teach me Arabic 22 years ago – a great teacher. He now has a senior post in the Embassy. He is a sad man. His children have grown up and emigrated. His brother was murdered in the presence of his mother.

My driver and bodyguard take me through the rush-hour traffic to the old British Council office. The bodyguard does not let me out of his sight. I meet Hassana and then former members of the British Council staff. Tawfiq of Shemlan used to be a miserable old git. The house he had prepared for his old age in the village of Shemlan has been totally destroyed, the furniture and contents pillaged. He has become deaf from the shelling. A former secretary, Renée, briefly back in Beirut, now lives near Marble Arch with her two sons.

Hassana takes me on some calls. We go to the American University and I talk to the Jordanian Vice-President in an office with signed portraits of Theodore Roosevelt and Mark Twain on the wall. Then on the Maqasid Foundation, and its hereditary head, the totally bald Tamam Salam, son of the former Prime Minister, Sa'ib Salam, now aged 86 and living in Geneva. The Maqasid Foundation was set up as a charitable and educational institution in the 19th century as a Sunni Muslim response to the foreign missionary schools. Initially it specialised in girls' education. I am their guest for lunch. We are served wine and spirits. I then go on a tour of the bombed areas of the city including the Borj, the old central square, which marked the dividing line during the civil war. It needs to be seen to be believed. Handsome buildings are shattered. None is undamaged. Byzantine and Crusader churches are battered.

Tuesday, 17 November

Hassana takes me to call on the Minister of Education, Michel al-Daher, a lawyer and Deputy from the north. We talk in French, lapsing occasionally into Arabic. I suggest to Hassana that we walk to Hamra Street to get a new film for my camera. Hassana, the bodyguard and I stroll along a road that was once very familiar. She tells me afterwards that I was the centre of attention: few foreigners venture there.

Wednesday, 18 November

I am on the road back to Damascus with the Defence Attaché and his wife – and a driver and bodyguard and two escorting Land Rovers. We hoot our way through the traffic and jump lights. The Defence Attaché's daughter earned some money as a model advertising something or other and her picture is on advertising hoardings all round the town. On another hoarding is a poster, announcing a new Lebanese wine, "Le Nouveau Kefraye est arrivé".

Thursday, 19 November

Ian Blackley asks me to call in at his office. He hands me a telex which says I am to have an OBE in the New Years' Honours. Although I have toyed with the possibility in the last months and years it comes as a most agreeable shock. I am asked to give my consent by 22 November.

"I always thought this was something that happens to other people," I say to Ian as he congratulates me.

"Well," he says kindly and warmly, "You're now one of the other people."

I feel in a glow all day. Theresa is absolutely delighted and we have a bottle of champagne. I am already planning the celebrations for the investiture and a dinner afterwards.

Friday, 20 November

We drive to Bosra, through Suwaida and Resas, where Freya Stark stayed in 1928. As we approach Bosra we have a puncture, which is repaired in the town by a *gommaji* – a lovely portmanteau word, the first part Italian, the second part the Turkish agent suffix.

In Abu Dhabi Peter had organised an exhibition of photographs taken by Wilfred Thesiger of the Emirates in the late 1940s. He had the idea of a similar exhibition of photographs taken by Freya Stark in the 1920s and 1930s. He wrote to a godson of Freya Stark, Malise Ruthven, about the idea. Freya Stark was still alive, aged 99, in frail health, living in Italy.

Saturday, 21 November

On the way back to Damascus we go through a suburb full of Iranian pilgrims, who have come to the Sayyidna Zaynab mosque. The suburb has an Imam Khomeini Hospital.

Sunday, 22 November

I have a letter from Malise Ruthven, helpful and cordial. Freya Stark's photos are in the library of St Antony's College, Oxford. John Murray, himself aged 83, holds the copyright.

Theresa, Nat and I go to see a film, *Al-Hail*, with Marina and Adam Ereli. The film has won prizes at the Carthage Film Festival and is historical, about the last days of the Mandate and the 1948 war in Palestine. It is directed by Muhammad Malas who makes a brief speech. The audience are appreciative, rapt and dour. There is none of the preening or power-broking of a comparable British event. Producers do their work, and critics, artists and audience seem much closer together.

Wednesday, 25 November

At the weekly Embassy "prayers" the Consul reports that he is receiving lots of visa applications from would-be Iraqi dissidents, all with a note from Julian Walker on an old business card. Julian, who was British Ambassador in Yemen when I was British Council Representative there, is working in London on Iraq and is using up cards from previous postings he had.

I am rereading *Dombey and Son* with huge enjoyment. Theresa is reading Freya Stark's *Letters from Syria*, and says that Freya reminds her of ourselves in our twenties – intellectually self-sufficient and really arrogant. Nobody else perceives things as she, Freya, does.

Friday, 27 November

Nat and I go to Bab Touma and call on Bouchra. Ahmed is working in Brooklyn. She has no idea when he will be back. She is having the flat redecorated in his absence. The eldest son, Husam, is in prison.

I gasp. He is doing his military service and was absent without leave and has 16 days "sentence". He is at the barracks in Mezze but is able to come and go during the daytime, so conditions are not too harsh.

Saturday, 28 November

Theresa and I go for a walk up the Barada valley which used to be the main road to Beirut. We follow the railway track past mosques, deserted railway stations, crumbling old villas, handsome Ottoman structures and unsightly modern breeze blocks. We stop at a newly opened restaurant. The waiter is Kurdish. Theresa used to be able to count to ten in Kurdish and he teaches her the words again.

Monday, 30 November

We host our first party. The guests are of three kinds: official colleagues; internationals, including Christa, an American researching food, and Andrew who is researching coups; and Syrian official contacts, such as Burhan, who was at Sandhurst in 1950, and Muhiuddin, Deputy Minister of Education.

I have invited Bouchra and Hunaina who is also called Hanan, and I despair of them turning up. But they do arrive just as we are eating, together with Reem.

"Have you any music?" Reem asks.

I have been playing some Caracalla – Lebanese dance music – but Reem goes out to the car they came in, brings in a tape, removes the Caracalla and plays her music. Then she dances superbly to it. Bouchra joins in with a lovely belly dance. Food is knocked back or abandoned and we all join in.

The music is loud, some of the women ululate and the party is transformed from an official gathering to a joyous spectacle.

Tuesday, 1 December

We receive two notes of appreciation. Ian Blackley found the party quite unlike normal diplomatic functions and the Defence Attaché's wife loved the spontaneous enjoyment of what she calls "orientals".

I spend much of the day number crunching. I must get a teaching operation going. If I have to postpone this it makes no sense of my being here. I would not relish a further year squatting in a cupboard in the Embassy.

Thursday, 3 December
The Ambassador and I call on the Minister of Culture. The courtesies are in English this time. We invite her to go to Britain in March. Ramadan is no problem. She coos at the idea of a visit to Edinburgh, her alma mater.

In the evening Bouchra phones. I invite her and any others to come round – there is still food left over from the party. She arrives with the two little girls. While Ahmed has been away she has arranged for builders to do work in their flat. She is dreading Ahmed suddenly coming home, while workmen are in the house. There is still a week's work to be done. Her sons are staying at the flat while she and the little girls are camping at Hanan's. Ahmed left lots of money in the bank for her to live on, but it is being spent on the building work.

In December 1962 Peter, on his first visit to Syria, had gone by bus to Saidnaya, 30 kilometres north of Damascus. He had visited the Catholic nunnery and was shown round by the Abbess, La Mère Maria. He had then walked on a dusty track to Maloula.

Friday, 4 December
Nat and I go to Saidnaya. The road is quite unrecognisable. I vaguely recall rural villages with copious greenery. Now there is a string of small ugly breeze-block citylets. We go to the nunnery. I have no

Mère Maria to guide us, but I note that the steps were built, according to an inscription, during the abbacy of Mère Maria, whose family name was Ma'luf.

I am wanting to see how far I walked that day, 30 years ago, so we drive north on the paved road to Maloula. Nat, who has never seen snow before, wants to experience snow. We see some in the hills of the Anti-Lebanon range, and pockets of snow in the fields by the road. We stop and I take a picture of Nat in the first snow of his life. He finds it far colder than expected. He wants to see more, so we push on and reach a cold, poor, remote village called Hawsh al-Arab. They had snow last week and people in the village tell me that snow can sometimes cut the village off for two weeks. It is well past three, the shadows are lengthening and we return to Maloula and the main road. I walked 38 kilometres that day in 1962.

Saturday, 5 December
Bouchra comes to the house at 1 with Mayas and we all go off to the Abu Kemal Restaurant. I am apprehensive for her reputation. And for mine. What conclusions do people draw? Anyway, we talk at length about the work being done in her flat. Ahmed would never embark on such a project and was always postponing things. He has never been away for such a long time and if he returned to see the flat in such a state "he would go off to the court and divorce me." She has had one phone call from him and is very nervous. Her sons are on her side but find the disruption inconvenient. Ahmed makes all the decisions in the house, does all the shopping and is increasingly authoritarian. Shortly after they got married she went with him to Vienna. She got a job – slave labour – fitting parts on to televisions. They lived in one room, knew nobody and came back to Damascus after four months. She quietly fumes about the submerged role of domestic women, but is resigned.

Monday, 7 December

I tell the Ambassador of my idea of a Freya Stark exhibition which he thinks is brilliant. I tell him of the idea of getting sponsorship from Shell. "I'll have a word with Alan, the local agent," he volunteers. "I've thought of going higher, to Sir Peter Holmes, sending him a copy of *Thesiger's Return*, the book I wrote about the exhibition of photos taken by Wilfred Thesiger of the Emirates."

I am reading some stories by Abdul Salam al-Ujaili: superb. He is the writer I am most impressed by. I would like to translate some of his work.

I go to a party at Warqa Barmada's bourgeois house in Malki. She has gathered an interesting group of guests. The novelist, Hanna Mina, is there: a short man, looking much older than expected. He chain-smokes and we talk of translations. His work has been translated into French, German, Russian and Persian. Another guest is an absurd Aleppine who has a PhD from the University of Havana and a runny nose. He is all for the purification of Arabic, the mother of languages. What rot, I think, reflecting on the beauty of words like *gommaji*, meaning the man who repairs punctures.

Wednesday, 9 December

I am searching for new premises and I negotiate with Haidar Bouzo, a former Minister of Labour, from a well-off Kurdish family. We talk in Arabic with occasional lapses into French, English and even Turkish.

Friday, 11 December

Nat and I go off and wander around the villages east of Damascus. We look at a Roman temple in Dumayr. Beyond the town of Dumayr are the ruins of a classical city, including one charming broken arch which I photograph. A couple of miles away is a military airfield which I take care to have at my back. A youth approaches us over the ruins. I think he is a lad wanting to sell old coins or to practise his English.

But he is a soldier and I have been taken photographs in a military zone. He escorts us back to a small hut where two or three other soldiers are on duty. I am questioned, remaining throughout courteous, calm and patient. And repentant. There is an oil stove by two beds. Yes, it is cold here at night. A report is made. I only took one picture. I promise to bring them a copy when it is developed. Name. Number of diplomatic card. Car registration number. All are recorded as we drink Yerba Mate tea – brought back from South America by returned Syrian migrants – and Nat befriends an affectionate kitten. We are allowed to leave and I give one soldier a lift to the clinic where he has an injection in his nose. On to Damascus. I feel a bit of an ass about it all. I trust no more will be heard about it.

Nat is not feeling well – he had five glasses of the Argentinian tea which "first I liked and then I hated".

Monday, 14 December
I collect some photographs from a store round the corner. The photographer is a grandson of Abdul Rahman al-Kawakabi, the Arab nationalist ideologue of a century ago.

I then go on to a dinner hosted by the head of the Army Medical Services, General Mahmud Zughaiby, at the Orient Club, Nadi al-Sharq, built in the 1940s, an opulently vulgar watering hole for the fat cats of the town. The General asks about my Arab world experience and I tell him about my first visit to Syria 30 years ago. He is fascinated. I tell him of the teacher of English at Palmyra I met. "I'd love to meet him again." The General, gruff, friendly but occasionally a bit alarming, says "I'll phone the Head of Security there tomorrow morning and we'll see if he's still around."

Tuesday, 15 December
The other day I met, by chance, Hanna Batatu, the Palestinian political scientist whose huge book on Iraq I bought a year or so ago.

He is briefly in Damascus and he comes round to dinner. Hanna is delightful, a quiet, elderly man with a ferociously intensive enquiring mind, linking otherwise unconnected aspects of the world – like the Druze and Druids. He has been reading David Hume lately. He spent a year in Iraq, going through intelligence reports from 7.30 am to 11 pm. The Iraqi authorities did not appreciate the value of the documents. He supplemented this with interviews with prisoners and later inspecting British intelligence documents. I get him to sign my copy of the great book[3].

Wednesday, 16 December

There has been quite a bit of snow in the night. Two inches. Nat is overjoyed. I am first to be up and out on the road. Schoolchildren go off to school at 7.30 but offices and shops do not get going until 9 or 10.

We have a lunch at the Ambassador's Residence for a visiting Medical Studies consultant. All the invited guests turn up, including General Zughaiby and the Deputy Minister of Education. The Ambassador is clearly pleased and at the end of the meal makes a speech. "Gentlemen," he starts. He talks about Syrians who have studied in England. "And Wales," I add, putting my hand on the General's arm – he is a graduate of the University of Wales. He talks about how the British Council has opened doors. "Wide," interpolates one doctor.

Thursday, 17 December

I see another landlord who wants us to pay five years' rent in advance, including all the taxes due. He is in short wanting us to be his accomplices in defrauding the tax office. Why is there not a real socialist revolution in this country? Why don't these people just get dispossessed?

---

3 Hanna Batatu, *The Old Social Classes and the Revolutionary Movements of Iraq*, University Press, Princeton, NJ, 1978.

Friday, 18 December

We all go up to the village of Bloudan and stop by some trees. *Le tout Damas* seems to be there, throwing snowballs at each other. Our boys join in the snow fun, exchanging snowballs with a middle-aged man in the next parked car. Other people have made snowmen on the bonnets of their cars, complete with hats, and stones for eyes. They slowly melt as we reach the lower, warmer plain. As people drive back to Damascus, their cars still have snowmen on the bonnets. Youths pelt passing cars with snowballs. Youths inside the cars lean out to snatch snow from the snowmen on their car bonnets to hurl at overtaking vehicles.

Sunday, 20 December

The proper way to clean carpets, according to Pamela Blackley, is to take them out into the snow, put them face down and get children to run up and down on them. You should not use too much water. Carpets should be dampened but not drenched.

I call on the Institute for Music and Drama. The Director, Solhi al-Wadi, shows me round. Thirty of the instructors are from the former Soviet Union. It all seems a very serious set-up. There are pictures of Solhi and his Welsh wife, Cynthia, with President Hafez al-Assad, the latter looking slim, dark-haired and youthful. He has been very supportive of the Institute.

Monday, 21 December

I am exhausted by unpleasant negotiations with grasping landlords, with their false bonhomie.

I spend a quiet hour reading *Letters from Syria* by Freya Stark. Broumana, Damascus, Jebel Druse, now all familiar places.

Thursday, 31 December

The four of us set off for Palmyra. We pause at the police post and I show them the photograph I took of the ruined column. This led to the detention of Nat and myself at the police post for a few hours three weeks ago. All is smiles, handshakes and offers of tea – but we press on.

We check into the Zenobia Hotel, built in 1924, where I stayed 30 years ago. One of the staff, Abdul Aziz, has been there since 1973. His father, Nuwas, was there from 1930 to 1969 – I must have met him in 1962.

Theresa and I go for a walk in the ruins. When we get back the boys and Theresa present me with home-made congratulations cards. I still have that element of doubt about the OBE. I am tired, ignore the New Year and am fast asleep by 9 o'clock.

Ayoub

1993

Saturday, 2 January 1993

We go to the Museum in Palmyra. A man comes up to us, wanting to sell us old coins. I tell him that my son, Nat, is the expert, so he sidles up to Nat. "The police will get you and kill you," he says and slips away. Nat is in tears. When the man reappears I round on him and say loudly in Arabic, "You have frightened my son. It is against the law to sell antiquities. I shall report you to the Director." He becomes obviously frightened. "Allah, Allah," he pleads, "I have six children." I enjoy his discomfort.

Sunday, 3 January

We drive back to Damascus.

The phone rings. It is Muhammad al-Murr, the Dubai writer whose short stories I have translated[1]. He is phoning from a restaurant just round the corner. We join him and talk of Syria. Sultan Oweiss, the Dubai pearl merchant and poet has a house here. They tell me that the Syrian playwright, Sa'dallah Wannous, is dying of cancer.

Wednesday, 6 January

I call on the Minister of Culture to arrange details of her visit to

---

1 Muhammad al-Murr, *Dubai Tales*, translated by Peter Clark, Forest Books, London and Boston, Mass, 1991 and Motivate Publishing, Dubai, 2008.

Britain in March. She is excited at the prospect and will stop off in Paris on the way to collect a gong from President Mitterrand.

We go to another party hosted by Nafiz and Joumana Shammaz. Their families are originally from Antioch and Joumana's mother has a Turkish passport as well as a Syrian. We chat a little in Turkish. Gordon Campbell, Professor of English at the University of Leicester, tells us about the importance of studying other literatures and begins to recount a story he heard on his car radio, called "Jazzmen". Theresa and I listen quietly: it is the story "Yasmin" by Muhammad al-Murr, one of the stories I translated for *Dubai Tales*. There is a delicious irony when Theresa reveals the identity of the translator. I give him a copy of *Dubai Tales* so he can read the text.

Peter goes to London for consultations at his headquarters.

Friday, 15 January

I go on to *The Guardian* offices and see Duncan Campbell. He invites me to join him and Julie Christie to see a film in St Martin's Lane. We meet Julie outside. She is wearing severe glasses and a woollen bonnet at a rakish angle and stretches her arms out in greeting. The film is French – "2627" or something about drug-busting French police. I could not have better companions for watching a film – the Crime Correspondent of *The Guardian* and a famous film actress. Julie has studied comparative religion over the last year. She studied them all.

"Well, who's right, then?" I ask.

"Oh, the Buddhists," she replies without a second's hesitation.

Tuesday, 19 January

I take a train to Oxford and go to St Antony's College. Derek Hopwood tells me that Albert Hourani died on Sunday morning. I feel a sense of shock although I only met him twice.

I then look through the albums of Freya Stark's photographs. My objectives for an exhibition of her photographs are precise and limited: Syria in the 1920s and 1930s. Most of the 28 pictures I select have not been published. I am aiming at a variety – people, portraits, landscapes, townscapes, activity and regional variation. Sometimes I think if she had moved a little to the left or the right she would have achieved a much better effect. And she did not know what to do with shadows. There are some pictures that are of historic interest but which I cannot use: one of the Glubb family with Faris as a three-year-old in keffiyeh and burnus; pictures of Jack Philby in the 1950s at Shemlan, with James Craig recognisable, and another of Philby with his Saudi wife and family.

Thursday, 21 January

It is good to be back in Damascus.

There are lots of letters, many congratulating me on my OBE. Hugh Leach writes with photocopies of two letters he received from Freya Stark in the 1970s, including a reference to a Dr Azm with daughters here in Damascus. Freya plays at being a marriage broker.

My Office Manager, Ayoub, is fasting for four months. Four months! He has a helpless look, resigned, and makes an upward gesture with his hands.

I go to the University and have a cordial half-hour with the Rector, Dr Riad Shuwaiki, who insists that he is independent of the Ministry of Higher Education. This is strange, for he used to be Minister himself.

Friday, 22 January

Our friends, Robin and Rebecca, and their two children, Kate aged eight and Owen aged six, arrived last night. I take them for a walk round central Damascus, the first time since we arrived that I have wandered in the old town.

Fati Darwish phones. In her late seventies, she was born in Manchester to a Manchester Syrian family and is very upset at Albert Hourani's death. He was, after all, the doyen of the Manchester Syrian/Lebanese community. She spoke to the Ambassador who thought Albert had died years ago. I tell her my impressions of that saintly man (Albert, not the Ambassador) and she breaks down. She is going back to England shortly to attend a commemoration for Albert – whom she regularly met when she was in England.

Sunday, 24 January
Back to the grindstone. I go through my in-tray and write a careful letter to Sir Peter Holmes, head of Shell, asking him for £9,000 for a Freya Stark exhibition. I send him a copy of my Thesiger book.

Monday, 25 January
I go with Ayoub to the Post Office. The building has not changed, it seems, for 50 years. I seem to remember buying postage stamps here in 1962. I am sure it has not been cleaned since then. We eventually get a man to witness my signature, enabling me to open a post office box.

Freya Stark will be one hundred in May. Malise Ruthven told me that she was physically strong but her mind had gone. As Hugh Leach says, "She has gone off the air."

I am reading Robin Fedden's book on Syria. I first got to know it before my first visit to Syria, and as I read it I am aware that there are phrases, sentences and ideas that have echoed in my mind for 30 years.

Tuesday, 26 January
The Ambassador says to me, "I have some business for you." He has been to see the Chamber of Commerce, who want some English classes. "Great," I say, and add, "I would like to explore the Ba'th

Party." There is a look of shock on his face. "*Al-hizb* [the Party]?" he says. "We'll talk about that later." But the Party is a centre of power and authority in the country and that cannot be ignored.

I drive to Lattakia.

Wednesday, 27 January
I go along to the office of Ahmad al-Isa. He is the Deputy Dean of the Faculty of Arts at the University and did a PhD at the University of Warwick on Henry James. We chat with Mahmud al-Khair, Head of the Department of English who did a PhD at the University of Exeter on Tennessee Williams. Then Ahmad is called away. Apparently, Ahmad attempted to discipline a student who was cheating. She defied and challenged Ahmad in front of four hundred students. She is a niece of President Hafez al-Assad and the bodyguards, ten armed men, now want to see him. After a moment's hesitation, he leaves, obviously scared stiff. Mahmud and I talk together. I wonder whether my presence has made things worse or better for him. Ahmad returns, quaking, looks at me and says, "I blame you for this. I learnt the importance of integrity and standing up for what is right in Britain." His hands are ice-cold.

I ask Mahmud why he studied the work of Tennessee Williams.

"I was in prison in 1967 and discovered a prison library and read the plays in Arabic translation."

"Why were you in prison?"

"I don't know."

I meet up with Robin and Rebecca. We have dinner at Spiro's Restaurant. I have invited three from the university but none of them turn up. Are they being watched? Do they fear talking with foreigners about what happened this morning? Am I a marked man? One of my objectives here is to promote the values of an open society. How do I do this when, in the course of my duties, I encounter such an incident?

There is a power cut at the hotel we are staying at. When the lights go out, the manager says, "Thank you, Hafez al-Assad."

Friday, 29 January
Hani al-Rahib comes to lunch. Hani is a novelist and was a colleague of Robin's at the University of Kuwait. He was on leave at the time of the Iraqi invasion of Kuwait and, unlike many Syrian intellectuals who were covertly pro-Saddam, vigorously denounced the action. He is a graduate of the University of Exeter where he wrote a thesis on the portrayal of Zionism in English fiction. His attempts to coin words in English, like notoriate, were thwarted by his British supervisor. The thesis was published by Zed Press.

Sunday, 31 January
It is Freya Stark's one hundredth birthday.

Koko Mazloumian has died. Poor old man! He was not enjoying old age.

Monday, 1 February
I am seeking an office away from the Embassy. The premises issue continues to be nail-biting. We have insisted on certain provisions to protect ourselves but Mr Bouzo, the landlord, has refused. I do nothing without the backing of the Embassy's lawyer and, at the end of the day, I send a letter saying we are withdrawing and looking for alternate premises.

I see more prospective premises. One is a basement flat belonging to Nazir Bagdanus ("Mr Parsley"). We have coffee with him and his sparkling wife, Nadia al-Ghazzi, daughter of Said Ghazzi, a Prime Minister in the 1950s. She is a writer and we talk literature and translation. This makes the search for premises so much more agreeable.

Tuesday, 2 February

I receive a handwritten letter from Mr Bouzo accepting all the conditions we demanded yesterday. Total capitulation.

Wednesday, 3 February

We have a small dinner party. The guest are Umara and Fayyez Kazak, and Maisun and Hani al-Rahib. Fayyez was the star of a much-praised Syrian film. Both Hani and Fayyez are Alawites – "the elite", as Hani says. Hani tells us how, at a meeting of the Writers' Union, he was critical of the state of things in Syria. At such meetings there are always representatives of the security forces. Shortly afterwards he was dismissed from his post at the University of Damascus and under house arrest for 20 months. He managed to get a job at the University of Kuwait and, because he denounced the Iraqi invasion when he was on leave in Syria, he fell out of favour with anti-regime Syrians.

Thursday, 4 February

I call on Bouchra. Ahmed got back last month, was a bit upset about the redecoration of the flat but soon got used to it. When she was a little girl Bouchra knew Nadia al-Ghazzi.

At 11 I go over to Mr Bouzo's house. There is a charm offensive. All is splendid – juice, chocolate cake, coffee and polite conversation.

Friday, 5 February

Bill Badley, a young British lute-player, is with us for a few days. He is 31, the son of an army officer, and, like Faris Glubb, ran away from Wellington. He is related to J H Badley, the founder of Bedales School. He studied English and History at the University of Exeter and then the lute at the Royal College of Music. We take him to lunch at Bloudan. As we drive back we run a gauntlet of snowballs thrown by all manner of people, old and young, men and women.

Saturday, 6 February

I take Bill Badley to the Higher Institute of Music and Drama, and we call on the Director, Solhi al-Wadi. We meet the resident lutenist, an Azerbaijani, Arif Abdul Hamid. Solhi is impressive. He is relaxed with staff and students, and there is a dynamic atmosphere about the place.

Sunday, 7 February

I see Warqa Barmada, the director of the English Language Centre at the University of Damascus. She advises me to call on the Ba'th Party official in charge of Higher Education, Wahib Tannous, a Christian Arab scholar with an East European PhD.

My headquarters is rejecting my plan for a teaching centre. I consult the Ambassador and I draft a letter to my masters in his presence.

"That sounds petulant," he says.

"I feel petulant," I say.

"You have every right to feel petulant," he sympathises.

Monday, 8 February

Bill Badley and I call on the Minister of Culture. He finds her cuddly!

Tuesday, 9 February

I call on Abdul Latif Abdul Hamid at the Al-Kindi cinema. He talks about the film, *Al-Rasa'il al-Shafahiyya*, (*Verbal Messages*) of which Fayyez Kazak was the star. It was made by the Ministry of Culture and has been the most popular film in Syria ever. It has run for five months and has been seen all over the country. One person has seen it 60 times.

Wednesday, 10 February

I am feeling depressed by my headquarters' negative approach to my plans for a teaching centre. But, as I say to Ayoub, the Palestinian

Office Manager, "I've only lost a teaching centre. You lost Palestine. Let's keep things in proportion."

One bit of good news. Hisham Yaziji of the local Shell office tells me that Sir Peter Holmes is interested in a Freya Stark exhibition. "How should the £9,000 I have asked for be spent?" I am asked. Well, that is fine. I can start on something I believe in, can control and know will be a success.

We have dinner at the flat of Allen Hibbard, the American Fulbright Lecturer in English. Allen writes stories, is an expert on Paul Bowles and has co-translated a story by Ibrahim al-Kouni.

Thursday, 11 February
In the evening I am taken to call on the writer, Abdul Salam al-Ujaili, a well-preserved septuagenarian. We chat, in French, about literature and translation.

Friday, 12 February
I spend the day with Bouchra and her family. I go to the flat. With her family, other relations and neighbours, we pile on to a hired bus and set off from Bab Touma and go up to Rukneddin and collect more people – about 30 of us altogether. We go west up the Barada valley. People have brought sandwiches and start dancing in the aisle of the bus to the taped music of a singer called Khalid. At a police checkpoint, the music is switched off and the coachload chants in unison, *bi qalb wa bi ruh, nifdak ya Hafiz* – "with heart and with soul, we pledge to thee, O Hafez", and *ramz al-thawra al-'arabiya, Hafiz al-Assad* – "the symbol of the Arab revolution, Hafez al-Assad". When we pass the checkpoint, Arab music and dancing in the aisles are resumed. I notice that at the checkpoint the driver hands over some cash to the policeman. I learn later that it is only 25 Syrian pounds – about 35p.

We reach Bloudan and go into the churchyard and all have a wonderful snowball fight. Abu Yasir, a balding man about my age, and Bouchra's aunt Amira (who is fasting during this month of Sha'ban, an act of supererogation, *nafl*) are fooling around as much as everyone else.

Sunday, 14 February

We go to a party given by our Filipino maid, Cecilia, and her Tanzanian boyfriend, Peter. I feel bored until I get talking to a Ghanaian student of Arabic. We talk in Arabic and I ask him who his favourite writers are. He says, the Lebanese who went to America, the *mahjar*. We talk about the Lebanese abroad, including those who went to West Africa.

Wednesday, 17 February

At the Embassy "prayer meeting" the Ambassador raises the matter of the death of the President. Apparently the bright young Embassy interpreter has gone through the list of recent Presidential engagements. It emerges that he only has appointments in the middle of the day. Much of his activity is telephone conversations with other heads of state. It is as if he may be confined to bed, and allowed to exert himself only for an hour or so each day. I press for a discussion on it. I am fascinated by the procedures, the precautions, the announcements. Will he die and be kept in a big fridge for a few days before his death is announced? His son, Basil, is being groomed to succeed but could there be a struggle for power among Alawite generals or uncle Rifaat? The first sign of something up might be roadblocks, but there could be a curfew and it will be prudent to stock up with water and provisions. And King Hussein is not well. And Sheikh Zayed in Abu Dhabi is slowing down. Could 1993 see the deaths of all three?

Assad lived for another seven years and died in 2000; King Hussein died in 1999 and Sheikh Zayed, the oldest of the three, lasted until 2004.

Friday, 19 February

Near Bab al-Sharqi I meet an old boy, Hassan, who tells me something of his life. A fascinating story. As a lad of 15 or 16 he was a batman (or batboy) to a British soldier in Aleppo. He went with him to Libya and was captured by the Germans, and taken to Berlin, where he saw Hitler. Still only about 16, he was asked why he was with the British.

"My father is poor," he explained.

"Here's an air ticket and some money. Go back to your mother."

Hassan also claims to have seen Montgomery, went to England after the war and spent nine years in Liverpool, studying and working in silk textiles.

Sunday, 21 February

We go out to dinner with Vanda Harmaneh and her husband, Nabil Batal. Nabil points out that the central character in the film, *Verbal Messages*, wees in his bed, is stupid and then … joins the army!

Monday, 22 February

I call on Dr Najah al-Attar, the Minister of Culture, and talk about the visit to Britain we are arranging for her next week. We go through the programme. She will be seeing her opposite number, the Secretary of State for the Department of National Heritage, Peter Brooke. She knows about his predecessor, David Mellor, but feels that the name of Peter Brooke is familiar. It dawns on me suddenly that she is confusing him with the theatre director, Peter Brook. She also asks about one of my predecessors. Would you like to meet him? I ask. No, she says firmly and decisively. He was proud and arrogant.

Tuesday, 23 February

Twice in the last few days serious Syrians have talked very

optimistically about the peace process with Israel. One of them tells of a rumour she has heard about a Damascus Jew who has bought a house which he is keeping for an Israeli Embassy!

I have a letter from Sir Peter Holmes agreeing to £9,150 sponsorship of the Freya Stark exhibition.

Wednesday, 24 February

At the Embassy meeting, the Ambassador raises the issue of what to do if the President dies. Apparently the Defence Attachés of four NATO countries (UK, US, Canada and the Netherlands: France and Germany are not included) have regular meetings to discuss the contingency. They have devised a series of codes in the event of death or civil insurrection.

Thursday, 25 February

I hear the *musahhir* cannon fired at about 4 am, announcing that Muslims should eat now before the Ramadan fast, and the dawn call to prayer at about 5.

Friday, 26 February

Theresa and I wander around Midan and Qanawat. We look at the late Mamluk monuments in Midan Street and then go through a low archway into the curving Qanawat Street by the Roman aqueduct. The houses around were built in the late 19th century and have the charm of the living antique. We push on south to the cemeteries, centres for Muslim pilgrims, especially Shi'i from Iran. There is no sense of Islamic exclusiveness, and we are welcomed to see the alleged tombs of Fatima, the Prophet's daughter, and of his granddaughter, Sikkina.

Although it is the first Friday of Ramadan people squat outside mosques munching away. We are invited into the "popular" Islah hotel. In the courtyard is a tower, part of the city walls, built by

Nureddin in the 12th century. Guests in the hotel invite us to drink tea with them, but we protest, muttering "Ramadan karim" and press on.

Saturday, 27 February

I am up early, put on a suit and drive to the airport to see off the Minister of Culture, en route for London.

Sunday, 28 February

Outside the Bagdanus flat the pavement is piled high with wreaths. Nizar Bey, whom I met on 1 February, died last night. I go upstairs to the wake and sit in silence with the men.

Monday, 1 March

British Council London phones to say Director General John Hanson will come to Damascus in October. He will stay with the Ambassador: they studied Arabic together in Lebanon. Will I have him to myself at some stage – to discuss the Embassy or to talk about our love for this country, how every day we have some experience that stimulates the mind or the senses, the imagination or the emotions?

I call on Comrade Dr Wahib Tannous, the Secretary General of the Regional Committee on Higher Education, at the Ba'th Party headquarters. He studied in Russia and his office is better appointed than that of the Minister. The forecourt has more Mercedes cars than anywhere else in the country.

Later we drive to Lattakia, and have dinner at Spiro's with friends from the university. We learn a new joke about a man from Homs. A curfew is in force in a Syrian town. People have to be indoors by 5 pm. At 4.30 a Homsi soldier shoots one citizen dead. "Why do you do that?" asks another soldier, "There's still half an hour before the curfew." "But I know he lives two hours away."

One of the friends is Ahmad. He tells us that after his encounter with the bodyguards of the President's niece, some members of the family came to see him to apologise.

Tuesday, 2 March

I call on the Rector of the University, Dr Hallaj. Wahib Tannous has already been in touch to say we are good chaps. Very interesting. I realise that the Ba'th Party is all-powerful in day-to-day decision making.

Wednesday, 3 March

I call on the Rector of the University of Aleppo, Dr Ali Houriya. He talks of the diversity of the city. Among his students are orthodox Jews. One refused to write an exam on the Sabbath but was allowed an amanuensis to whom he dictated his answers.

I walk into the centre of the city, call at the Baron Hotel and see Sally Mazloumian, all in black. She is clearly distressed, having been married to Koko, as she says, "for 44 and a half years". We have coffee in the front room which used to be Koko's museum. There are familiar portraits of Koko's parents and books on Armenia. Koko's photographs are in a state of disorder.

I then wander off to the Umayyad mosque. It is crowded with people of both sexes and of all ages. One man is cheerily singing the Koran as children mill around. I look in at the Halawaiya madrasa, the former Byzantine church, and into the souks, past a medieval loo, and look at famous khans – Khan al-Wazir and Khan al-Sabun, and then south to the Arghum Bimaristan, an eerie place that used to be an asylum for lunatics, in use as such to the beginning of this century.

Thursday, 4 March

I return to the university and sit through three hours of insufferable boredom, a seminar on English-language teaching. There are

English-language teaching professionals from other universities, including a Greek Aleppo girl called Phedra. I sit through it all and make a gracious speech at the end.

Saturday, 6 March

I take a visitor from my headquarters to call on the head of the English Language Unit at the University of Damascus, Warqa Barmada. She is a mixture of the sweet and the scheming. She can be very illuminating on many aspects of Syria. The University of Aleppo, she tells us, is freer than the University of Damascus. First, because it is not the capital, and secondly, because the Rector, Ali Houriya, is married to a sister of the wife of Mustafa Tlas, Minister of Defence. In Damascus, President Assad's daughter works – or rather has a job – at the University and acts as a channel of information to the President.

Sunday, 7 March

The weather is miserable. Our tortoise seems to be dead. Its body is beginning to stink and Theresa asks me to bury it. I give it a nudge and his head stirs and peeps out. Poor thing! Being buried alive is not much fun, even for a tortoise.

Tuesday, 9 March

I take a guest to Homs and we call on the Rector, Dr Abdul Majid Sheikh Husain.

In the last few months I have been putting out feelers about Ibrahim Abdul Nur, the young teacher of English who was so kind to me when I met him at Tadmor/Palmyra in 1962. Someone told me that he was in retirement near Homs. Abdul Majid has traced a student, Abeer Ibrahim Abdul Nur in the Faculty of Arts. She is brought to see me at 11 and I go off with her to Fairouza, a Christian village and virtual suburb of Homs. The village has close links with

Los Angeles and thousands have migrated there, more people than are in the village today. They return periodically for wedding parties.

I arrive with Abeer at their concrete house and meet Ibrahim, wizened, bald, patriarchal and gentle. He greets me with kisses on both cheeks, and introduces me to the family. Ibrahim does part-time work as a "sworn translator", assisting in the documentation for the emigrants who go to Burbank, a northern suburb of Los Angeles. He used to go to a Protestant church in Homs as a lad. As there is no Protestant church in Fairouza he goes to the Catholic church. He was a teacher from 1957 and did a degree in the early 1960s. The eldest son, Bassam, is an engineer here, working at the petrochemical plant. A second son, Ghassan, is in Burbank, married to a Fairouza childhood sweetheart who works as a cashier. Shadi, the youngest, is very bright. He got 287 marks out of a possible 290 in the Syrian ninth-grade exams, losing one mark in English and two in Religion. Ibrahim remembers snippets of conversation we had 30 years ago. We are served a syrupy home-made wine at the house. (They also make their own araq.) Bassam and Shadi take me to the old quarters of the village and also to the neighbouring village of Zaidan, whose inhabitants have close links with Jacksonville, Florida, similar to those Fairouza has with Burbank.

In the evening Abdul Majid takes us out to dinner. He has been a member of the Ba'th Party since 1956. As a secondary-school student in the 1950s he lived by himself in Nabk. The monthly rent for a room was 35 Syrian pounds – about three and a half UK pounds. His father, a policeman, gave him an allowance of two Syrian pounds a week. His grandparents migrated to Argentina but returned.

Wednesday, 10 March

I go off early to have a look at Homs, seeing the walls and visiting the Zinnar church, housing a belt that allegedly belonged to the

Blessed Virgin Mary. The church has been extended, thanks to donations from Homsi communities in New Jersey and Detroit.

Thursday, 11 March

I drive off through a blizzard to Damascus airport to greet the Minister of Culture on her return from her visit to the UK. She is full of excitement. "I did not realise what a great organisation the British Council was," says her husband, the General. The trip to Edinburgh where she met her old supervisor, Professor Montgomery Watt, was a huge success. She and the General had studied there and the place was full of "romantic souvenirs", as the General puts it in his Gallic English.

Friday, 12 March

We go to Hanan's for lunch. Hanan is trying to get her daughter, Reem, married to a nice Christian doctor from Saidnaya, who is also present with his amazingly youthful-looking mother, whom we first think is his sister or wife.

We have friends round for dinner. At 11.30 the doorbell rings. It is our neighbour, Ghasan ("God bless you; call me Gus"), garrulous, with a whisky bottle and glass in his hand. I manage to manoeuvre him out after half an hour.

Peter paid another visit to Beirut to see Hassana Jabr Salam who had been looking after British Council interests.

Peter had worked in the Beirut office for two months in 1970 and knew Beirut and Lebanon before the Civil War.

Monday, 15 March

I visit Lebanon. On the border I am met by the Management Officer of the British Embassy, who has served in China and Pakistan and loves Lebanon. We move off in convoy – two Land Rovers, lights on, charging past checkpoints, and driving past Tell al-Za'tar, a mass of rubble and breeze blocks.

Tuesday, 16 March

In the evening I have dinner with Farid Tabib, who taught me Arabic at MECAS in 1970 and is now a senior member of the Embassy staff. He thinks the United States is determined to get Syria to sign a peace agreement with Israel, and, knowing this, can call all the shots. Most of Assad's time is spent on Lebanon. I ask about the village of Shemlan. It is a Christian village but surrounded by Druze villages. "It is all controlled by Jumblatt now. I want to go back to my house there but it would be dangerous. 'You can have a barbecue,' we are told, 'but cannot spend a night there.'"

Wednesday, 17 March

My first appointment is with the Minister of Higher Education, Michel Eddé, a plump man, born in Lattakia. I am five minutes late, Hassana is ten minutes late, the Minister 15.

I go on to the museum which in the Civil War was one of the crossing points from west to east Beirut, *le passage*. Most buildings in the area have been battered. The tall, scholarly Director, Kamil Asmar, takes me round the museum, with its statues still enclosed behind cement barricades. Roman pillars are pitted like cheese. Different armies occupied the museum and soldiers' graffiti adorn the walls.

I have lunch with Hassana and her husband, Fuad Salam. Fuad is a joker and I listen to a recording of Hassana's speech, accepting her MBE. She was rehearsing it beforehand in the house and Fuad secretly taped it. We look through photographs. One is of Hassana's father, Abdul Halim Jabr, with Atatürk at Mersin in about 1920, a solemn group of men, with Mrs Atatürk, Latifa, in a headscarf.

Thursday, 18 March

I call on Najwa Nasr of the Lebanese University. She lived through all the Civil War. During the worst of the troubles she was trapped in her house and spent her waking hours translating a Barbara Cartland novel into Arabic.

Tuesday, 23 March

Damascus. It is the Eid, marking the end of Ramadan. Sermons are loudly broadcast. There were fireworks last night and a cannon fired off a dozen or more times after sunset. The citizens can be in no doubt that Ramadan is over.

Theresa, Nat and I leave Damascus and drive to Deir ez-Zor. The Furat Cham Palace is to the north of the town, overlooking a broad Euphrates that sluggishly drifts southwards. We go for a walk along the banks of the river. People are friendly and courteous. In a field a group of young men invite us to share their brown gin made at Homs. It is foul. We follow a branch of the river where some youths are shooting at birds. The frogs make a huge din.

Wednesday, 24 March

We set off on roads new to us – always a stirring and exciting experience – to the south. A chain of small villages derive water and sustenance from the Euphrates and are en fête for the Eid. We reach Dura Europus, with walls intact and with dry wadis around the citadel. The synagogue in the Damascus museum comes from here. The river sweeps along in broad curves with flat green patches of cultivation. I am reminded of the Sudanese Nile.

We go on to Abu Kemal, only a few kilometres from the Iraq border, and then double back to stop at Mari, a site going back to the third millennium BC. The site has been the preserve of the French – a man called Parrot was in charge of excavations for over 40 years.

Thursday, 25 March

We return across the desert to Palmyra and on to Harbaqa Dam. This is a Roman[2] construction, built in the middle of nowhere, over three-hundred-metres wide and surrounded by dusty hills. A swamp and intensive cultivation bear witness to the fact that the people of the nearby villages must have cause to bless the Romans. We pause, gaze and marvel.

Saturday, 27 March

Ayoub invites us round for tea. He lives in the Palestinian suburbs of Damascus. After feasting on the first day of the Eid, he is now fasting for a further six days. He has five children. We do not meet Haitham the eldest. But three younger ones are there – Muhammad aged ten, Ahmad aged eight or so, and Hiba aged six. Ahmad is a little tough guy. Muhammad a softie. Hiba is a spoiled brat who at one point lashes out at Muhammad who suffers uncomplainingly. The eldest daughter, Reem, joins us and then Nadia, Ayoub's wife, a distant cousin. When Ayoub is not in the room she is voluble. "I want a bigger house, but Ayoub doesn't. We are near the school and there have been cases of Palestinian children being kidnapped for medical experiments. I was 14 when I married Ayoub. He is very good. Everybody thinks the world of him. I don't think people should marry their cousins." And so on. But when Ayoub returns she becomes quiet and subdued.

Sunday, 28 March

I appoint a cousin of Bouchra – Bassam al-Usi – as driver/messenger/gardener from 13 April. I met him when he was eight in Yabrud – when I first met Bouchra. It is my first bit of Syrian nepotism.

2 No longer generally accepted as Roman.

Tuesday, 6 April

I take a letter to the Ministry of Culture at 8. All the doors are open but nobody is around on the ground floor. The Minister's room is wide open. I hang around for a minute, find nobody, so slip in and place it on her desk.

During the morning we have a visit from the new European Ambassador, Alan Waddams, his wife, Brigid, and younger daughter. The older daughter, aged 17, is sulking at the hotel. The younger one has been expelled from Wells Cathedral School and the parents do not know what to do with her. Theresa and I offer pastoral and educational advice.

Wednesday, 7 April

We go to lunch at 2 with Jane and Andrew Green. The other guests are the Minister of Culture and her husband, Majid al-Azmeh. They are very much a couple. He is a giggler, devoted to his garden and his vines. Although he has the rank of General, basically he is a doctor, having been head of the Army Medical Services. She is very professional, as she must be after 16 years in the same job. I suggest that she gives a press conference on her visit to Britain. She deflects that deftly. It is clear that she enjoyed her visit to Britain and is grateful to me.

Thursday, 8 April

At 5 or so we go for a Maundy Thursday tour of the Christian quarter. We wander with a group from church to church. At the Church of Ananias, a group of Africans come in with one white-haired gentleman. It is Julius Nyerere, the former President of Tanzania. There are only four or five in the party: two smart young Tanzanian diplomats are obviously bodyguards.

Saturday, 10 April

We drive up to Selinfe in the hills. It used to be the hill resort and summer headquarters of the Alawite State during the French Mandate.

Back in Lattakia we have dinner at Spiro's Restaurant with Tim Mackintosh-Smith and Jay Butler, who used to teach with the British Council in Yemen. Tim is writing a book on Yemen[3].

Monday, 12 April

We drive from Lattakia to Jisr al-Shughur and south through the flat Orontes valley. We locate Burzay Castle, park the car and walk up. And what a walk! The path is clear and makes its way through rock and a flower-bestrewn valley. We go round the back of the castle, perched above us. We come upon a little plain, with ruined houses and a few shepherds. Then one final heave up to the ruins of the Crusader castle. After that a slow walk back to the valley and the car. A young girl urges us to go to her house. She is insistent – an example of the tremendous warmth of the people here.

Thursday, 15 April

I take Tim and Jay to the airport. Tim tells me that Saddam Hussein, who was called "Keith" by the British expatriates in Baghdad, was in Sana'a. Tim, on his bicycle, was caught up in Saddam's motorcade. He made eye contact with "Keith" and they exchanged salutes. No doubt Tim, a tall, gangling figure on a bicycle, must have been a conspicuous figure.

At 9 I put on my dress suit and we go to the Sheraton Hotel for the wedding reception of the son of our landlord. There are about 200 guests and the bride and groom parade in at a quarter past ten. The couple cut a cake of *11* tiers with a sword. We are first to leave, after one.

---

3 Tim Mackintosh-Smith, *Yemen, Travels in Dictionary Land*, John Murray, London, 1997.

Friday, 16 April

We go to Bouchra's flat. A little later a bus turns up. We slowly pick up other relations and set off for Bosra – not Yabrud, as planned: the driver does not have permission to drive to Yabrud. We are joined by Hanan and her father, Abu Sulaiman, and by Nazmat, a writer of geography textbooks.

At Bosra there must be 40 or 50 coachloads of people. It is as if it is the first day of spring and all Damascus is abroad. We go into the Roman theatre. Pushing our way in is like leaving a football match. In the theatre groups dance to drums. One lad has a set of bagpipes. We clamber all over the place.

Back in Damascus we quickly change and are driven with our sons to the farm of Majid al-Azmeh and of Najah al-Attar. Their ophthalmologist daughter, Arwa, is also present. The Ambassador joins us. Our hosts have a pen of animals – brown Damascus goats, a baby lamb, one-week-old, with loose bowels. A peacock that opens its feathers for us. Guinea fowls. Turkeys including one elder statesman of a gobbler. Majid refers to Najah as "the second Zenobia" – the only previous Syrian woman to have achieved high political office.

Monday, 19 April

I call on Mahmud Zughaiby, Director of the Army Medical Services (and successor to Majid al-Azmeh). His daughter has a British passport and is a graduate in English at the University of Damascus. She has done a secretarial course in Leeds.

Tuesday, 20 April

High winds blow away the intense heat of the last few days. Rubbish swirls around the streets of the capital – and our back garden.

I call on Adam Ereli in his office at the United States Embassy and meet Hassana al-Azm, one of three sisters, whom Freya Stark wanted to marry off to Hugh Leach. I show her the picture taken in 1927 by Freya of two ladies sitting in the sun in the latest Paris fashions. They are still alive, aged 87 and 95. What fun it would be to have them at the opening of the exhibition of Freya's photographs!

Friday, 23 April

We go to dinner at the house of the Belgian Ambassador. We seem to have entered the First Division of social Damascus. Other guests are heads of missions. Our Ambassador seems surprised to see us there. The Minister of Culture is present and thanks me for the charming letter our sons sent her after the visit to her farm. I meet some of Damascus's filthy rich and find myself talking in four languages – I must make an attempt to improve my Turkish. There is a recital, after which we eat in the garden. I talk to a businessman from Deir ez-Zor about Abdul Salam al-Ujaili, a great man in those parts. He was a Minister in the 1950s.

Sunday, 25 April

We go to a recital at the Orthodox church in Qasa', the guests of Momchil Georgiev, the Bulgarian flautist at the Higher Institute of Music. We are just in time and are ushered to the front and sit next to a Greek Professor of Theology and two Orthodox priests, with beards and black gear, looking very orthodox and very priestly. What a bother for them if they have to go to a public urinal.

Monday, 26 April

In Homs, my host is the Deputy Dean of the Faculty of Arts, an authority on John Fowles. He complains of the poor standard of Soviet degrees. If you were accepted there you always got a degree. In Britain people failed. Standards were maintained.

I give a lecture on translation to about 250 students in a hall-theatre, tiered with seats. There is no microphone. Or rather, there is, but there is no electricity, so I have to shout and summarise my prepared text. Afterwards there are a lot of questions – pompous academic ones from the staff, intelligent, probing ones from students.

We go on to Fairouza and call on Ibrahim and his family. Abeer is newly engaged to George, who comes from the Fairouza community in Burbank. They both turn up. George is off to the United States tomorrow. He has a liquor store on a freeway. Older and very amiable, he invites us cordially to Burbank. They will get married on 11 July and have a honeymoon in Cyprus and Argentina. Ibrahim is not looking his best. He is a little deaf and is diabetic, which means his eyesight is failing. His wife, Insaf, tells me that he used to hunt sand grouse and was the best shot in Fairouza.

Wednesday, 28 April

I read a story by Hanna Mina – "Ala al-Akyas", "Among the Bales", which he suggested should be put into English. It is a charming tale, based on his childhood in Iskenderun. It ought to translate well. I would need to work on it and polish it to get the right degree of accuracy and innocence. It is strange how some tales are right for translation, others are not.

Meanwhile Theresa goes to the airport to meet her mother, Phillippa, and her daughter, Katie.

We rush around, getting ready for a party – 30 guests, a nice mixture of Syrian, British and American. Hazar Awad, the film actress, comes with her fiancé, Brendan. She is a great hit, sweet, poised, modest. Hassana al-Azm brings her brother, Qais. Hanan and her daughter, Reem. The Ambassador. Randal Keynes and his wife, Zelfa Hourani.

Friday, 30 April

I take Zelfa and Randal to Bloudan where we eat with a splendid view from the restaurant over the broad valley. This is part of Syrian life. Syrians have the capacity for enjoying life. Families of three or four generations enjoy their food, drink, each other and the view, and sing and dance to the beat of a drum.

Saturday, 1 May

I suggest to Zelfa, who is commissioning editor of Quartet Books, a translation of some of the short stories of Abdul Salam al-Ujaili. She is not encouraging and says, "He's old. He's male. And they are short stories." She wants another Hanan al-Shaykh. I must find a young female novelist.

Sunday, 2 May

I say farewell to Zelfa who is off to Beirut in a shared taxi. She will see her father, Cecil, who is due to call on President Hrawi, to ask for his grandchildren, Sammaya and Iskander, to have Lebanese nationality, a commodity not in great demand these days.

Tuesday, 4 May

I have a call from Eddie Peltenberg, an archaeologist at the University of Edinburgh. We talk of the British School of Archaeology in Amman, which I was involved in setting up years ago. "Yes," he says. "Your fingerprints, I have heard, are all over the Middle East."

I now have new teaching premises and I plan to start English classes on 1 August. British Council London will have to recruit a Teaching Manager. Meanwhile I have to furnish classrooms, recruit staff, send people off on training, select books. I hope I can soon have a Senior Teacher, but if necessary I will do it all myself.

Thursday, 6 May

I go to a concert and sit next to Christa Salamandra and Mary Tahhan. Mary is doing research on Syrian writers under Roger Allen at the University of Philadelphia. Mary tells me about Ulfat Idilbi – a woman's writer of value. I must get some of her fiction and see if it will work in English. I am determined to make a contribution to Syrian writing in English while I am here.

Friday, 7 May

Nat tells me that a nephew of the President, a 17-year-old slob, is at the American School. He has four bodyguards and has been throwing his weight around with the Principal. Nat feels strongly the injustice of it all. Good for him.

Outside the school I give some money to a beggar-woman. Just as I get a wan smile from her I am hit by a car, or rather, brushed by a car driven by a well-dressed woman on to the kerb. Some soldiers are standing by. I expostulate in Arabic that the pavement is for pedestrians. I wonder whether she is an Assad. I lose sight of the beggar-woman.

We go to Bloudan to have lunch with Jenny and Hanna Khoury. He is a psychiatrist and she is a potential English teacher with the British Council. There is an old building in Bloudan I have often wondered about. Hanna, who is from the village, tells me that it is the former British Consul's summer residence. It is known locally as *'unsuliyat 'Ud*, Wood's Consulate, presumably named after Sir Richard Wood, that wily old bird who, one hundred and fifty years ago, fixed for the British the Consulate – now the Ambassador's Residence – in Tunis. That information gives me much pleasure.

Monday, 10 May

There could be aid money from the Overseas Development Administration (ODA). When the Ambassador was taking up his post, he saw the Minister, Mrs Chalker (as she then was before the General Election) and asked for some aid money for Syria. "It will help the British Council," he said. "Our job," she replied, "is not to help the British Council."

In the evening I have dinner with Haitham al-Kawakibi, whose grandfather was a pioneering Arab nationalist a century ago. Haitham has been a teacher of mathematics, is a make-up artist for Syrian television, has written a book on behaviour, and campaigns against smoking. He feels strongly about language, disapproves of switching from one language to another and hates expressions like "Bye Bye" that have crept into Arabic.

Wednesday, 12 May

I call on the local Shell representative. Sir Peter Holmes approved the money for the Freya Stark exhibition, but the local office is having to find the funds. I apologise for going over his head. It has caused him embarrassment, but I am not really sorry. I exploited a connection and have got what I wanted.

I have been inveigled into organising a tea party at the Meridien Hotel to celebrate Florence Nightingale's birthday (today). Some nurses, General Zughaiby of the Army Medical Services and the Dean of the Faculty of Medicine at the University of Damascus turn up. The cost of the tea party in the superb Kassioun Room is the equivalent of two months' nurses' salary. But the excellent Sister Bridget of the Italian Hospital puts the Dean on the spot about the status of women and nurses.

Thursday, 13 May

Newspapers arrive. Freya Stark died on Sunday. There are obituaries by Malise Ruthven and by John Julius Norwich who recalls her going around Krak des Chevaliers in 1982 at the age of 89.

I phone my headquarters for authority to sign a lease on some offices. A is at a meeting. B has gone home early. C is off sick. D is on tour. I ask for someone to phone back. But nobody does.

Saturday, 15 May

I settle down and read 68 pages of Ulfat Idilbi's Damascus novel. It is a powerful tale and could be translated. It describes a Damascus family – actually from Saruja. A maiden aunt looks after an ailing grandfather who has been semi-paralysed for ten years. She organises a festival to commemorate 40 days after the death. This is elaborate and shocks her brothers and, more particularly, her sisters-in-law. They do not want to pay, but she has sold a carpet to cover the costs of the party. The rest of the family want to sell the old man's house and put the maiden aunt into a small room in a neighbour's house. She has loved the family house, has cultivated the garden, and looked after the cage birds. All for nothing. After a stand-up row when the aunt tells the family what she thinks of them, she hangs herself. And that is chapter one!

Tuesday, 18 May

I have a visit early from Mary Tahhan. We gossip for an hour. She is an American Aleppine who came back to Syria 20 years ago. Her family wanted to marry her off to a young man called Yusuf. An aunt was in charge of the process of winning her over, but she constantly said No. "What happened to Yusuf?" I ask. "He took Canadian citizenship and has been very prosperous working in oil in Saudi Arabia." We also talk about Ulfat Idilbi and her book.

Wednesday, 19 May

I have a letter from Malise Ruthven. John R Murray phoned him with the news of the death "of the old lady". I also receive copies of the photographs of Freya Stark I have selected. They look good. I look at them repeatedly.

Theresa and I go to tea with Nadia al-Ghazzi. We are casually dressed but her first guests, and Nadia herself, are dressed, as only westernised Arabs of the Levant can be dressed, up to the tens. I talk to a nice doctor about Hanna Mina. He says the mixture of Christianity and Marxism in his novels produces an interesting tension.

Thursday, 20 May
I receive a letter from Buckingham Palace, full of Tudor English, "Sir, I am commanded to request your presence at an investiture."

Saturday, 22 May
Theresa, Nat and I go for a walk along the northern walls of the city, looking in at the citadel and noting each successive gate, the different styles of the walls and the material used. The Aqsab mosque has a square minaret and Gothic windows. The 14th-century Sultan Hammam, where I used to go for a Turkish bath 20 years ago, is now a furniture store.

Ahmad al-Isa, one of those Syrians who speaks with a gorgeously plummy Oxford accent, calls to introduce one of his fourth-year students, whose uncle bicycled to Turkey and wrote a book about it. We are invited to dinner at a rich Syrian house, which strikes me as utterly vulgar. Rich, malcontent, grasping, ugly.

Sunday, 23 May
I take the train to Aleppo. It is dirty. The first class is undoubtedly comfortable and stress-free. The line skirts Damascus and bypasses both Homs and Hama. It seems to be a custom for the train to run a gauntlet of stones, thrown by small boys. Several windows have been shattered and I am conscious of pelts and blows aimed at the train, which moves steadily at about 40 miles an hour.

Monday, 24 May
I call on the Rector of the University of Aleppo. We talk about the Muslim Brothers. In the late 1970s members of the University staff

were assassinated by them. "You must have been a target," I say. "Yes, and I am authorised to have a pistol here," and he shows me a small gun, hidden to view, by his desk.

I call on Ismat Mudarris. He is the Netherlands Consul. His son, Husain, has a wonderful collection of old postcards – hundreds and hundreds – of Syria. He also has postcards of old 1920s film stars, and others from the same era with sentimental love messages.

In an antique shop I buy a fascinating three-volume guide (in French) to Antioch and the region, written by a French soldier, in 1931.

Tuesday, 25 May

I locate what used to be the old Altounyan Hospital, now a school and in a poor state of repair. A school official shows me around, apparently unaware of its glorious past and literary associations[4].

I call on the Chamber of Commerce and meet the Embassy's Commercial Attaché. We meet some of the big merchants – cotton, plastics and so on. In February the Chamber of Commerce sent a delegation to Adana. I see the brochure of the visit which is all in English. Strange, for the merchants of both cities probably speak both Turkish and Arabic.

At the Baron Hotel I have a drink with Sally Mazloumian. We look at some splendid photographs taken by her late husband, Koko. There is one of Freya Stark that I would like to use for the exhibition catalogue. Sally talks of Freya, how she could be kind, thoughtful and full of human sympathy. She (and Koko) used to cheat at Scrabble. When confronted, Freya would say, "I wondered when you'd catch me out."

I walk to the railway station and meet Hugh Leach, tall, pipe-smoking, alert. He has recently been camel riding in Sinai.

4 See Taqui Altounyan, *In Aleppo Once*, John Murray, London, 1969 and Taqui Altounyan, *Chimes from a Wooden Bell*, I B Tauris, London and New York, 1990.

Wednesday, 26 May

I give a talk to the staff of the English Language Advisory Centre at the University of Aleppo. The Director, Ghias Barakat, is active in the Party, secretary of the University branch. He has access and leverage in all sorts of matters. We go on to have lunch at the Teachers' Club with the fat cats of the Party and academia.

The Commercial Attaché and I host a reception for 50 or more guests: Aleppo millionaires, Ba'th Party functionaries, Kawakibis, Mudarrises, academics.

Thursday, 27 May

The University has lent me a car and a driver for the day. Hugh and I take advantage of it and travel out to Qal'at Sam'an, the monastery and shrine dedicated to St Simeon Stylites. The road goes through a suburb of sensibly designed housing, not too high and making use of the local cool, white stone. Then through rolling countryside, olive plantations, with outcrops of rock and fields full of peasants. The villages are attractive too – not too much concrete or breeze blocks. Syria has changed less than any other Arab country over the last generation.

Friday, 28 May

Hugh and I wander along to an antique shop. We pass an ancient Citroën on the way. Now Hugh likes old cars and marvels at it. The owner is nowhere near but Hugh opens up the bonnet and, to the encouragement of male passers-by, inspects the works. In the antique shop, he finds a bugle and, to the amazement of the shopkeeper, plays a Sudanese reveille on it.

We then call on Ismat and Husain Mudarris and pore over old photographs. Ismat mentions that the flag is being raised on the new Armenian Consulate at noon today and we think it might be a good idea to go along. Ismat puts on a smart suit – as Honorary Consul he is representing the Netherlands – but we are less well dressed. We all go together to the Armenian cathedral in an area called Villat. The whole district, including the balconies, is thronged with people. We are ushered to the front of the packed church though we feel as if we are there under false pretences. Many superbly dressed bishops are on parade. Incense and pretty girls, and then a splendid oration from a Bishop all in Armenian, of which we understand not a word. We next find ourselves in a procession and move slowly out of the church. A band plays vigorously outside and we walk three hundred yards along the road. Every balcony is crowded. We are shoulder to shoulder right across the road. Women ululate. Sweets, rice, coins and flowers are thrown by people applauding and crowded on the balconies. The Armenian Ambassador in front of the procession greets people with a clenched fist. At the Armenian Consulate a rather tatty cardboard box is raised aloft and a dozen doves are pushed out. Portraits of President Assad and of the Armenian President, Ter Petrossian (who, I am told, was born in Aleppo) are held high. The band enthusiastically plays the Syrian National Anthem and then, to tumultuous applause as the flag on the Consulate is raised, the Armenian National Anthem. All deeply moving. There are three million Armenians in the Armenian Republic and six and a half million in the world. Aleppo has the largest Armenian community in the Middle East – 200,000. Hence the significance of the occasion which neither of us would have missed witnessing for worlds.

Ismat later tells us that the Kurds are the largest minority in Aleppo. There is an Assyrian community in the area called Siriani. They migrated from Mosul in Iraq and Mardin in southern Turkey. He also tells us of a massacre of Bengal Lancers in 1919 north of the city. After Damascus fell to Lawrence and Faisal in the winter of 1918, the Turkish commander, Mustafa Kemal, later Atatürk, was withdrawing his defeated army and said to the pursuing Bengal

Lancers, "I do not want a fight. I am retreating." But the Bengalis persisted. So he took them on, ten miles north of Aleppo and massacred them, at a place known as Maqbarat Ingliz.

Saturday, 29 May

Theresa and Nat have joined us. After a final call at the University we are ready to set off in our car, but it seems I have lost the car key. Panic! Gloom! It is nowhere to be found. With the help of the hotel we consult the Peugeot dealer. "There is only one man who can help. That is Malik al-Mafatih ("King of the Keys"), Muhammad Tahir al-Bili. We find him and have no alternative but to accept his price. The window door is slightly open and Hugh, with a piece of wire, manages to open the door. Then the King of the Keys is soon at work, an obvious professional. We go to his workshop. He has a master key that can get the car moving. Theresa takes Nat to the souk. Hugh is interested in acquiring a new skill – lock breaking. I have a sense of responsibility and stay with the car. The King removes the ignition lock altogether and takes it to pieces on his workshop bench, reducing it to smaller and smaller components. Meanwhile people come in with emergency jobs and the King takes time off to deal with them. He reassembles the lock, provides us with a key, and reassembles the car, all the time with the key in his mouth, glasses pushed up on his head, a pencil behind his ear, screws in his hand or between his lips. We are at last able to drive off.

We drive east to Jerablus and meet the team from the University of Edinburgh. Jerablus is right on the Turkish-Syrian border near the site of the Hittite city of Carchemish, excavated by Leonard Woolley and T E Lawrence in 1911 or so. We can see the huge tell of Carchemish on the Turkish side of the frontier formed today by the railway, the Berlin to Baghdad line, which crosses the Euphrates by a fine suspension bridge. We walk along a track to it and then by the river and come across a primitive awning structure on the riverbank. It is a bar and we stop for a beer. What a perfect location, the best bar any of us have ever known! The man who sells us beer is a Turk who used to work in Beirut, having a café in Hamra until the Israeli invasion. As well as beer – at a very good price – he could also provide food – fish from the Euphrates. We stay to watch the sun set and stroll back to Jerablus. As we walk through the village we meet an old man who is very depressed – old age and various ailments. "I'm 82," he says. "You'll be a bridegroom next year," I cheerily say. He puts his hand to his crutch and says, "*Ma fi.*" ("Nothing there"). We stay overnight with the team who occupy a house in the village. Next door is a family of a woman and seven children. Father works in Beirut as a taxi-driver.

Sunday, 30 May

It has not been a comfortable night in a stuffy room shared with silent mosquitoes. We are only aware of them after they have taken action.

After breakfast we go to the archaeological site, a tell near the river. We are given a tour of their work which has unearthed stuff from Uruk to Hellenistic times.

We push on, over a pontoon bridge over the Euphrates and through villages on the eastern bank. Many houses have raised platforms in their gardens – for sleeping? Stores? We reach a main road, double back to Membij and then to Qal'at al-Najm. This castle is on a spur overlooking a bend of the Euphrates. We clamber over the ruins and enjoy the views. I have a postcard-size copy of the photograph Freya Stark took of the castle and we find the exact spot from where she took it. Hugh is able to work out what kind of camera she used. We drive down to the riverbank and inspect huge metal tubs, called *khal*, that are used as ferry boats. People nip across the river in them at great speed.

We go on to al-Raqqa for the night.

Monday, 31 May

We have to return to Damascus. Hugh goes on to Deir ez-Zor. He has enjoyed Syria – "Asia's best-kept secret," he says. Theresa's daughter, Kate, recently wrote, "I don't want to talk to anyone who does not know Syria." What is so lovely is that the country has not changed substantially or significantly since the 1960s. People are warm, friendly, hospitable. There is a balance of town and country, and the provincial towns are as charming and undemanding as ever.

Friday, 4 June

I read some stories by Nadia al-Ghazzi. They seem to be based on cases that have come her way in the course of her legal work. They are full of feminine consciousness, with women as victims. The language is ornate and I do not think they are suitable for translation.

Hugh returns. He has had a full time, meeting Armenians in Deir ez-Zor, the Hungarian Ambassador to Alma Ata in Palmyra, and leading Isma'ilis in Salamiya.

The Defence Attaché is back from Britain. They returned on a Lufthansa flight. While they were airborne the Chief Pilot had a heart attack, slumped over the controls and the plane lurched all over the place. The cabin crew were called to the cockpit – Emergency – to prise him off the controls. He was taken out on a stretcher at Brussels. The largely British passengers were cool, nervously looking at their newspapers.

Saturday, 5 June

We go out to dinner with Sulaiman Ahmed and his wife, Sa'da. The English of them both is perfect. He talks about "service" without a trace of cynicism. He has a command of English expressions such as "the school of hard knocks" and we look at his edition of *Two on a Tower* by Thomas Hardy, of which he is rightly proud. He earns 11,000 Syrian pounds a month. They have no car but do have a place in Tartus.

Tuesday, 8 June

I write to Zelfa Hourani at Quartet Books, offering to translate Ulfat Idilbi's book, *Dimashq Ya Basmat al-Huzn.*

During the morning Allen Hibbard drops in with a copy of his book on Paul Bowles. *The Cimarron Review* is to produce a number focussing on Syrian literature and I offer to translate some characteristic stories.

Wednesday, 9 June

The Office Manager, Ayoub, passes his driving test. I congratulate him on joining the army of potential murderers.

At home we have a surprise visit from Bouchra and Mirfat Urfa, a demure, attractive girl wearing neat and correct Islamic dress and reeking of jasmine perfume. The smell lingers on in the house for several hours after they leave.

Thursday, 10 June

We have a problem about recruiting people. Apparently the British Council has no formal identity and newspapers will not accept our advert unless countersigned by the Ministry of Culture. I am told I cannot use the name The British Council because it does not exist.

Friday, 11 June

I read in the courtyard, *hawsh*, of our flat, though there is the whiff of the drains. I did think that while Theresa is away later in the summer I would sleep each night in the *hawsh*, but the drains and the mosquitoes have changed my mind. And the cats. They lurk, the villainous and the endearing, on the walls and have not deterred a rat I saw a week ago. I do not fancy sharing my bed with a strange cat or have it slept on during the day by mangy beasts.

Saturday, 12 June

We go to Kanawat, having read the section in Freya Stark's *Letters from Syria*, in which she writes of her visit in 1928. I take with me a photograph of Ahmad al-Hajari, the Druze sheikh she stayed with, another of his son, Ibrahim, and grandson, Husain. If Husain is still alive he would be in his late sixties. The museum curator takes us to a majlis in the village. A portrait of Sheikh Ahmad al-Hajari dominates the wall and we meet women from the Hajari household. Husain, we learn, died as a boy. The present head of the family, Sheikh Ahmad, is another grandson of Freya Stark's Sheikh Ahmad. We meet him in his majlis, with pictures on the wall of his father: one with an ancient Lebanese Druze, another with Crown Prince Hassan of Jordan.

Back in Damascus we have dinner with the Hibbards. One of the other guests is Husain Omran and his wife. She is a cousin both of the wife of the Lebanese leader, Walid Jumblatt, and of Nadia al-Ghazzi. Husain tells me that the Hajaris are one of three Syrian Druze families that provide religious leaders. The Druze political leaders have come from the Atrash family.

Tuesday, 22 June

At 6 we go to the Queen's Birthday Party at the Ambassador's Residence. It is, I work out, the 25th I have attended. Someone (I cannot remember who) gives me a signed copy of short stories by Muhammad Ibrahim al-Ali, a senior army/party figure. I talk literature to the Palestinian representative. Mustafa Tlas, the Minister of Defence, is present and Hanan introduces me to him.

Friday, 25 June

I buckle down to translating Ulfat Idilbi's novel. During the day I translate 3,000 words, using four dictionaries.

Saturday, 26 June

I buy some flowers and take a taxi to Muhajirin and call on Ulfat Idilbi. She is a tremendous lady, 81, alert, fit and articulate. We are soon chatting away in Arabic about her work. She shows me translations into German, Russian and Chinese. She comes from Midan, married young and became involved in the Women's Professional and Cultural Movement, although she herself had no profession. She wrote some short stories for the Movement's magazine, and in the 1940s won a prize from the BBC Arabic service. Meanwhile she had three children. One son is an Oxford graduate. Another works in London with Wafic Said. She gives me permission to translate *Dimashq*, which was first published in 1980, when she was 68. I am with her for over two hours – I thought it would be only 45 minutes!

Allen Hibbard and I are taken off late at night by the actor, Jamal Sulaiman, to an amazingly seedy nightclub somewhere in the suburbs of the city. It is full of decadent young Saudis and Gulfis. Girls come onto the stage to dance. There is no grace and they keep their clothes on. It is all very boring. Home at 3.

Sunday, 27 June

Having moved to new premises, I am now able to recruit some more staff. We have over 80 applications for three posts. They include five PhD holders – one has two PhDs – and they range in age from 22 to 62. I work out priorities and whittle the number down to a shortlist of 15.

Monday, 28 June

I go to the Spanish Cultural Centre to see an exhibition of paintings by Hala al-Faisal who greets me warmly. She is 35, has been an actor, is a poet, was educated in Moscow and is off to Paris next week. I buy one of her paintings, of two women, together, but not communicating with each other. Hala is a vulnerable but active woman.

Tuesday, 29 June

We now have 150 applications for jobs. I go through them all carefully. Riad Ismat calls. He is interested in the senior job. He has published volumes of short stories and studied drama in Britain. At present he is earning 40,000 Syrian pounds as Press Officer at the Kuwaiti Embassy. He tells me that Hani al-Rahib has made a statement defending Salman Rushdie. I learn also that Hani, when he was teaching at the University of Damascus, compared Assad to Sadat and was transferred to a post as a secondary-school teacher. He was lucky, I am told. Hani comes from Qardaha, the President's village. He could have been imprisoned, or even executed.

Wednesday, 30 June

I settle down to translating more Ulfat and do 2,500 words. It all flows easily and I am able to work at speed.

Thursday, 1 July

In the end we have had 209 applications for three posts. 206 people are going to be disappointed. How to make 206 enemies!

Saturday, 3 July

Ian, the new Director of the Teaching Centre, Ayoub and I interview a procession of candidates for the post of Registrar of the Teaching Centre. We are all impressed by one woman. But Ayoub corners me later. He does not want a woman. "They burst into tears when under stress. They are emotional."

Monday, 5 July

I spend the morning interviewing people for the post of Assistant to the Director, (me). Riad Ismat is an outstanding individual but lacks the qualities required. One man wants to retain his job as Lecturer in Bioengineering at the University. One woman has done her homework and is obsessive about facts and figures about Britain, but she fails to impress, especially as she tells me there are 46 universities in Britain. (There are, since the upgrading of Polytechnics, now 96.). But Motaz Hadaya is smart and presentable. I know and like him. He ought to be all right.

Tuesday, 6 July

I do some more interviewing. Some exclude themselves – a semi-veiled girl, an unshaven youth, a shifty young man. But the first candidate is an impressive girl called Souha Hajjar.

I go to Douma for lunch with Nabil Batal and Vanda. I get Nabil talking about Syrian politics. Since 1968 he has been a member of the Ba'th Party which he compares to the British Social Democratic Party. There are branches of the Party everywhere and at each level: a *far'* for the University, a *sha'ba* for each Faculty and a *firqa* for each Department. He is aware of a large number of politically conscious people from his village, Deir Attiyeh, who have been detained. Likewise Alawites. He talks of the junta of Alawite generals who are more important than the Assad family, most of whom are rubbish. The President is very ill and all eyes are on the future. He has bad blood that needs to be constantly changed. His lungs and kidneys are not responding. Khaddam is the most likely successor: a Sunni from Baniyas.

President Assad lived another seven years. He was succeeded by his son, Bashar. Vice-President Khaddam left the country and spearheaded opposition to the new President in 2005.

Peter went to Britain for a fortnight in July, primarily to collect his OBE at Buckingham Palace.

Wednesday, 14 July

Theresa, my son Paul and I are up at 7 and on the road from Ealing to Central London. There is a slow build-up of traffic and it takes us an hour to get to Trafalgar Square, where we collect my sister, Stella. We go on to Buckingham Palace, queuing up outside, with a special sticker on our windscreen that lets us through the gates and into an inner courtyard.

There are 130 other recipients. I am separated from my guests and go into a long corridor full of paintings and meet fellow-recipients. I fall into conversation with Michael Aspel, a television personality. We are then briefed by Palace flunkeys who tell us exactly what to do when we receive our award from the Queen. Then, in batches, we proceed in a long, slow line into the ballroom where our guests are seated, facing a stage where some officials are seated. The slow line of recipients is full of worthy people and I wonder to myself, "Am I part of all this?" At one point I am overcome with emotion, almost in tears. My parents would have been so proud. To pull myself together I concentrate on details – on the John Gielgud-like flunkeys. We are courteously moved forward by these officials, as each of us has his or her 12 seconds with the Queen. When it is my turn, I advance to a few feet from the Queen, turn to face her, bow, go up to her. She pins the OBE to my lapel with the words, "It gives me great pleasure to give you this." She asks me where I am now serving. "Syria, Your Majesty," I reply, "but I was in the United Arab Emirates, where I had the honour of looking after your son." When she speaks her tone is one of intimacy, almost of coquetry. She gives a very good act of being interested. She shakes hands – no gloves – and I withdraw, walk backwards, bow again and proceed out to join the others in the body of the ballroom. It is all done smoothly and with a minimum of fuss. The ballroom is an attractive room, with a gallery where a band is playing tunes from musicals, the conductor facing the Queen. Then the National Anthem is played and one of the officials, the Lord Chamberlain apparently, asks everybody to stand. The Queen leaves, and so do we for pictures to be taken in the courtyard.

I have lunch with Stella, her husband John, Paul and Theresa in the Travellers' Club.Later on we host a reception at the British Council. I keep my morning suit on, but do not wear the top hat! The first to arrive is my Uncle Dick, aged 90. Then other relations, people who have known me since childhood. I am so pleased with these links from the past. Three Ambassadors and lots of colleagues and friends. To my surprise Edmund Marsden makes a speech. I reply saying that I am basically a backpacker.

Monday, 19 July

Back in Damascus, I have heaps of work to do. I have the Freya Stark photographs, enlarged for the exhibition, and arrange them in the sequence they will be displayed. I withdraw one of Broumana, which is not Syria. After all I am including one of the source of the River Jordan on the occupied Golan Heights. That is unequivocally Syria. I look through the Freya Stark books and plan a weekend tour to visit places she went to.

Wednesday, 21 July

At the Embassy "prayer meeting" I meet up with Brian Stewart, the new Number Two in the Embassy, after five years. He has been dealing with drugs and AIDS since leaving Tunisia. I propose a dinner party in his honour, inviting my particular friends and people I would like to know better – Hala al-Faisal, Riad Ismat, Hani al-Rahib, Nadia al-Ghazzi and so on.

I have a phone call from my headquarters. I have written a minute in which I talked about extra cash being "dosh off the back of a lorry". I am told off: "we are not to talk in language like that."

Thursday, 22 July

I write up my Acknowledgements for the Freya Stark catalogue. I will have to write a brief introduction and intitulate the pictures. Freya Stark is full of quotable maxims. Some are pearls of wisdom, others are utter crap. An example of the former is her observation that it is not what you see, but how you see it, that matters.

I fill the car with books and set off for Tartus. I check into the Daniel Hotel (200 Syrian pounds for a double room). I am fed up with luxury hotels with grossly inflated dollar charges. There is a whiff in the bedroom on the fourth floor, but otherwise all is satisfactory.

I go for a walk along the cornice. Tartus is becoming a Syrian resort for the urban middle class. Plastic toys, rubber dinghies and blown-up plastic fish make the place very different from what it was in 1939 when Freya Stark was here.

Other guests at this hotel are young and French.

The bill for my Investiture party of 14 July comes through – over £1,000. Thirty-two bottles of champagne were consumed.

Friday, 23 July

I go to explore the citadel part of Tartus, and find it enchanting. A small square is surrounded by buildings old and new, with medieval structures being used, added to and adapted for domestic use.

I then set off for Khawabi. I have to ask the way all the time. The road drops into ravines and through exciting mountain country, rugged yet gentle, olive-clad and secluded. Khawabi was one of the Assassin castles Freya Stark photographed. The castle still has houses with people living in them. I have with me a photo taken by Freya Stark, and try to take a picture from the same spot. I meet an elderly man, Salih Ahmad Raqiya, who identifies a man in Freya Stark's photograph as Sheikh Muhammad Adawiya. He was the imam and taught Salih how to read Arabic. I have coffee and a chat with Salih on the roof of his house.

I then go to the village of Alleika. Some village lads take me round the ruins of the castle. We look at the picture Freya Stark took in May 1939 and work out the point from which she took it, not from the fragment of ruins, but from the position of a walnut tree. There are some little girls in the Freya Stark photograph and I ask about some older person in the village who might be able to identify them. Hamdan Ramadan, I am told. His house is pointed out. In the garden I meet a group of folk sitting under a tree. A mother and her 19-year-old daughter are sewing tobacco leaves to a thread for compulsory sale to a branch of the government, still referred to as the *Régie*, which was an instrument of oppression in the 1930s, according to Hanna Mina's novels. They are a wonderful family. Not very helpful with identifying the children in the picture, but we chat for an hour. One son is a teacher. His grandfather, Hamdan, is 88 and remembers Freya Stark. "She took a picture of me, and promised to send me a copy. She never did." I find myself defending her explaining that war broke out shortly after her visit and it might be that post could not get through.

I drive on to Hama and stay at the Cairo Hotel

Saturday, 24 July

Yesterday my Alleika friends gave me a lot of apples. I left them in the car overnight. This morning the car has a lovely apple aroma.

I go to the Bishriya waterwheel – *noria* – which Freya photographed in 1939. It is one of 24 in Hama.

I do not linger but drive on to Shaizar where I am greeted by a score of kids. I spend half an hour scrambling over the castle that overhangs the Orontes by 50 metres. The castle housed a village until the 1940s.

Then on to Apamia, a wonderful classical site. The museum is a magnificent Ottoman khan and there is an Ottoman mosque on the hill leading up to the castle, which is still a crowded agricultural village. Little can have changed for centuries. I wander round and then, sadly, head south.

Monday, 26 July

I go to the United States Embassy and see Hassana al-Azm and show her the photos taken by Freya Stark. She coos with pleasure and brings in her sister, Lina, who also works in the Embassy. The land behind the Bishriya *noria* in Hama was "ours", she says. The khan in Homs "belonged to us". The pictures of two aunts "were taken on our estates at Raihan".

"So many people have entered politics and become rich," she observes. "We were rich and moved into politics. But now we have nothing."

I do not believe that for a moment, but do say,

"I suppose you have to take the long term view. You had it good in the 18th and 19th centuries."

Lina says that Freya borrowed some Yemeni manuscripts from her uncle, Nazih. These were not returned.

Tuesday, 27 July

I join the Ambassador, the Commercial Attaché and other Embassy staff on a series of visits to people in Homs. We are in two or three cars and are escorted by a man from the Homs Chamber of Commerce. First the Acting Governor, who is also the Chief of Police. Then, with six bodyguards in attendance, we call on the regional secretary of the Ba'th Party. This is an innovation for the Ambassador. Is this my influence? I have told him that a man is to be judged by the size of his retinue. So eight or ten of us are tagging along behind him. The third call is on the head of the University.

Homs is a city with over a million people – 1.3 million according to the Chamber of Commerce. Traditionally it has had strong links with Tripoli in Lebanon, only 90 kilometres away, nearer than either Damascus or Aleppo. Wednesday is a special day in Homs – *waqfa Humsiya* – when Homsis can do whatever they like. There is total freedom of speech and it is an excuse for any aberrant behaviour.

We all have lunch as the guests of the Chamber of Commerce. It is an exhausting marathon. The main course comes – after three earlier courses – after four o' clock. I am longing for an hour to sleep and an hour in the bath. Mercifully we get back to the hotel at about half past five.

The Ambassador hosts a reception at the hotel. About a hundred turn up, mainly commerce and the University. Guests appreciate the attention paid to Homs. Samer of the Department of English is getting married to a spivvy Aleppine businessman called Tariq. I am invited to a wedding celebration afterwards and stay till half past one. I dance with the bride and sit with the men who include Abdul Majid, head of the University. Someone tells me a Homs joke. A Homsi was in the United States and, looking glum, he is asked whether he is homesick. He replies: "How do you know I come from Homs?"

Wednesday, 28 July

The Embassy team have lunch at the hotel and I talk to the manager, Ibrahim Sheikh Yassin. Tomorrow night they have a Lebanese singer, Walid Tawfiq, who, with his backing of ten, will cost the hotel half a million Syrian pounds. Tickets will be 2,000 Syrian pounds a head – just over £30.

Friday, 30 July

I translate over 6,000 words of Ulfat Idilbi's book. It is most enjoyable to do this, regardless of other people, commitments, time, anything else. All I am concerned with is teasing out a meaning, transforming the squiggles in the Arabic book into meaningful squiggles in my huge notebook. There are plenty of puzzles and some uncertainties. I mark these and will go over them with one of my colleagues.

Saturday, 31 July

I travel south and call at two sixth-century churches at Ezra, St George and St Elias. I am invited to have some lukewarm coffee with Father Farhan. He offers sweets. "Take three," he says in Arabic. "One for the Father, one for the Son and one for the Holy Ghost."

Then on to Resas, which Freya Stark visited in 1928, shortly after the suppression of the Druze Revolt against the French Mandate had left the village in ruins. One of Freya Stark's photographs is of a family, a branch of the Atrashes. Some of the children in that photograph may still be alive. The central man in the picture is Mut'ib al-Atrash. In Resas I find for the Atrash house. It is full of nubile girls, giggling and friendly. I should see their father, Hamza, they say. They outline the Atrash family tree to me. I am taken to a room on the walls of which is a photo of the splendidly venerable Sultan Pasha al-Atrash, leader of the Druze Revolt. Hamza, they say, will be here at 4 – three hours later. I go off to the small town of Salkhad and take a photo of the Ayubid citadel, roughly from where Freya Stark took hers 65 years ago.

Hamza bin Hail bin Mut'ib – and therefore a grandson of Freya Stark's Mut'ib – was born after 1928 but he identifies all the people in the photo I have brought. Only one is still alive, Ha'ila, the smallest pretty girl on Mut'ib's lap. She currently lives in Damascus. Other people in the younger generation emigrated, as did many from Jabal Druze, to Venezuela. Two of the children in the photograph were children of Hassan al-Atrash, a brother-in-law of Mut'ib. Hassan was married (twice) to the charismatic singer, Esmahan, who died in mysterious circumstances in Egypt in the late 1940s. I translate what Freya Stark wrote about the family in *Letters from Syria*. "One of your uncles was deaf from childhood." ("Yes, yes.")

Monday, 2 August

I throw a few things into a bag and an Embassy car takes me to the Lebanese border. I am met by the usual two vehicles and a British security man (Craig). Does this mean that the security is upgraded? I ask him what the effects of the war have been. The Israelis fly supersonic jets over Beirut each day, breaking the sound barrier and creating a big bang. There are daily Hizbollah funerals that turn into large demonstrations. And there is a flow of refugees from the south, but they are not allowed into Beirut.

Traffic in Beirut is worse than ever and it takes an hour to get from the outskirts to the Embassy. I have no programme for three hours, so I go with my driver, Tony, to Bikfaya, to see Marie-Reine, who was my Lebanese Personal Assistant in Abu Dhabi. Her father, Musa, is poorly, shaking and helpless, needing constant attention. Musa's brother and family have been visiting Bikfaya for the first time for ten years or more. He has been a trader in Mauritania but has now retired to Las Palmas. I am a witness to tearful farewells as the brother and his family go off . . . for another ten years? Who then will be still alive? Marie-Reine is thoroughly happy pointing out things around the house – her childhood room, the garden. We stroll around the village. The house of Maurice Gemayel. Sheikh Pierre's house. Her father was a pharmacist and used to work for Pierre. The village square where girls and boys used to meet and eat ice cream together.

Wednesday, 4 August

On my return to Damascus, I propose to the six bodyguards (or BGs, as they are called) that we return not through Beirut but over the hills by Bikfaya and Zahle. We climb up the quieter mountain road that has a 1950s or 1960s feel to it. We pass near Zarour, a Shi'ite village, and Aintoura, that used to be a major Maronite religious centre. At Zahle I want to buy some araq. We stop at a shop and two bodyguards shadow me as I go inside.

Friday, 6 August

I buy some flowers and take a taxi to Jisr al-Abyad, to the Azm villa. The house is full of Azms, even though more of their property has recently been confiscated. I am taken in to see Amat al-Latif, the "Handmaiden of God" in Freya Stark's *Letters from Syria*. She is frail and bedridden, the very picture of old age – she is 95 – and I sit at her bedside, while Hassana and other relations buzz in and out of the room. We talk of Freya Stark and she becomes quite animated. "Freya took some documents from my brother Nazih to copy," she tells me. "They were about getting to Marib. Nazih went to Yemen with Charles Crane. She never returned them." I show her an enlarged photograph (which is in the book). The "squire", referred to by Freya Stark was Najib Ghazzi, her maternal uncle. "There's my handbag," she says, pointing at the photograph. I had not noticed that before. I feel as if I am a character in a Dickens novel, hearing a deathbed confession or extracting some vital and melodramatic bit of information before she slumps back and dies. I am next taken in to see the younger sister, Ni'mat, aged 89, also bedridden, having recently broken her hip. She is even brighter and I hope will be well enough to come to the opening of the exhibition in October.

The rest of us go on to the balcony. Ni'mat, I am told, was going to be married to Zaid, the youngest son of Hussein of the Hijaz, the nominal leader of the Arab Revolt. Her sister, Sara, was married to the 1930s Syrian nationalist leader, Dr Abdul Rahman Shahbandar. She was known as "Umm al-Suriyin", Mother of the Syrians. Dr Shahbandar was imprisoned and when he was released there was a reception in this house. There are floor tiles sunk into the ground, the result of the pressure of people who came to greet him. Freya Stark used to refer to "the sheikh", Hassana's father. He was Dr Yasir Muayyad al-Azm and was probably in his early thirties when Freya Stark first met him in 1928. There is much Freya talk. Dr Yasir and she used to greet each other – "Ya Fareya!" "Ya Sheikh!" After graduating from the American University of Beirut, Yasir worked with the Sudan Medical Services for a couple of years. I am told that in the 1930s he had an affair with a British lady who was somehow connected with the Royal Family.

Saturday, 7 August

I go to the Midan area of Damascus, south of the city. It used to be the area where the pilgrims camped before setting off for Mecca. Shops, catering for their needs, used to line the road. But where did the Midan wealthy live?

I have tea with Georgette Jabbour and meet her brother, George. He is a political scientist and involved in human rights. He has just published a little history of his home town of Safita, which he would like me to translate.

Sunday, 8 August

I have an unpleasant night, coughing away and spluttering.

In the afternoon I am taken to the Shami Hospital, and am told I must come in for 24 hours. I am diagnosed as having viral bronchitis.

I collect some personal effects and go back into hospital at seven and become some kind of package. Routine things are done to me – blood pressure and X-ray. Things are stuck to my feet and my arms. I am institutionalised with the hospital pyjamas and am given an intraviral drip. A Dr Usama Tawil who has practised in Worthing is my minder.

Monday, 9 August

I am in hospital all day. It is a mixture of hotel and prison. People, nurses, come in before eight to probe me and inspect me. I am hardly aware of what is going on but patiently (yes, that is the word, patiently) submit to everything.

My room has a view that looks on to the hills, a view that includes Ulfat Idilbi's house. I read three of her stories.

I also have visitors. Half my British Council colleagues come and see me at 10. The other half at 2. Bouchra comes also at 2 with Lilas. She tells me she dreams of me and thinks of me a lot. It is a responsibility to be thus considered. It is also interesting that she tells me.

Minutes and hours go by. I finish Freya Stark's *Baghdad Sketches* and at the end of the day am totally exhausted. The Big Doctor, the owner of this private hospital, Dr Shami, comes round at 9.30. One of the other patients is a son of the President's brother, Rifaat al-Assad.

Tuesday, 10 August

The hospital has shortfalls in matters of customer care. The medical, catering and cleaning departments are not coordinated. A nurse comes in to see me before 6 to see if I am still alive. My pulse rate is taken and recorded on a clipboard and other checks are made. But breakfast does not come for another two hours. It is the best meal of the day, but that is because the other meals have been so awful. Perhaps they think the intravenal drip provides sustenance. It is attached to a bottle, and I am surprised to see it gradually empty itself.

Dr Shami breezes through and I give my card, and urge English classes at the British Council for his staff.

Thursday, 12 August

I drive to Homs and call on Ibrahim Abdul Nur and his family in Fairouza. Ibrahim has lost the sight of one eye and is largely blind in the other.

Friday, 13 August

I drive to Masyaf and on to Deir Soleib, an isolated Byzantine church, ruined but in pretty good condition, especially the apse roof. I drive on to Abu Qubais, a valley full of coffee houses and restaurants. Busloads of Friday trippers bestride the stream and falls. I go in search of the Crusader castle and walk up with Abu Ali, a 71-year-old with six daughters and three sons. I leave him at an Alawite shrine below the castle that is on a peninsula overlooking the Orontes valley. I ramble around and then pick my way down again, collecting Abu Ali at the shrine. I understand little of what he says but, undeterred, we chat on. I sit with him for half an hour, chewing raw figs and watching his three-year-old grandchildren, twins, at play.

I drive on to Qadmus, where there is an Isma'ili castle. Qadmus is a small town and the castle is still inhabited – or at least there are houses there. I am hailed from one of them and accept an invitation to coffee and fruit – pears and apples. My host is Tamir, a photographer who owns Studio Qadmus. We sit and gaze over the hills – to Jabal Sis to the south and the hilltop *maqam* or shrine of Maulay Hasan to the south.

I leave. I am wanting to get to Kahf, another Ismaili castle. I give a lift to a man to the town of Shaikh Badr. He tries to deter me from going to the castle. "The road is rough. There are snakes. And wolves. And wells in the castle." Is he rationalising a fear of djinns? I do get there. It is not easy to find, but what a place. It stands out like an island in a thickly wooded plain, and looks across at another Alawite *maqam*. I fight my way through thick undergrowth into the castle which used to be the base for "The Old Man of the Mountain". The sun is sinking fast, alas, and there is no sign of the Department of Antiquities.

I drive on to Lattakia and meet Ahmad al-Isa for dinner. He is an Alawite. Ibrahim Abdul Nur taught him once. Ahmad's mother, according to Ibrahim, was "the most beautiful woman in the village *in her time.*"

Saturday, 14 August

I leave Lattakia and drive on the Aleppo road, into the hills and turn off to Shughur al-Qadim, to see a Crusader castle. The dusty, friendly village is only a few kilometres from the main road, but seems much further away. I meet the teacher of English, Abdul Karim, who is busy producing thread from goats' wool.

A 15-year-old lad called Zaki accompanies me to the castle, which is only 50 metres from the village mosque, but across a ravine. It takes us 20 minutes of tough walking to reach it. But the views from the castle are fantastic. You look down a sheer drop of hundreds of metres to the valley of Nahr al-Abyad. I explore the ruins, in the company of Zaki, four lads aged about 12 and ten goats. Then down to the village where I meet Abdul Karim again. I go to his house and we have lunch – eggs and eggplant in a stew, then fried eggplant and green peppers. Abdul Karim graduated from the University of Aleppo in 1979. He likes silly jokes, for example:

"Why does a Homsi walk on two legs?"

"Because he cannot walk on one."

I have to leave and drive on to Ma'rat al-Nu'man, stopping at the ruins of Ruwaiha, one of the Dead Cities – early Byzantine. A few families live in the ruins. I talk to some who wonder whether the book I am carrying[5] has a key to where there may be water. All water has to be brought in. They live in poverty in the middle of these extraordinary ruins going back fifteen hundred years. They refer to the big church as Qasr al-Sultan, the Sultan's Palace.

I get back to Damascus before sunset.

Monday, 16 August

Rana, the Palestinian receptionist in the Embassy, asks about the possibility of working in the Teaching Centre. She is able, ambitious

---

5 Ross Burns, *Monuments of Syria*, I B Tauris, London and New York, 1992.

and not professionally fulfilled in her present job. She is quite coldly calculating about what she wants. This seems to be a Palestinian trait. I like it. I like her.

In the afternoon Vanda, Motaz and I go to call on Ha'ila al-Atrash, who was the baby in the lap of Mut'ib al-Atrash in the photograph taken by Freya Stark in 1928. She and her family live in a scruffy part of southern Damascus. We meet the brother and sister-in-law before she comes in. She is about 66, unsophisticated, in peasant dress. We bring in the enlarged exhibition-size photograph taken 65 years ago and she bursts into tears. We learn that her mother died when she was very small and that her grandfather, Mut'ib, was mother and father to her. She knows nothing of Freya Stark, and knows nothing about this photograph. It is as if we have brought her late grandfather back to life.

Tuesday, 17 August

Motaz and I call on the Minister of Culture. We are having problems with the fitting of a generator on the outside of our new teaching centre. We need the Ministry to help us out. Motaz is far better than I am at picking up the nuances of the situation. We are directed to the office of the Director of Public Relations, a stern lady called Hana. I must get my relationship right with her. She could be very obstructive or very helpful. Motaz suggests afterwards that we might arrange for her to go to Britain. We tell her about the classes, hand over copies of the textbooks to be used – they have to be cleared by the Ministry. She says, "You cannot start until you are open." We devise a formula whereby we are in principle open from 1 September, and we are officially open from 11 October.

Wednesday, 18 August

I go to the Military Hospital and see the Director, General Mahmud Zughaiby. I have been negotiating for permission for Syrian doctors to enter for Part One of exams for the Royal Colleges. I linger and chat, and arrange to visit his Alawite village near Tartus in ten days' time.

I call on the Ambassador at the Residence and stay for two hours. We discuss the visit of my Director General, and I outline how I see things developing in the next year or so. I tell him I shall be staying at the house of an Alawite General next week. He is impressed and asks me to try and find out the answers to two questions. First, is there an Alawite Higher Council? And, secondly, what is expected to happen when Assad dies? I tell him about Nabil's having been a member of the Ba'th Party since 1968. "He must have joined for career purposes," the Ambassador says. "But then, there is something square about him." I am mystified.

Thursday, 19 August

I have lunch with the novelist Hani al-Rahib. He does not think much of Ulfat Idilbi as a writer. I should be translating Ghada Samman. Ulfat is backward-looking and reinforces western stereotypes. Hmmm. He is wanting to give up teaching – he is a Lecturer in English at the University of Kuwait – and start a photography business. We discuss modern literature and Syria.

In the evening I go out to a restaurant in the Barada valley with Hikmat Shatti, designer, Fitna al-Rayess, niece of the publisher, Riyad, and two film directors, Muhammad Malas and Umar Amiralai. Conversation is all in Arabic, but it is searching and exhausting. We return, after much araq, at about half past one.

Saturday, 21 August

I work on translating *Dimashq Ya Basmati al-Huzn* by Ulfat Idilbi, and work out the words for different rooms in a house – there are over ten words.

I am invited to a "Hawaii" evening at a house of one of the British oil executives. Precious and beautiful people. I wear shorts, the shirt

I bought in Carnaby Street in 1968 and a floppy hat. I have a long chat with the helpful Adam Ereli. He loves suckled pig, and is far more aware of Alawite politics than anybody in the British Embassy. He is also aware of the strengths and weaknesses of the Ba'th Party. The member of the Party Command in charge of higher education, Wahib Tannous, is an old-style Communist sympathiser.

Monday, 23 August

I go to the Embassy and read the Ambassador's carefully written paper on what happens to the Peace Process if Hafez al-Assad dies. It is interesting, but suggests that there could be the possibility of a civil war, and of Islamic fundamentalists taking over. Of course both are possible scenarios. But a civil war? There are numerous factions and confessions in the country – as in Lebanon – but there has not been the build-up of private armies, with war lords. If there were a civil war where would the weapons come from? Iraq overland? Libya by sea? Kurds? Before the level of weapons became dangerous there would be ample time to secure the borders. But I think plenty of people are mindful of what has happened in Lebanon. There are plenty of forces against a civil war. Similarly there is a coalition against the Muslim fundamentalists, who could claim an alternative legitimacy. Hopes for the Peace Process do rely on the survival of Hafez al-Assad. All that is a sobering thought for our activities.

We are getting a hundred enquiries a day about English classes.

Tuesday, 24 August

I have dinner with an Embassy colleague. There have been serious electricity power cuts. "After 30 years of the Ba'th party, they can't get the electricity right." This is saloon-bar political analysis. Syria, like any other place, is an aggregate of individuals. One of my Syrian colleagues tells me that her mother-in-law, who comes from a village in the north, was married when she was 11, and screamed as she was raped on her bridal night. In her older age now she hates men, all men.

Wednesday, 25 August
Salah Jadid, one of the rivals of Hafez al-Assad 25 years ago, has died.

At five in the afternoon I set out north and drive to Tartus. I buy some chocolates for my hosts and go into the labyrinth of roads in the hills, asking my way to the village of Qarqifta. The Alawite villages are full of people walking out in the evening – men, women, girls, courting couples. I reach Qarqifta and a young man shows me the way to Mahmud Zughaiby's house. After a shower, Mahmud takes me off to a beach café near Baniyas where there is a party full of young people. It is 1 am before I get to bed.

Thursday, 26 August
A day in the life of General Dr Mahmud Zughaiby is full of interest. I observe and absorb. Throughout the day, people come to call on him, bringing their problems for him to solve. A disputed Ba'th Party appointment in Baniyas. A sick child. A young man in search of a job – his parents have recently died. Mahmud listens to everyone. He is affable and humane. Often he scribbles a note, such as to the manager of the local cement factory. I meet all sorts of people during the day. The village *mukhtar*, a poor man who registers births, deaths and marriages, whose brother was killed in the 1973 war against Israel. Butros Germanos runs a cafeteria in the adjacent Maronite village of Dhar al-Safra; his cousin is in the French army and was involved in intelligence during the 1991 Gulf War; his brother is a Professor at the American University of Beirut.

We go to Mahmud's farm which brings in an income of a million Syrian pounds a year. Oranges, grapefruit, olives, apples and pears. Nearby is a swimming pool, freshly filled with water. We then go for a drive through wonderful countryside to the shrine, *mazar*, of Sheikh Muhammad Riahi. It is a picnic spot but becomes a pilgrimage site at weekends: for Muslims on Fridays and for Christians on Sundays. There are about five hundred having picnics and barbecues. Many have come in busses parked close by. Drums and singing demonstrate the Syrian capacity to enjoy life. The saint's life and circumstances are lost in the past, but people come here from as far as Beirut to seek and find a cure for neurological disorders. We carry on through a ravine of utter beauty, with terraces (*silsilat*), the result of much hard work, on the slopes above. From time to time we come upon a fine villa, belonging to somebody who has made it.

We return to the house at Qarqifta. After a rest we set off again. Mahmud's driver, Nabil, a Christian from Marmamita, drives us in the army Mercedes, at 160 kilometres an hour, and in disregard of traffic lights, to Tartus, to meet Mahmud's merchant cousin, with the same name. We take a small boat, a *shakhtur*, to the island of Arwad. It is the last weekend of the school holidays and plenty of boats are sailing to and from the island. There are Saudi tourist families, the women enjoying themselves by whacking each other with their handbags! The water around the island is full of swimmers. We return to Tartus, to the merchant's villa, which could have been transferred from Abu Dhabi. We sit on the balcony, drink araq and discuss politics. Assad will not sign a peace agreement, General Mahmud thinks.

Saturday, 28 August
Over breakfast Mahmud tells me the Minister of Electricity has resigned. "It was not his fault. The government made a mistake in the policy of extending electricity to every village. The Turks have taken our Euphrates water. And there are problems with generators." The cost of electricity is heavily subsidised by the government and there is no mechanism for economising. In some ways, I suggest, the

power cuts have imposed rationing by force. Mahmud is critical of Syria's intervention in Lebanon. The relationship between Assad and Lebanese Christians is interesting. Apparently he was looked after by a Christian as a child. And the Lebanese Maronite leader, Sulaiman Franjieh, after massacring some Christian rivals in a church in the 1950s, sought refuge with Alawites in Baniyas. Mahmud is critical, to the point of abuse, of the "syphilitic and AIDS-ridden ruling families of Kuwait and Saudi Arabia".

I leave Qarqifta before seven in the morning and drive north to Lattakia and on, north, through wooded hills, with trellised restaurants fringing the road. I turn off to the popular Syrian holiday resort of Ras Basit, where chalets and tents are rented out. Mattresses are laid out, lining the tents, near cooking pots and fires. Public toilets and showers are available for all. I go to the Tourist Hotel for breakfast. It is run-down and there is a sense of it being the tired end of the season. I stroll around, return to the car and drive on to the beautiful Armenian village of Kasab, which is a cross between the prettier parts of Switzerland and Yemen.

Peter went on to southern Turkey for a few days.

Monday, 30 August

It is Army Day in Turkish Antakya. From my breakfast window I see a series of marchers, some in antique uniform as if they were Crimean veterans or the last of the Janissaries. One Ancient Pistol periodically fires off a salvo.

I drive on to the Syria-Turkey frontier. Leaving Turkey is easy, and, coming to the Syrian immigration post, I am told that the chief inspector is off for lunch. My heart sinks. I glance at the register and note that only one vehicle has passed from Turkey to Syria all morning. Such a busy morning calls for a leisurely lunch followed by a nap. But he turns up and I am let back into Syria in record time.

I drive straight back to Damascus. As I pass the hills above Tartus, I glance up and think, "A part of me is up there."

Tuesday, 31 August

A crowd has gathered outside the teaching centre at a quarter to eight as I pass. The doors are not due to open until nine.

The organisation for the registration of our first students is first rate. There are no hitches, no awkwardness. It is all smooth and streamlined. Customer care. The feel-good factor. All the qualities of the service economy. The first student to register is Mrs Bouzo, wife of the landlord. Is it to check up on how we use the premises? At least we are getting some of the rent back. The vast majority of the prospective students are Syrian, patient, courteous, friendly. I stay around all day, helping out. The novelist, Hani al-Rahib, calls with his daughter, Hala.

Hani calls back later and we go to the house for a beer and a chat. He tells me his wife is from Qardaha, the President's village, and her father is an old chum of Hafez al-Assad. When she and her father went to pay a condolence call, after the death of his mother in July last year, the President asked her, "Is Hani still writing novels against me?" That worries Hani. He suggests that a feature of Assad's personality is a feeling of guilt about picking off his former colleagues one by one. All in all, there is the appearance of a negative man, unsure of himself.

Thursday, 2 September

The registration for English classes continues. Ninety-five per cent are Syrians or Palestinians based here. I am content that few object to our high fees. Many, it appears, are Palestinians who were in Kuwait and wish to pursue their international migratory career. The arrangements have been smooth, with orderly consideration for everybody. There are constant comparisons, explicit and implicit, with the American Teaching Center. One left an "advanced" class there, thinking he was advanced. On our scale of assessment he is intermediate. During the last week 700 have been assessed. All will have a favourable impression. We have so far taken about a million Syrian pounds. The first class will be at 3.15 pm on Sunday: a historic moment.

Friday, 3 September
The new Director of Studies, Ian Arrowsmith, and his wife have taken a penthouse flat belonging to the Jarudi family. The landlord seems to want a connection with us as a cover to acquire a satellite dish and access to international television. The building is next to the office of Vice-President Khaddam who would be Acting President if and when Assad goes. Across the road is the office of the President's brother, Rifaat. I calculate the chances of the flat being caught in crossfire. A small chance, but not one to be excluded.

Saturday, 4 September
I go to the Sheraton to celebrate Qatar National Day. I miscalculate and arrive too early. It takes over an hour for food to arrive. I sit on the edge and watch waiters rushing in with glasses of non-alcoholic drinks and plates of nuts and fruit. I then wander around and talk to the Deputy Minister of Education, Muhiuddin Isa, and one or two others. This is the kind of function I can happily do without.

A gentle breeze brings in the pleasant perfumes of jasmine. Ah, Damascus!

Sunday, 5 September
I go along to the teaching centre to see the first students arrive. We have five teachers. Two professionals (Annie Stewart and Renu Arrowsmith) whose husbands have been posted here, and three (Jenny, Tracey and Debbie) whom I have had trained. The latter are

nervous but geared up to facing their first classes. All are looking fresh and well groomed. "You've done well, Ian," says Jenny. "In only three weeks you've got this going. It's taken me three weeks just to get these lessons prepared."

The students are docile, mostly professionals. We have a portrait of President Assad near the door as you enter and one student is heard to wonder whether he is the director of the centre!

After five hours the teachers are looking exhausted. Ian has brought in a bottle of champagne and I bring some sticky cakes, and we eat and drink to celebrate.

Monday, 6 September

Towards the end of the morning I have a phone call from Mark Allen, Counsellor in the British Embassy, Amman, and chum of Wilfred Thesiger. He would like me to look up a tribal friend, Nuri Sha'lan. There is some problem about the education of his son. Mark travelled by camel from Jordan to Abu Dhabi around 1970 with Said Salman, and has written a book on falconry.

I write to Andrew Green on leave about the start of the teaching operation. All targets are being met and exceeded. There is no reason why we cannot go to 1,000 students by this time next year. This would really mean a substantial impact on the country.

Tuesday, 7 September

I go to two social functions. The first is Brazilian National Day. I do not stay long, but talk to the Ambassador of the United Arab Emirates and to Mahir al-Hamdi, the Palestinian representative here. I ask him about the Oslo agreements reached last week between the Israeli government and the PLO. He fears it is a trap and is against mutual recognition. Most Palestinians are against it and think it will not work.

I go on to dinner with my colleague Vanda and her academic husband, Nabil. I arrive at nine, fearing that I am late, but her relations do not turn up until much later. Nabil is actually very political and knows George Habash well.

Wednesday, 8 September

I spend more time translating Ulfat's novel. I get into a rhythm and am pleased with the way it is going. I am turning the stilted English of my first draft into what I hope sounds like English, as if it were originally written in English.

I call on the Sha'lan house. A majlis of chairs is laid out in the courtyard of a rather tatty house by the mosque in the area of Damascus called Sha'lan. I have coffee with the only member of the family, Sultan, present. The head of the family, Nuri, is in Amman.

Friday, 10 September

I work in isolation at the office. Ian Arrowsmith calls in. He has done an analysis of the students of the teaching centre. 75 per cent are aged between 18 and 25, the median age being 23. The oldest student is the landlord's wife; she is 61. Many have learned some English elsewhere.

I read half of the little history of Safita by George Jabbour. I will not translate it. But it is interesting. He is concerned that local history is seen as a challenge to Arab unity, and that local families may be upset by the exposure of their differences.

Sunday, 12 September

There is a crisis. A neighbour in the block where the teaching centre takes up a floor, has been in, complaining that we are taking up three parking spaces when we have no entitlement to any. We are not diplomatic and have no right to a police guard. I even hear that he has threatened me with violence. I must meet him. He has been along to the Ministry of Foreign Affairs asking them to send a letter to the police to that effect. It is all very un-Syrian.

I have a visit from Kamal Abu Deeb, Professor of Arabic at the School of Oriental and African Studies, a Syrian. He is translating the poetry of Adonis. We talk for an hour. I tell him what the British Council is doing in Syria. He invites me to give a lecture at SOAS on translation.

Monday, 13 September

The crisis with our neighbour is resolved. I talk to Brian Stewart, Chargé in the Ambassador's absence, and he will take it up with the Ministry of Foreign Affairs. I then arrange to call on our neighbour, taking Motaz and Ayoub, who – in spite of his gentleness – is largely built and can look intimidating. The man lives on the top floor. I take the initiative in shaking hands. We go to his sitting room. He is Abdul Razzaq al-Jabi and, according to his own account, a businessman in Riyadh and close to one of the Princes. He has four cars here. I tell him he should have been in touch with me first. He speaks good English and was at Broumana High School in Lebanon. He is full of slightly embarrassed politeness. We have coffee together. As Motaz says when we leave, "He's got the message".

Tuesday, 14 September

In the evening we have dinner with Ghasan Shannan, one of the army doctors. There are some interesting guests. I talk to Abu Nuwar, Jordanian, kinsman of Ali who had a huge row with Glubb Pasha in the 1950s. And to a member of the Syrian parliament, representing the university. He is confident that Syria will sign a peace with Israel and that Arafat will be praying at the Aqsa mosque "before Christmas". It will be strange that Arafat might find himself escorted by Israeli soldiers as he commutes between Gaza and Jericho.

Wednesday, 15 September

I have dinner with my American opposite number, Fernando Gonzales.

There I meet an adviser to the Ministry of Finance who has been to the States on a one-month course on privatisation. And also a bright young American who studied Arabic under Kamal Abu Deeb at Columbia University. And an official from the Ba'th Party. The Americans are streets ahead of us in understanding the country.

Thursday, 16 September

We are fixing up a course for a doctor in the Army Medical Services, provided he gets a satisfactory score in his English test. He will be going to a paid job worth £23,000 a year. This is amazing money and Zughaiby is disbelievingly pleased. It is a great boost to our standing that we can be offering such perks. It is, of course, not British Council money.

Theresa and I pack and drive to Safita.

Friday, 17 September

Safita is a small regional centre. There is a large Christian community – the Bachours and the Jabbours – as well as Muslims and Alawites. From the hotel balcony we look over densely populated countryside, across to Krak des Chevaliers and to Akkar.

After breakfast we walk through the town to the fort. I take a photo of the entrance from the position Freya Stark took her photograph in 1939. In front of the fort is a car with a Dubai number plate. A sign of the times – inconceivable in 1939.

We drive to Arima, a Crusader fort, now a rugged ruin in three sections on a hill and near a small well-kept Alawite shrine or *maqam*. We clamber up through the undergrowth. Strange stirrings turn out to be caused by well-camouflaged tortoises doing their thing.

We then go on to Yahmur, with another Crusader fort in an orchard by a small village square, occupied by a family and also – it seems – by the village rubbish dump.

After that we set off into the hills through Dreikish, along winding lanes. We have to ask everywhere – there are no road signs – and eventually reach Husn Suleiman. This is a classical ("Syro-Phoenician") temple site in a fold in the hills by a spring. It has been a place of worship for millennia. Like the Temple of Bel at Palmyra, there is a cella within an enclosure. It is totally overgrown. The whole setting, quiet and remote, is staggeringly beautiful. Every hilltop has a bright white Alawite shrine. Breeze blocks have not reached here.

Saturday, 18 September

On our way back to Damascus we go to Deir Mar Musa, near Nabk. A dusty track takes us from Nabk into the hills. We park at the end of the track by a stone building and walk along a narrow path down a valley and reach the monastery which is on the edge of a cliff overlooking a broad plain. The priest in charge is a young man, Father ("Abuna") Paolo. Some young people are helping with restoration work. We go into a small chapel where there are 11th-century frescos of the Resurrection as well as of the usual saints and Fathers of the Church. A young couple are sitting on the carpeted floor, one of them strumming a guitar. The monastery was abandoned in the last century and has been undergoing restoration since 1984. There is a pervasive malty smell, coming from the barley stalks and mud of home-made bricks. In the surrounding hills are anchorites' caves. There is only one hermit today, an Italian in a yellow caravan.

Sunday, 19 September

I hold a meeting of staff and talk about the forthcoming visit of the Director General. I get each member of the staff to contribute something. I am excited by the fact that we are on an upward escalator. Business, activity, impact. The other day my German opposite number said to me, "You are the talk of the town". Well, that is fine, but I am hoping that the official opening, the Freya Stark exhibition, and the possibility of work with the Ministry of Petroleum Resources will all make us the deafening shout of the town. I want the British Council to be the leading cultural centre in Damascus. I am also developing my own style of management. Control, delegation. Most staff have the individual task of advising me on some aspect – information technology, English, etiquette and so on.

After work and a heavy sleep I return to the teaching centre and talk to a couple of classes, with the idea of letting them know me and emphasising what we are doing. With one class I talk only in Arabic.

Monday, 20 September

Hassana al-Azm tells me that her aunt, Ni'mat, who knew Freya Stark in 1928, and who seemed so compos mentis in August, has gone into a decline. She will not be able to come to the opening of the exhibition.

Wednesday, 22 September

The journalist Peter Mansfield is in Damascus, and I invite him to the press conference we are holding. This is the main event of the day. A dozen journalists turn up, including Tony Touma and Christopher Dickey who wrote the book, *Expats*, and with whom I was in correspondence about Wilfred Thesiger. I speak to the journalists all in Arabic about the British Council and the official opening, about the Freya Stark exhibition and the visit of the Director General. I am flanked by Ian Arrowsmith and Motaz. I talk into a microphone and learn later that I am talking live to the BBC

World Service. I also give a separate interview into the mike of an American journalist.

We are invited to drinks with a Serenissima Tour group, which will include the Duke of Wellington "who will be revisiting Syria for the first time since the war when he liberated Aleppo".

Friday, 24 September

I go with some of the teachers to Bloudan where one of the teachers I have trained in Britain, Jenny, and her Syrian husband have a second home. They lived in Britain for the first few years of their married life, before coming to Damascus in 1978. Hanna is a successful psychiatrist, and has his own television programme. He has an orchard here and loves to watch the fruit grow. He is so busy that the fruit often rots before he gets round to giving it away. We are given a box of apples. After lunch we go for a walk and I take pictures of the old building, known as *'unsuliyat 'Ud* – Wood's Consulate. Richard and Isabel Burton stayed here. Unfortunately the building is in a ruinous state and threatened with demolition. Today it is used as an informal public urinal.

Saturday, 25 September

We drive out to Salkhad and I take a picture on the spot Freya Stark took hers in 1928. The 12th-century citadel is a military area. People look at us from the citadel but we are not questioned.

Back in Damascus we have a drink with the journalist Alan George whom I used to know in the 1970s. He has known Syria since 1967 and thinks Assad will sign a peace treaty before Christmas. He also thinks Syria is on the brink of an economic take-off. He specialises in "nasty" countries – Syria, Iraq and Libya.

Sunday, 26 September

We have more registration for classes. There are problems as potential students jostle for the places that are soon all taken. A son of the Minister of Foreign Affairs and another son of a General object that they have not been given preferential treatment.

Monday, 27 September

We go over the hills down to Beirut. I have an appointment with Hassana Jabr Salam, and we talk over prospects for the renewal of British Council work in Lebanon. We go to lunch with her lovely family. One daughter is based in Houston, Texas. A cousin, Salma, is a speech therapist who trained in Montreal. She is a great-grand-daughter of Hajj Amin al-Husseini, the former Mufti of Jerusalem. Husseinis of Jerusalem married Jabrs and Salams of Beirut. I also meet Fuad, Hassana's second husband, a brother of Sa'ib Salam, the former Prime Minister.

In 1973 Peter was in Beirut, having breakfast in a small restaurant near the Borj, downtown Beirut. He had noticed that the names of a lot of fruit in Arabic were derived from French – firez for fraise (strawberries) for example, but grapefruit was the word for grapefruit. Peter asked fellow breakfasters why this word broke the pattern. Suddenly an argument broke out which became so animated that one man threw a bowl of hummus across the café at another man. There was a deathly pause. Would knives or guns be brought out to resolve the issue? Peter was alarmed. What had he started? Should he dive and hide under a table? He quickly fumbled for some cash to pay for his breakfast, threw it on the cash desk and slipped out with such dignity as he could muster. He never found out why grapefruit could be such an explosive issue, until …

Fuad, I learn, has been a fruit farmer specialising in citrus fruit. I venture to ask him when grapefruit entered Lebanon and with it the English word for the fruit.

"1934," he tells me. "It came to Palestine first with Jewish settlers from California."

So the row 20 years earlier may have been about the role of Jewish immigrants. Grapefruit and the Palestine question!

Tuesday, 28 September

Hassana takes me on two calls. The first is Ibrahim 'Id who has two jobs. He sells whisky, but is also a consultant, advising the government about traumatised and war-battered orphans of Beirut. The second is Wafiq Ajouz whom I first met in Abu Dhabi at the majlis of Sheikh Nahyan bin Mubarak al-Nahyan. He has had an interesting career. He was head of Public Relations for Middle East Airlines, but he has also been the President of the Arab Youth Hostels Federation, and is still a keen swimmer and wrestler. He is connected by family to the former Syrian Prime Minister, Said al-Ghazzi, but owed his career in the Airlines to the patronage of Sa'ib Salam, the first General Manager.

Wednesday, 29 September

I attend a dinner party given by the Ambassador, Maeve Fort. One of the guests is Zaid Baidun, a Palestinian with impeccable English, the result of being educated at St George's School, Jerusalem; St Luke's College, Haifa; the American University of Beirut; and the University of Oxford. Another is a lady who helps to organise the Baalbek Festival. She does not know whether she is a widow or not. Her husband was kidnapped seven years ago, and has not been seen since.

Maeve Fort was a note-taker at a meeting between Margaret Thatcher and Kurt Waldheim. Thatcher ignored her. Waldheim was a solemn bloke and the two made speeches at each other. There was no conversation.

Thursday, 30 September

Based in Hassana's office I have a series of visitors, including two environmentalists – separately. The second rubbishes the first. "He does not even have a doctorate and only pretends to know about environmental issues." He tells me that the Druze leader, Walid Jumblatt, is keen on green issues. On his land there is a copse of cedar trees that have been under threat. Approach is monitored. Away from the official approach to the copse, the land is mined.

Hassana and I go to Musaitbey and have lunch with Cecil Hourani and his daughter, Zelfa. They live in an old house, rented since the 1960s. It is a hundred yards from Sa'ib Salam's house. The area, with its narrow streets, has its own distinctive character. One of his other guests is an ancient cousin, Labib Hourani, Principal of the school in Marjayoun, homeland of the Houranis. Cecil tells me that ginseng is grown on the slopes of Mount Hermon, and that goat paths on the mountain were used to smuggle arms to the Palestinian resistance. The Arafat Trail, it was called.

My bodyguards escort me via Aintoura and Zahle back to the Syrian border. I bid them farewell. During the Lebanese Civil War they were murderous gangsters in militias, shooting up other militias. More recently they have been recruited as security guards by Embassies and others.

Saturday, 2 October

Theresa and I are invited to meet a tour group, brought out by Serenissima. The manager, Serena Fass, introduces us to the party, misleadingly, as "very close friends of John Julius Norwich". The party includes Anthony Eden's widow, the Countess of Avon; the Dowager Duchess of Grafton; the Duchess of Beaufort; the Duke and Duchess of Wellington; and four Americans. I talk to the Duke of Wellington about his war experiences here, greeting him with "Welcome back to Syria". The rich are incredibly penny-pinching, arguing about the exchange rate and the price of whisky. I point out that this room, on the ninth floor of the Meridien Hotel, is the most expensive bar in town.

Theresa talks to the Duke about when he was in Palmyra during the war.

"I went out one night," he says.

"To look at the ruins in the light of the moon?" suggests Theresa.

"No," barks the Duke. "To look for the enemy."

Serena shows me the service sheet of Freya Stark's funeral. It includes a lovely picture of Freya Stark with John Julius Norwich at Krak des Chevaliers in 1982.

Sunday, 3 October

At seven in the morning, I collect the Duke and Duchess of Wellington from the hotel, and take them to the Commonwealth War Graves at Mezze. On the way, the Duke, sitting in the front passenger seat, talks of a beautiful princess of the Atrash family. It is Esmahan he is talking of. "I had a bit of a walk out with her," he says. "It was before we were married, and she" – he indicates the Duchess sitting at the back – "knows about it." The Duchess is a daughter of a General who worked under "Jumbo" Wilson in Palestine during the war, and they were married in Jerusalem. I have brought a chair with me and we use it to climb over the wall into the cemetery. They gaze at the names on all the graves. It is clearly very meaningful for them. "Lots of Warwickshires died on 21 June," he observes. He is looking for the grave of a Corporal Fowler "whom I first buried at Palmyra. I know exactly the spot."

Wednesday, 6 October

The British Council driver, Bassam, spent last night sticking up Freya Stark posters at every bus stop and available space in town. Only Hafez al-Assad has more of his pictures around the city. I drive to see Bouchra, and see Freya Stark's smiling face on every available hoarding. What would she have made of it?

I arrange with Bouchra for her two little girls to present bouquets to the Minister at the opening of the Freya Stark photography exhibition. A bouquet has been ordered that will be the colour of the British Council logo! Every detail is being considered.

In the evening we go to a party hosted by Razek and May Memerbachi. There is champagne to start with and then a piano recital given by Geoffrey Saba, an Australian of Lebanese origin, now living and teaching in London. May is an authority on Indonesian textiles, and restores old houses.

Thursday, 7 October
I check everything for the next few weeks. Guest lists, programme, briefing notes – all are carefully and repeatedly checked. I have my local mission statement ("The aim of the British Council in Syria is to serve the people of Syria and to make friends for Britain") framed and hung in every room. The framed photograph of the Queen giving me my OBE is above my desk. Extra lighting is placed in the exhibition room making the pictures stand out, looking really good. Potted plants are distributed everywhere making the office look like Kew Gardens.

Saturday, 9 October
The Duke of Wellington has a throat infection, and we are able to fix up a doctor for him.

There is a terrible traffic jam on the way to the airport, but we have given ourselves plenty of time. We have a beer before going to the VIP lounge. Hasan al-Kirkukli is the master of ceremonies for the Ministry of Culture and we are joined by senior staff from the Ministry. By Solhi al-Wadi from the Institute of Music. By Jane and Andrew Green. The Director General, John Hanson, and his wife, Margaret, arrive five minutes late.

Sunday, 10 October

I take John Hanson on a tour of Ministers. First, Dr Saliha Sanqar, Minister of Higher Education. We are early and are immediately ushered into her room. The Ambassador turns up a bit later – actually on time. Then on to the Minister of Culture, Najah al-Attar, for a cordial meeting. Finally to the Minister of Health, Dr Muhammad Iyad al-Shatti. At each meeting we have the press and television cameras. John is very good at talking on his feet.

At 2 Theresa and I collect the Hansons for an outing to Burqush. John, Theresa and I walk up. John tells me that the film crew who made *Desert Journey*, the film about Freya Stark's voyage down the Euphrates when she was 84 had it in for Mark Lennox-Boyd (Freya Stark's godson who accompanied her on the trip), and deliberately showed him up as an upper-class twit.

Then on to the Cham Palace for dinner with the Minister of Culture with about 30 others, including the novelist, Hanna Mina, with whom I have a word. The meal is dry so Ayoub comes along. But Solhi al-Wadi has brought with him a hip flask of whisky.

Monday, 11 October

I am round at the Ambassador's Residence for breakfast. John wants some points for his speech. I suggest that one of the first Archbishops of Canterbury, Theodore of Tarsus, may well have spoken Arabic, and that Arabic was taught at British universities and at Westminster School in the 17th century, and – more facetiously – that the British helped to liberate Syria from the Turks in the First World War and from the French in the Second.

I take John to the Institute of Music to see Solhi al-Wadi. We then have 20 minutes before meeting the Minister of Culture again. So I take John up Jabal Kasiyun for the view of the city. "We have 20 seconds to enjoy the view," I tell him. Enough time, just, to identify the Umayyad mosque. Then to the Ministry of Culture. The

Minister takes us – we are now joined by the Ambassador – through traffic jams to the Prime Minister's office. We are bang on time and go along carpeted corridors to the large reception room where John and Prime Minister Zubi chat away.

We take John to the Barada Valley Restaurant for a well-organised lunch. Solhi al-Wadi and I talk about Muhammad Fadl al-Jamali, the former Iraqi Prime Minister, whom I used to know in Tunisia. Solhi's father was the head of the diwan of King Abdullah of Jordan, his uncle the head of the family in Baghdad.

Then the official opening of the British Council, and the Freya Stark exhibition. Just as we are about to receive the Minister, a neighbour upstairs decides to wash the landing and the stairs and a flood of water pours down. We are able to stop that just in time. All goes well according to plan, my plan. The Minister is charming. Ha'ila al-Atrash is seated by the photograph taken of her with her family by Freya Stark 65 years ago. The Minister gives her a cuddle before the television cameras. The Minister unveils a plaque.

Tuesday, 12 October

Bassam drives me to Homs, picking up the Rector of the University of Homs, Abdul Majid Sheikh Hussein, on the way. He was offered the post of Ambassador in London just as diplomatic relations were broken off in 1986. We call at his village of al-Qara and have coffee at his brother's house. The economy of al-Qara is based on three things: first, remittances from emigrants; secondly, smuggling electric goods on donkey-back over the hills from Lebanon; thirdly, agriculture, and especially cherries. We go into the countryside and come upon a ruin. "What is that?" I ask. "A surprise," says Abdul Majid. It is, in fact, the remains of Deir Mar Ya'qub, a 12th-century monastery. We crawl all over it and see some frescos, half exposed, in what I suppose is the former church.

We continue northwards, passing by a memorial to martyrs who died in the uprising against the French in 1925. One of them was Abdul Majid's grandfather, who had already been to Argentina and returned. The village 40 kilometres south of Homs is Hisya, where the feudal family of Suwaidan used to have their base. My friend's father was a policeman and when Abdul Majid was a child, he was posted to Hisya where there is a shrine to Abdul Majid Suwaidan. The Suwaidan family claimed exclusive rights to the name and did not allow any boy in the village to be called Abdul Majid, and ordered my friend's parents to change his name, but his mother, a socialist, refused. That would have been in the early 1950s.

I return from Homs with John Hanson. I am ticked off for not doing enough financial checks. Back to the house for a farewell party for the Hansons. Fifty turn up. Imad, a breakdancer, starts the ball rolling and we are all dancing. The painter, Hala al-Faisal, is superb, flowing with movement. Everyone joins in.

Wednesday, 13 October
The Ambassador and I see the Hansons off at the airport.

Saturday, 16 October
The Azm House in Hama is now a museum. It was damaged in 1982 during the bombardment of the city, but reconstruction is taking a long time. What was it like ten years ago? We also look at the Umayyad mosque, also battered in 1982. Then to the elevated built-up ridge to the south of the citadel. At the topmost part we are invited in and on to the roof. The house belongs to a Christian family, a middle-aged lady and her daughter who has just qualified as a dentist. The area is called Bab al-Ibli (*Qibli*, south?) and is mixed, Muslim and Christian. A convent adjoins the main mosque. Hama is a city of great interest. Far more than meets the eye.

Sunday, 17 October

Muna, my colleague, has read my draft translation of *Sabriya* and I go over some chapters with her. I have made some mistakes and she has a lot of suggestions for improvement. For example, I have translated an expression literally, "The morning brings fresh breezes". She suggests – and it is so simple – "Tomorrow is another day".

I have some visitors, some of whom I could do without. The Brazilian Counsellor quizzes me about how the British Council works. A young Iraqi wants me to sponsor a group of Shi'ite Iraqi exiles in a production of a Shakespeare play in Arabic. A British amateur actor wants advice (and sponsorship) on an old-fashioned music-hall evening he and some friends are planning.

I read some of the novel, *al-Waha*, by Hani al-Rahib. And start to translate Abd al-Salam al-Ujaili's story, "Sultan Euphrates".

I have a phone call from my headquarters. How would you spend an extra £50,000? Half an hour later I send a fax reply: £20,000 for a visit from the Regent's Park theatre people to put on *The Taming of the Shrew* in April, perhaps culminating in a gala performance at the Azm Palace on Shakespeare's birthday.

Monday, 18 October

In Aleppo Ian, the Director of Studies, and I find the British Consulate and meet up with Tony Akhras and his son, Iskandar, Alexander. They work from a scruffy office dealing with ginning and other commercial work. They take us off to look at possible premises for a British Council operation in Aleppo.

It has been a good year for cotton, and property – we are told – is changing hands a lot in Aleppo. "People do not rent," says Tony. I find this hard to believe but we see a couple of places. Tony is a Maronite and his family has been in Aleppo for four centuries. Father and son seem to prefer to talk to each other in French. Alex studied at the University of Sheffield. They have a large family house in the city which Tony wants to sell for not less than four million US dollars.

At sunset Ian and I call on Sally Mazloumian at the Baron Hotel. "Could we have a few more of the Freya Stark catalogues? One for Patrick Leigh Fermor and another for Xan Fielding's widow."

Wednesday, 20 October

At 10 I go to the University and, in the absence of the Rector, call on Dr Abdul Rahman Ibrik, a stooping veterinarian educated in France. We talk university affairs and then switch to discussing the Arabian horse, something he is passionately interested in.

Meanwhile Ian has been looking at possible premises. "I've found them," he says. We go to look at them. They are in the area called Muhafaza and were actually the building containing the British Consulate until it was closed in 1967. Ian went with Alex, and not with his father. There are, according to Alex, plenty of places to rent in Aleppo.

Friday, 22 October

Our sons are with us and we all go south to Ghazala and follow up T E Lawrence's exploits just before the fall of Damascus. A bridge by a cement factory was one target. Then on to Dera'a. We wander round the railway station, look at an old (1914) railway engine and a lavatory, called locally a *cheshme*, the Turkish word for fountain, long neglected but with just a glimpse of a fin de siècle Ottomanism. Then on to Mazarib, to the railway station. After a picnic we make our way to Tell Shihab, where the landscape changes dramatically. The railway line – to Haifa – is in a narrow cutting beneath the ruins of a classical site. We meet the local mayor, Isa Ya'qub, and he takes us along a footpath round the curve of a hill overlooking the river Yarmouk.

Saturday, 23 October

I am at the office early and at precisely 9.30 we hear the screaming of sirens, and Douglas Hurd, his detective, and the Ambassador arrive, followed by members of his entourage – Richard Culshaw in charge of the press and his Principal Private Secretary, John Sawers, whom I last saw in Yemen in 1980. I take Douglas Hurd round the exhibition of Freya Stark's photographs and he talks to some of the staff. He also signs my copy of his novel, *The Palace of Enchantments*, which was already signed by the co-author, Stephen Lamport, in Abu Dhabi. And that is that. The party disappears and so do we.

Douglas Hurd has called on the President, with Andrew Green. It is the first time Andrew has met him.

Sunday, 24 October

I am in the office very early. The Hurd visit has been seen as a success. A tide is moving in our favour, an enhancement of Syria-British relations. Meanwhile the situation in Algeria gets grimmer by the day. The country is slipping into confusion and foreigners are being kidnapped and assassinated. At this rate the British Council will withdraw and there may be extra funds for Syria. Every cloud has a silver lining.

Tuesday, 26 October

I have a visit from three Syrian journalists. We are becoming newsworthy! I give an interview in English to *The Syria Times*, one of the worst newspapers in the world. I am asked about my perception of Syria before I came and how I have adjusted my views. I admit to being biased in favour of the country which I have known for 30 years. So I cannot answer that question. I am also asked some searching questions in Arabic. They verge on the political, so I have to think quickly and formulate appropriate answers.

Wednesday, 27 October

I call on Ghasan al-Umari, our drunken American neighbour, who claims descent from Umar al-Khattab, one of the first Caliphs. His father has written several volumes of memoirs on the King Faisal period when he knew T E Lawrence.

At 6 I go along to the Assad Library for a *takrim* (a celebration, an honouring) for Ulfat Idilbi. The little lady sits next to Najah al-Attar, the Minister of Culture. There is a full house – over 300 people. Among the several speeches is a lovely one by Abd al-Salam al-Ujaili, who compares Ulfat to a fragrant magnolia flower. Najat Kassab Hassan talks about translations and mentions that *Dimashq Ya Basmat al-Huzn* is being translated into English by the Director of the British Council in Damascus. At the end Ulfat comes forward on to the stage and speaks clearly without notes in beautiful Arabic. There is not a dry eye in the audience. I see her and give her my own congratulations afterwards. The audience is mostly middle-aged and middle class. She has been "politically correct" in Ba'thist terms but she also relates to European liberalism.

Saturday, 30 October

Returning from a weekend with the boys in Lattakia, we go to Jabala, an old port, with a magnificent Roman theatre, on to which has been added the solid masonry of a Crusader castle. There are other interesting buildings in the town – attractive, late Ottoman houses with traces of provincial gentility. There is also an intriguing run-down hotel – I want to stay there!

Sunday, 31 October

Dr Ahmad Sukkar takes me to the site of his proposed Heart Institute. It is planned to cater for elite patients, with a helicopter pad, and a special area for the bodyguards of the patients.

Wednesday, 3 November

An interview I gave is published in today's *Syria Times.* There are a few distortions. For example, I was asked why British people had a negative view of Syria and I said that it was because few British had come to Syria. This is reported as "because a few British had come". And I quoted the remark by Hugh Leach that "Syria was Asia's best-kept secret". This comes out as "age's best-kept secret". But it all looks positive and friendly. I do not think other cultural organisations have such coverage.

Thursday, 4 November

We drive north to Idlib and check in to the ungrand Grand Hotel. Services are adequate but the restaurant seems to cater only for hard-drinking men. A small elevated stage has a stage set of a small cottage with "Love" in English written over it. A whiff of piss assails you on the stairs. There are two other kinds of hotel in Syria. The smaller hotels like the Cairo Hotel in Hama are perfect: clean and friendly with a family atmosphere. The only drawback is its proximity to the town clock with its loud regular chimes. (It is unusual to find a public clock in the Arab world that is working.) The other kind of hotel is the abominable Cham chain. It aims to be of an international standard, with prices to match. But they are run like prison camps.

Friday, 5 November

The hotel seems to be deserted when we get up and we appear to be locked in. But by pushing on one door we manage to escape. Friday in Idlib.

We drive towards the Turkish frontier at Bab al-Hawa, and go off the road to look at the remains of a sixth-century monastery, tucked into the mountainside. Olives and heresy sustained this outpost. The dry-stone ruins are in an excellent state of preservation. We go on to another of the Dead Cities, Baqirha, totally deserted, with no nearby village to plunder and recycle the ruins. One arch lies, arch shaped, on the ground, as if an earthquake caused it to break off from the building only a few days ago. Then on to Bamuqqa. A grove of trees covering a few acres is dotted with Roman farmhouses and an Alawite saint's tomb, draped in green and with fragments of clothes hanging on nearby trees.

The road winds into the hills, looking down on to the plain with the Turkish town of Reyhanli, the frontier watchtowers and the Antioch-Aleppo road along which Theresa and I, separately, in the 1960s came for our first taste of the Arab world. It is like looking down from Heaven. We had no idea that these limestone hills were full of ruined cities. We come to the attractive town of Harim: light-blue-washed houses and the crumbling Ayubid fort. We go in search of food. One restaurant provides nothing, but thanks to a man called Husni, who would like us to be his guests, we find al-Sahil al-Akhdar, the Green Coastline, by a stream, and have a fish lunch. We are invited by some women to the rooftop of a nearby house. It belongs to the mayor of the town, Ghasan Babush. We join his wife and her sisters. Giggles and warmth.

We tear ourselves away and go on to Qalb Lozeh, a beautiful Byzantine church in a village full of horse-loving Druze. And finally back to Idlib.

Saturday, 6 November

The plains surrounding Idlib have, for two thousand years, been famous for the cultivation of olives. We buy a bagful of olives at the olive souk near the museum. Inside the museum are some of the more tangible finds of the site of Ebla, including the tablets that reveal a sophisticated literate society of three or four millennia ago.

We drive on to Ebla. The site is unmistakeable, a long raised perimeter with gaps for gates and a mound in the centre. A "royal palace" has been partially reconstructed and one has a slight idea of how it must have looked.

Ma'rat al-Nu'man, a few miles away, is much more obviously interesting. We go into the town and park by one of the two khans, that of Murad Pasha, a museum full of splendid mosaics taken from neighbouring sites. The town itself is absolutely crowded. The main road stretches to the west, gradually rising, and closed to traffic: one busy busy market. Hundreds of people have come in from the desert and the villages to buy and sell: fruit, vegetables, fish (from Tartus and from the Euphrates), pipes, triangular ladders for picking olives, coffee pots, paraffin stoves – winter is coming. We walk right to the top of the town, go into the mosque and see, in the distance, the ruins of the citadel.

We return to Damascus and find invitations to a reception hosted by the Minister of Culture at the Ebla Cham Palace. The Minister is with her Lebanese counterpart, Michel Eddé. Solhi al-Wadi and his orchestra play some music – "Smoke Gets in Your Eyes", the overture to Rossini's *Barber of Seville* and Solhi's orchestration of a Muhammad Abdul Wahhab song.

Sunday, 7 November

I am having difficulty with my local car insurance which was up for renewal yesterday. The insurance company insist that I have a Syrian driving licence. To get that I need a statement from a doctor that I am fit to drive. I have got that – no problem. I also need a statement from the police. They will only issue that if I have not left the country in the last three months. This is impossible, unless I lie.

Monday, 8 November

I try to phone my headquarters about a possible contract with al-Furat Oil Company to arrange English classes. One person is off sick. Another is down with food poisoning. A third is away because of a bereavement. Can anyone in London still stand up?

Tuesday, 9 November

In Aleppo I meet up with the Ambassador to make calls on the Rector of the University, the local secretary of the Ba'th Party, the Chamber of Commerce and the Governor. He brings the Embassy interpreter, Rana, who is generally very good. But she is not thinking of the context of what she is translating and renders "encouraging tourism" as encouraging *irhabiya*, "terrorism". The Ambassador gets the Governor to agree to open a branch of the British Council in Aleppo, where, as I say, we will "resume activities". (There was a British Council in Aleppo from 1943 to 1956.)

The Ambassador hosts a party for business and university contacts, and British wives of Syrians living in Aleppo. At one point I want a pen. Nobody has one. "It is because we are all in our best suits," someone says, "and have left our pens in our second-best suits."

Wednesday, 10 November

We buy some Syrian champagne – not bad, at £1 a bottle.

We return to Damascus and I go to the office. My Line Manager is due here next week. I feel I have the reputation in my headquarters of administrative incompetence. There may be hints that I take early retirement. "Interesting bloke. No financial administration," will be the verdict.

Saturday, 13 November

My Line Manager comes into the office to meet the staff. We arrange a collective breakfast with food brought in from the Marouch Restaurant. It comes in late and Vanda has to spend time chopping up tomatoes and cucumber.

My Line Manager and I call on the Minister of Culture. We talk about the idea of a British Council office in Aleppo. She points out that the law, as it stands, does not permit us to have a cultural centre there. Calamity! A change in the law requires the signature of the President and that is unlikely to be effected quickly. It looks as if I have to postpone or abandon my dream.

My Line Manager and I fly together to Larnaka, for a "Regional Team Meeting" on a scruffy and dirty Syrian Arab Airlines plane. There are no safety warnings or lifebelts and bits of the plane seem to be falling off.

Thursday, 18 November
We go to a ghastly dinner-dance organised by the British Women in Damascus. There is no imaginative organisation about it. Loud music all the time except for ten minutes when the Ambassador announces the results of a raffle. The food is mediocre. Tracey, who persuaded us to come "and make up a table", arrives late and leaves early.

Friday, 19 November
Theresa and I wander around Straight Street and call in at a shop that sells antiques and also copper plates. It is run by two Jews, David and Elias, who have brothers in Canada and the United States. There are Hebrew writings on sale. It would be nice to get something to defy the shamophobes. We wander into the Jewish quarter. There is not a lot to note – shops with very un-Muslim names. To the south is an UNRWA building and the whole area is called Palestine – a symbolic recognition of an exchange of populations?

We also see the Anbar School, built in the 1860s, a smart building with a series of courtyards, like – as Theresa observes – Oxbridge colleges. One leads on to another. The decoration is baroque. The house was originally the home of a Jewish merchant, and then, at the end of the 19th century, became a school from which many young Damascene nationalists went on to the Istanbul Law School.

Saturday, 20 November

We spend another few hours wandering around the centre of Damascus. We walk to the Umayyad mosque.

We enter the Shi'ite shrine that houses the head of Hussein, grandson of the Prophet Muhammad. There are plenty of women pilgrims from Iran. One couple are reading prayers together – a nice domestic touch. I return to where I have left my shoes. They are gone. This is outrageous, and we both feel that so many rules have been broken – sacrilege, inhospitality and so on. I have only my stockinged feet to walk in. I complain loudly to everyone. People do not wish to know. One Iranian pilgrim offers sweets. Theresa goes back to the house to get another pair of shoes. For I fear they are lost. Someone has gone off wearing them. They were comfortable walking shoes. I have had them for four years. I walked up Ben Nevis in them, and have tramped in the hills of Nepal and on the South Downs in them. There is something distressing about it all.

Monday, 22 November

Theresa and I call on Ulfat Idilbi at her flat. I discuss the title of her novel I am translating, *Dimashq Ya Basmat al-Huzn*, which, translated literally, is *Damascus, O Smile of Sadness*. That does not sound right, and I am proposing the title in English to be named after the central character, *Sabriya*, with the subtitle, *Damascus Bitter Sweet*. "After all," I tell her, "there's *Emma* and *Madame Bovary* and *Anna Karenina*." Ulfat has her two sons with her, Ziad and Yasir, both prosperous men in their fifties. Ziad works with Wafic Said in London, and is, with Sir James Craig, a Trustee of the Karim Rida Said Foundation, Wafic Said's charity, named after his son who was killed in an awful car accident. Yasir works in Paris. Ziad went to Broumana High School and, on their recommendation, to the Quaker Leighton Park School, and then on to Oxford. Their father,

Dr Hamdi Idilbi, was a friendly rival of Dr Yasir Mu'ayyid al-Azm. Both were the first radiologists in Damascus.

Later in the day Motaz and I call on Midhat Ukash, a Circassian, who, in 1958, founded the magazine *al-Thaqafa* which he still edits. It has managed to retain its independence all the time.

Tuesday, 23 November

I have a meeting with two visitors from the Royal College of Physicians. Dr Mahmud Zughaiby, Director of the Army Medical Services, wants to get two hundred of the army doctors to take the Royal College exams. The number is unrealistic. The visitors have been impressed by Zughaiby, seeing him as a bright Alawite peasant from the mountains with excellent political contacts who rides roughshod over the more sophisticated third-generation Damascene professionals. He has been brought up short by the Minister of Higher Education who reminds him that examinations are the concern of her Ministry.

Motaz and I later call at the Chamber of Commerce, meeting Ratib Shallah, the smooth Broumana-educated Director. With him is Abdul Rahman al-Attar, pipe-smoking Anglophone. Their style is very different from the Chamber of Commerce in Aleppo, who seem to be Ba'th Party hirelings. As we are about to leave, Ziad and Yasir Idilbi turn up: an interesting Broumana network there.

In the late afternoon Theresa and I go to the souk and spend an agreeable half-hour buying spices, checking names, smells and prices. They are sold by the oke, or 200 grams, an interesting Ottoman survival.

I go by myself to a lecture in French at the Assad Library, given by Anne Marie Blanqui on Damascus. Apparently the Baghdad Boulevard and the Inner Ring Road were built soon after the 1925 Revolt to seal off the city and to facilitate the movement of troops.

Friday, 26 November

We drive to Saidnaya and visit the nunnery with the ancient paintings. The place is crowded, for Muslims as well as Christians make the pilgrimage here. It strikes me as interesting that such a strategic site, on top of a rock, is a religious, not a military, site. I take a photograph of a sign on the wall that says, "Do not write on the walls."

We go on to Maloula and see the grave of St Thecla, in the nunnery of the same name, guarded by a Juliet's nurse sort of nun.

Saturday, 27 November

We wander around the Ghouta, driving east to the village of Haran al-Awamid, where three Roman columns stand isolated in somebody's courtyard. The village is built mainly of mud brick, with imposing doorways. There is a touch of Arabia about it.

We drive along small village roads. When we enter a village the road becomes a dual carriageway, as if this has to be an obligatory feature of a developing township.

Sunday, 28 November

I walk down to the Institute of Music and hear the orchestra in full blast, rehearsing something or other. I see Solhi al-Wadi, the Director, and we talk about doing the idea of putting on *Dido and Aeneas*. His daughter, Hamsa, is a pianist acquiring a reputation in northern Europe. She is the only one of his children with an Iraqi passport: she was born in Baghdad in 1957.

Momchil Georgiev invites us to the Greek Orthodox Patriarchate to a recital given by him and some fellow-Bulgarian musicians: a delightful mixture of Vivaldi, Haydn and Bach before a full house of the Christian bourgeoisie of eastern Damascus.

Wednesday, 1 December

We have dinner with Brigid and Alan Waddams. The other guests include Christopher Ross, the United States Ambassador. I chat quite a bit with him. He has a Greek mother and he is Greek Orthodox in religion. His parents were working in Beirut in 1954 and that was his first exposure – at the age of 11 – to the Arab world. He was at the Middle East Centre for Arab Studies and has served in as many Arab countries as I have. Warren Christopher is due here on Sunday.

I notice that Brigid has a copy of my edition of *Saïd the Fisherman* on the table. She has been reading it with enjoyment.

Thursday, 2 December

I have a visit from Sulaiman Ahmed, the Hardy expert. He is very cross about the university. There is no library. They have purchased no journals since 1979. They send their journals to other universities in the world, expecting a reciprocal arrangement, but only the University of Jordan responds. He despises the Rector who has blocked his proposal for a commemorative volume for Musa Khoury, a teacher of English whom he greatly admires. I ask him why he does not pursue his alternative career as a lawyer. "They are evil and corrupt," he says. "All the judges have got there by corruption or wrongdoing."

At 7 we go to the National Day party of the United Arab Emirates. As booze is not being served we do not hurry there. The Ambassador and his staff are lined up to greet us. I am wearing a tie with Ras al-Khaimah on it. "You see where my tie is from," I say to one of the officials. He reads it in Arabic and the whole row burst into laughter. Is Ras al-Khaimah the Homs of the Gulf? The Ambassador's wife is there – he is in Tel Aviv – and sidles up to us. "I'm trying to avoid the Minister of Defence," she says. "He is – as you know – a notorious lecher."

Saturday, 4 December

We go for another walk around the old city, visiting the Maristan of Nureddin, and the museum of musical instruments. As a museum it is feeble; as a building it is lovely. We then go to the Arab Academy around the tomb of al-Adil, son of Saladin. One room is dedicated to the memory of Muhammad Kurd Ali, the historian of Damascus and Minister under Faisal between 1918 and 1920. Opposite is the tomb of Baybars. Both are under heavy restoration, but nobody seems to be doing any work. Outside the old city is the Damascus City Museum, formerly the home of Khalid al-Azm, Prime Minister in the 1950s. There are faded and poorly maintained photographs of befezzed political figures of 40 years ago, as well as pictures of Abdul Nasser and Tito.

Monday, 6 December

I have a call from Mark Allen from the British Embassy, Amman. We talk about Wilfred Thesiger and Mark quotes Wilfred's brother who describes his sibling as "the biggest phoney in town". One of Mark's rooms in his Amman house is put aside for his falcon.

Friday, 10 December

I have a visitor from my headquarters and I take him to Zarzar Lake, a small but attractive stretch of water near the Lebanese border. We then make our way to the Druze shrine that marks the alleged tomb of Abel. This is perched high up, overlooking the Barada valley, with stunning views in all directions. We pause and look around under the eye of a magnificently bewhiskered gentleman who tells us that a moustache is a symbol of manhood, in which I obviously fail.

Sunday, 12 December

We go to dinner with the Ambassador. Bouthaina Shaaban has been invited but does not come. Her Iraqi husband does. They met at the University of Warwick. He was doing research on Shelley while she did her PhD on Chartist poetry. Other guests include David Browning and Ferhat Nizami of the Oxford Centre for Islamic Studies.

Monday, 13 December

I call on Hanna Mina to discuss the translation I have done of one of his stories. It is largely autobiographical, about a lad working as a docker in Iskenderun, where he was brought up. After working in the docks he became a barber's apprentice. He had no formal education after the age of 12. He gives me a copy of what he insists is the German translation of one of his novels. It is actually in Polish or in some other Slavonic language.

Tuesday, 14 December

We are registering the son of the Prime Minister in our English classes. Actually the Minister of Culture has asked us to do this and to send the bill to her. There are a couple of interesting points about this. She wishes to curry favour with him, and we are building up our reputation – and constituency – among the wealthy and privileged young.

Wednesday, 15 December

I attend an Embassy "prayer meeting". I note that only one person spontaneously laughs at my jokes. Everyone else seems to wait for a lead from the Ambassador.

Thursday, 16 December

We host a dinner party. One of the guests is George Jabbour. He has an idea of getting the Pope to apologise for the Crusades in 1995, the nine hundredth anniversary of his predecessor's call for what became the First Crusade at Clermont Ferrand. Interesting coming from a Syrian Christian.

Saturday, 18 December

I am smartly dressed and am at the Ministry of Culture at 10. The Ambassador arrives and we have a cordial 40 minutes. She is immediately on the defensive. "You've come to see me about Aleppo," she says. Well, not primarily, though it was on the agenda. I sense problems, perhaps with security or the Ba'th Party. There are three echelons of society that interpenetrate. First the public – our public – there are no problems there. Secondly there is officialdom, the Syria to which we relate formally – the Ministries. Then thirdly, there is the darker area of secrecy and paranoia. The Americans were refused permission to open in Aleppo. The Minister asks if we can find the terms under which the British Council operated in Aleppo before 1956. For the rest, all is sweetness and light.

Sunday, 19 December
We drive north with our three sons to Aleppo and check in to the Baron Hotel. A huge incontinent dog crawls around the reception area, and the hotel seems to be full of morose displaced Slavs.

Monday, 20 December
I walk up to the University of Aleppo to see the Rector. The anteroom to his office is occupied by his (male) secretary with ten people seated on chairs round the edge of the room. The secretary is on the phone. A minion is busy stamping letters. Two men hover over the secretary, ready to catch his attention as soon as the phone is put down. I catch his attention – "I have two letters for Dr Houriyeh". He then admits me through a locked door to the great man's room.

Thursday, 23 December
We go to a party at the home of a couple from the Australian Embassy. I talk to Carmen, the architect wife of a Spanish diplomat. She tells me of Fernando de Aranda, a Spanish architect who designed the Hijaz railway station, the Serail (now the Ministry of the Interior), and after the First World War, the Zenobia Hotel at Palmyra. He became a Muslim, married a Syrian girl and had two

children (one lives in Beirut, the other in Barcelona), divorced and married a Turkish girl. What a fascinating story, a mixture of personal drama and professional achievement.

Friday, 24 December

In the late morning I take my three sons to Burqush, the ruined Byzantine church on the top of a hill on the slopes of Mount Hermon. We stop at a soldiers' tent and have tea with them. We go up to the ruins. The air is crisp and clear. Snow covers the summit of Mount Hermon and pockets lie lower down in hollows that have not been reached by the sun.

At sunset we go to an old house in the Christian quarter near al-Bab al-Sharqi for a splendid Christmas singsong. We are all – 80 or so of us – in the courtyard around the fountain and a choir stands in the *liwan*, the recess, and we all bawl out our favourites. I reflect on the beauty of it all and tears well up in my eyes. The superb traditional architecture, the good humour, the western cultural insertion.

Tuesday, 28 December

Back to work. I interview seven interesting candidates for the job of cashier. We go for Tamara, a 27-year-old Circassian. Ayoub will have to accept the idea of sharing a room with a woman. I cannot allow his social conservatism to influence the appointment. Will Ayoub show resistance to sharing an office with a woman? He has to accept the idea of equal opportunities.

We go to have dinner with Helen Bachour. I talk to her lovely children, Rafiq and Na'ila. I learn that their home town of Safita is dominated by the Bachour and Jabbour families. They are interesting on Alawites who are liberal and not fanatical. Christian girls do not veil although there is steadily increasing pressure on Muslim girls to veil or at least wear headscarves.

Thursday, 30 December

I call on Solhi al-Wadi. Solhi was an exact contemporary of King Faisal II whom he knew well. In the early 1950s he accompanied an Iraqi parliamentary delegation and saw Winston Churchill in the House of Commons.

I have been invited by the Minister of Culture to go to Palmyra to spend time with her, her husband and two friends – doctors – from London. Accordingly, a glum Ministry driver collects me with Bashir Zuhdi, the veteran Syrian archaeologist who bears a physical resemblance to Groucho Marx. He was born in 1927 in Jisr al-Abyad and was a Primary School Principal at the age of 18 or 19. He is the author of many books on the antiquities of the country. He has an encyclopaedic knowledge of the history of Syria. The two doctors are in another Ministry Mercedes with Majid, the Minister's husband, and we drive off to Palmyra, cruising at about 160 kilometres an hour.

At Palmyra we are greeted by Khalid al-As'ad, the Director of Palmyra Antiquities. Khalid was born and brought up in Palmyra.

Friday, 31 December

Bashir takes us off on a tour of the Temple of Bel. I see things I have not seen before – the base of the friezes that stood at the entrance to the inner temple, the traces of Byzantine wall paintings indicating that it was once a church, the relic of a *mihrab*. We go to the rest house at the far corner of the enclosure of the Temple. The whole village of Tadmor used to live inside the Temple enclosure, worried about the Bedu and locking themselves up at night. This continued until the 1920s when the new town was built. The rest house is the only house that survived. It has a courtyard and fountain, a majlis and residential quarters.

Only 30 per cent of Palmyra has been excavated, the theatre uncovered only in 1963.

The Minister has arrived with her ophthalmologist daughter, Arwa, and we join her at the Cham Hotel for lunch.

Bouchra

Ibrahim surrounded by his family.

Hamdan Ramadan with his family. Freya Stark took a photo of him in 1939.

Peter with Motaz.

Hala al-Faisal.

Ha'ila by the photograph taken by Frey Stark in 1928. (Ha'ila is the little girl in her grandfather's lap.)

The Minister of Culture, Dr Najah al-Attar, reopening the British Council in Syria.

Douglas Hurd at the exhibition of Freya Stark's photographs

1994

Saturday, 1 January 1994
We go to a New Year gathering at the home of Adam Ereli. The United States Information Services are planning to buy 50 copies of *The Cimarron Review* with my translation of the story by Abdul Salam al-Ujaili to present to people to demonstrate the strength of the US-Syria connection.

Peter took his son Gabriel to England to take an entrance examination for Bedales School.

Wednesday, 5 January
Thirty-five children are taking the exam. Bright-eyed untraditional parents with a look of "we grew up in the 1960s" about them escort their children to the reception counter. Gabriel and I part.

He was accepted for Bedales. Peter returned to Damascus.

Monday, 17 January
I go to a party to say farewell to Jeremy Dumas and welcome to his successor, Dick Clarke. It is full of western Military Attachés who are a chummy lot, for ever kissing each other.

Thursday, 20 January

In the afternoon we go for a walk, due north, beyond Muhajirin and up the mountain. Jabal Kasiyun has slowly had the city encroaching upon it. We climb up roads that are at a gradient of about 1 in 3. The views over the city get more and more splendid – skyscrapers stand out, tall white buildings, with here and there to the west patches of green, all that is left of the gardens of Damascus. It is invigorating. We descend, passing by an office that is surrounded by dozens of black Mercedes cars and lots of security people. I learn later that this is where the Pesident has his office. It is a shabby building but one can, at least, walk within 20 yards of it, and the residential flats nearby in these leafy suburbs must be desirable.

We are invited to dinner with Dr and Mrs Drubi. He is a prosperous doctor from Homs. She has three daughters, one of whom is studying English at the British Council. Another was Miss Syria in 1986 and is now in Canada. I talk to Zelfa Samman, half-sister of and 20 years younger than the novelist, Ghada, who chooses to live in Paris. Zelfa's mother is a Shishakli, a niece of the former President, Adib. Her mother's mother is a sister of Akram Hourani[1], who is still alive, in exile in Amman, over 80 and frail. Zelfa's father was President of the University of Damascus and has been briefly Minister of Higher Education. Our host's brother was Minister of Petroleum. The older ruling official and the contemporary elites merge.

Friday, 21 January

We drive up the Barada valley, short of Nabi Habil. We find a mile or so of railway track in good condition and walk, away from the road and by the river, swollen by the melted snow on the distant

1 Hama notable and founder of the Arab Socialist Party that in 1953 merged with the Ba'th Party to form the Arab Ba'th Socialist Party that has run the country since 1963.

hills. Winter sunlight breaks through the trees. We walk gently up for a couple of miles, and then gently down.

On the 4 o'clock news we hear that Basil, the President's son – and as the BBC puts it, "heir apparent" – has been killed in a car crash. Attention turns to the President's brother, Rifaat. Hafez himself is likely to be personally deeply affected; his health is not good.

We go for a Chinese meal and bump into the Ambassadors of the United Arab Emirates, Oman and Kuwait having a jolly meal before going to Lattakia for the funeral.

Saturday, 22 January

We walk into the city centre. There are more people around than usual. Men in dark suits persuade shopkeepers to close up and by 1 o'clock all shops have their shutters down. Groups of youths process in hooting cars, carrying pictures of Basil. Newspapers with large photos are stuck on shop doorways and people pause to peruse. One paper has a long poem by the Minister of Culture. Yesterday people seemed to be too stunned to show any reaction. Today there are demonstrations. A human tragedy is perceived. Everyone can deplore the death of a child before his parent. Basil was writ large across Syria. His father, prematurely aged, must be shattered.

I hear there were troop movements all last night, including tanks in the city. The accident, we hear, was on the road to the airport, perhaps late on Thursday night. Basil was perhaps drunk, driving to see a Makhlouf cousin off to Germany.

Sunday, 23 January

I try unsuccessfully to get some guidance from the Embassy. I decide myself to keep the teaching centre closed today. We arrange to put a notice of condolence in the paper and to send a cable to the President. Yesterday there were manifestations of grief: fake, orchestrated and genuine. Today there are further demonstrations that border on the contrived. Shops and schools remain closed.

I think in years to come Syrians will look on Basil al-Assad as the herald of a golden age that never dawned. His early death will be an alibi for frustration or disappointment.

Monday, 24 January

William Lancaster of the British Centre for Archaeology in Amman calls with his wife, Fidelity. I show them the Freya Stark photographs. He tells me he is a godson of John G ("Jock") Murray. I work out that he must be the son of Sir Osbert Lancaster. There is the same plummy voice and the same short, pug-like look. I take them to call on the Minister of Culture who, remarkably, sees us without an appointment. She seems weepy and is clutching a hanky. All goes well but then she is summoned to Qardaha, though she was there only yesterday. She is very chummy with the President's wife and mother of Basil.

Friday, 28 January

We go for a walk, driving first to Zarzar Lake and from there into the hills. It drizzles miserably, as if we were in England. We take a track up a valley, which takes over portions of a Roman road. It is totally deserted and we have extensive views to the range of hills west of Zabadani.

We go to dinner with Renu and Ian Arrowsmith, Director of the Teaching Centre. The new teachers were visited by the secret police, and quizzed in the kitchen. Rachel was asked if she was Jewish. They were asked why they had come to Syria and what they thought of it. But all the teachers are in good humour, enjoying the country.

Sunday, 30 January

I give an interview to a nice Syrian journalist, Ghalia Qabbani, from

Aleppo. She spent many years in Kuwait. The interview is about my Thesiger book and translation work and is for a Kuwait newspaper.

Tuesday, 1 February
There is due to be a massive demonstration to mark the nation's mourning for Basil al-Assad. The weather is not encouraging. At the office I chat to the cleaner – from Qatana. A secret policeman looks in at us and we fear "our attitude has been noted". So when the cleaner goes I close up.

Theresa and I stroll down to Umayyad Square. Small processions gather, representing different unions or other groups. A platform for speakers is erected but all is damp and bedraggled. We walk back home and see a lot of people solemnly – and not so solemnly – march by.

Saturday, 5 February
We go to Burqush. It is a perfect day for such a walk. It is warm, and walking up the hill is bracing. Snow covers Mount Hermon and the neighbouring peaks, emphasising tracks and paths – old routes from Damascus into Palestine.

We have dinner with the Commercial Attaché and his wife who are to be transferred to Hong Kong. He tells me of the merchant families – the Shallahs and the Attars – who, through connections, have done very well. With the liberalisation of the regime the field is open to all and there is an emerging thrusting generation of merchants.

Sunday, 6 February
Our students – 793 of them – are an interesting lot. There are Muslim Brothers (and Sisters) and secret police. The Sisters refuse to talk to the men in their classes. They have also refused to acknowledge grief or mourning for Basil al-Assad on the grounds that his untimely death was the will of Allah. Opinions are frankly

expressed in spite of the presence of the *mukhabarat*. The teachers are occasionally embarrassed. One student started to compare the police in Syria unfavourably with the police in Britain. We have a Makhlouf nephew of the President's wife. Such people come with their bodyguards who are also enrolled in classes – not always the same class. One of the most outspoken students is the son of the Prime Minister who is brighter than we thought.

We have dinner with Haitham al-Kawakabi who used to perform in a circus, balancing tables and plates on his chin.

Tuesday, 8 February
A man is marrying a woman who has had three husbands and is still a virgin.

"How was that?"

"Well, the first was gay and was uninterested. The second was a poet and philosopher; his mind was on higher matters. The third was a member of the Ba'th Party who would spend all his nights marching up and down, saying, "We will fuck. We will fuck.""

Wednesday, 9 February
My request to start negotiation for opening an office in Aleppo has been rejected. It is a result of the success of our Damascus operation. We have provided an oasis for freedom of expression. We even offer choices to students! The *mukhabarat* fear opinions being expressed under our auspices in Aleppo. It is a bitter disappointment.

Friday, 11 February
It is the first day of Ramadan. I wake to hear the *musahhir*, the gun at 4 am or so, one hour before dawn, waking people up to eat for the last time for a dozen or so hours.

We go out of town, to Nabk, into the hills and park the car near some lads shooting at sand grouse. We walk down, a chilly walk, to

Deir Mar Musa. The priest in charge of the monastery, Father Paolo, is a big bearded Jesuit. He shows us the wall paintings in the church and a grotto outside where some modern paintings tell the story of the Seven Sleepers.

Saturday, 12 February
The Ambassador and I call on the Minister of Culture about the rejection of our request to open a branch of the British Council in Aleppo. She is as distressed about it as we are. The decision was made by the Central Committee of the Ba'th Party. Sulaiman Qaddah was the man against it. She advises submitting another request, scaling our ambitions down to the office being just an English-language-teaching operation.

She goes on to talk about Basil al-Assad. He was a good lad, a contrast to some of the tearaways around. He was being groomed for the Presidency. The cabinet is much concerned about spoiled rich kids. Their bad behaviour leads others to be intensely Muslim.

Sunday, 13 February
We are invited out to the home of Shafiq Fayyad. We listen to music from the time of his youth in Britain in the 1950s – all sorts of mostly forgotten names – such as Eve Boswell and Pat Boone.

Monday, 14 February
I call, as arranged, on the Ba'th Party headquarters. The Central Committee has 21 members that include the President, the three Vice-Presidents, the Prime Minister, the Minister of Defence, the Secretary General of the Party and representatives of different sectors. In theory they devise policy which Ministers execute. I can legitimately make calls on two – Wahib Tannous who is in charge of higher education, and Ahmad Dargham, in charge of culture. I see Wahib who is cordial and welcoming. I start by offering condolences

on the death of Basil and we move to talking about contemporary Syrian literature. We then turn to the idea of a British Council branch in Aleppo. He sees no objection. "And what about Homs as well?" he says. I then see Ahmad and go through the same drill with him. He is from near Homs and was trained as a teacher. The Party headquarters used to be the Teacher Training Institute where he trained and attended lectures! He also sees no objection. "What Damascus has Aleppo should have."

I report back to the Ambassador who feels he cannot call on Sulaiman Qaddah without having called on the Deputy Secretary General of the Party, Abdullah al-Ahmar. (The Secretary General is the President.) It will be odd to call on him, having neglected to call for three years. Yes, yes, it is all a game. They know it and I know it, but we keep up the pretence and the courtesies nonetheless.

Tuesday, 15 February
The other day a Syrian academic friend told me that when he was doing his PhD at the University of Essex he went out with an English girl who said after a while, "I can't continue with you. Your accent is too posh for me."

Thursday, 17 February
Ghalia Qabbani and her Iraqi husband, Fadil Sultan, take us to call on Sa'dallah Wannous. I impress him with my interest in his work, bringing him a copy of the play of his I saw 23 years ago at the Hamra Theatre here in Damascus. Sa'dallah is from Tartus and became interested in the theatre through reading. He studied in Cairo and then in France where he was greatly impressed by the work of Genet, Ionesco and Beckett. His wife, Fa'iza Shawish, is an actress. He is cordial, wears a polo-neck sweater, looks thin but not ill. He seems to have mastered the cancer. He tells me he has not met a European who speaks Arabic as well as I do. I am better than Jacques Berque!!

Friday, 18 February

I read one of the stories by Ghalia Qabbani from the collection she gave me. One is very good, a grim tale about people in a taxi and the car radio broadcasts a news item about an Amnesty International report about political prisoners. The passengers fall quiet and do not know where to look.[2]

Peter went for a few days to London, to meet colleagues and to give two lectures – on Freya Stark and on translation – at the School of Oriental and African Studies.

Tuesday, 22 February

I have a meeting with the British Council Music Department. Solhi al-Wadi is in London and comes to the meeting. As does Caroline Sharman. We talk about putting on *Dido and Aeneas* next year. Caroline will make a series of visits to Syria beforehand. She will be the artistic director of the opera project.

Thursday, 10 March

Back in Damascus after 20 days away. That included one conference, two training sessions, three lectures, one play, one concert, three films, one BBC interview and two days' walking in the Cotswolds. I receive a contract from Quartet Books for a translation of Ulfat Idilbi's novel, which I am calling *Sabriya*. I am getting a £750 advance.

Friday, 11 March

During the afternoon we go to see Karim, the six-day-old son of Motaz and Yara. He is called Karim because he is born in the month of Ramadan – the greeting for Muslims during the month is

---

2 Ghalia Qabbani, "What the Newsreader Said", translated by Peter Clark,
  Banipal 1, 1998.

"Ramadan Karim". He is multiply blessed for he is the first grandchild on both sides. And he has been born just before the Eid at the end of Ramadan when friends and family come to offer congratulations and gifts.

My sister, Stella, and Theresa's sister, Aggie, arrive on separate planes.

Saturday, 12 March
We think it is the last day of Ramadan and take the sisters to Aleppo. We divert to Krak des Chevaliers and I chat to a waiter in the restaurant, who is laying tables for a Japanese tour group. He has been to Homs, but never to Tartus, Aleppo or Damascus.

Sunday, 13 March
We drive to St Simeon's church and on to Basufan, a village inhabited by Yazidi Kurds. A ruined Byzantine church is in the backyard of the house of Muhammad al-Nasim who invites us in. He has four sons and two daughters, attractive, unveiled and relaxed. The 15-year-old is at intermediate school. Do you study English, I ask. "Yes," she says with an expressive toss of her head and a lovely smile, meaning, "Well, there are English classes. I don't take any notice of them so don't expect me to speak any English." And she does not, apart from one "Yes". One of our host's sons is a graduate of the University of Aleppo and is doing a postgraduate degree in Germany. Another son is also in Germany, a third in Greece.

Monday, 14 March
In Hama small children come up to us, all with the same observation – "Hama is beautiful".

We go on to Deir Mar Musa, and a young man points out details in the fresco paintings. We are puzzled when he says something about juices in the bubble, wondering whether this is a reference to a painting technique. We then realise he is talking about Jesus in the Bible.

Tuesday, 15 March
Back in Damascus, we arrange a dinner party, to celebrate my sister's 59th birthday. We have invited Warqa Barmada who has recently completed a PhD. Among other guests are Cynthia and Solhi al-Wadi. He and Stella get on very well, talking about birds. At Burqush we saw 50 or so migrating storks. "Ah," says Solhi, "the best place for birdwatching is Iraq."

Thursday, 17 March
I am reading J L Porter's *Five Years in Damascus*, in two volumes, published in 1855. It was in the Embassy library. The pages are uncut so I am the first to read it. It has the stamp of "Colonial Office Library" and was also in the library of the Arab Bureau in Cairo where T E Lawrence worked. Did he never read the book? Or had he read it before 1914? So many people have passed through the Damascus Embassy and have not read it. Strange.

Friday, 18 March
We take the sisters to Palmyra. Aggie and Theresa go to see the ruins. Stella and I go by the Temple of Bel – where, in Porter's day, 80 quarrelsome families lived – and to the salt lake to the south-east to see birds, but not with much success.

Sunday, 20 March
I make a condolence call following the death of the father of the economist, Nabil Sukkar. There must be 50 men in the double saloon. We mumble condolences and sit down. As people leave they give a curious hand gesture. The hand is raised to head level, but it is not like a military salute. It is very Syrian.

Monday, 21 March

I collect Stella and we head north and west, stopping at Baniyas for lunch. There is no suitable restaurant there and I ask for a *zarif* ("nice") restaurant. We are directed to Ras al-Ain, one mile inland up a valley. The open-air restaurant overlooks a stream that charges down from the mountains. This superb site is rather marred by rubbish that has been dumped on to the stream's bank.

We go on to Alleika to locate the house of Hamdan Ramadan and his descendants. His grandson, Hafiz, immediately recognises me and takes us to Hamdan's house. The old man is seated on the ground, smoking locally cultivated tobacco in a rolled cigarette with an amber cigarette holder. He is wearing a sort of army trench coat. I present him with a copy of the photograph I took of him and his family last July. He has been ill but his wife is as active as ever. Hafiz likes to practise his English: he is in his last year at secondary school. His sister is a student in the Faculty of Science at the university in Lattakia. One room has two portraits of Basil al-Assad. Are they Alawites? – I see no Islamic decorations. Hamdan asks me if I have brought the picture Freya Stark (whom he calls "your mother") took of him in 1939.

Tuesday, 22 March

Back in Damascus, Theresa and I go to a party for the Embassy staff to say farewell to Andrew Green. He gives a pretty speech, praising the British Council.

Wednesday, 23 March

I take my old teacher of Arabic, Leslie McLoughlin, to call on the Grand Mufti of Syria, Ahmad Kaftaru. His house is off the road to the airport and we sit in his garden, shaded by almond trees in blossom. The Mufti represents a liberal Islamic tradition and is at pains to emphasise this. He talks at length and has a twinkle in his eye. He tells us that he was in Japan and was asked how many Christians there were in Syria. "We are all Christians," he told his puzzled questioner. "We honour Jesus and Mary. We are all Christians."

In the evening I take Leslie to give a lecture. The hall fills up with about 120 people, including Muhiuddin Isa, Deputy Minister of Higher Education, and Ulfat Idilbi. Leslie speaks excellently. He says nice things about me, and talks about Syria being an ideal place to learn Arabic.

Thursday, 24 March

We arrange a breakfast for the British Council staff to say farewell to Jane and Andrew Green. I make a speech saying that, but for Andrew Green, none of us would have a job here. He has been the "midwife" of the operation. (Chortle, chortle.) We have benefited from Jane being here as a teacher. Indeed, Andrew can be regarded as a British Council spouse. (Chuckle, chuckle – but I do not think he likes the idea!) Jane is graceful and almost in tears. I remember her saying that teaching English is like hosting a dinner party. The ideal number is 16 and the host (like the teacher) has to ensure that everyone is involved. Like most Embassy wives, she has had a more interesting job than her husband.

Friday, 25 March

We have a little drama in the house. A stray cat has come into the garden and given birth to three cats on a fragile chair cover. We try to disturb them as little as possible and put out some meat and water.

I take Stella to Abel's tomb, 40 or so kilometres to the west of Damascus. There are two coachloads of – I work out – Iranian pilgrims. Inside the tomb are a score of praying veiled women from Meshhed . Then to Lake Zarzar. We walk all round the lake, meeting an army officer who attended one of Leslie's lectures. We avoid a pack of dogs, find a live tortoise and see the lake from all angles.

In the evening we go to a party at the Ghouta farm of Badr al-Din Shallah. He is 93, has a lovely, ready smile and shuffles around on a walking frame, wearing a spotless tarbush. He bought this place in 1939. I talk to Rafiq, husband of Randa al-Azm. Freya Stark's old friend from 1928, Amat al-Latif, has had a stroke and the family are not optimistic.

Ulfat Idilbi's son, Ziad, phones and we talk over points in the publisher's contract for my translation. He is keen that I should meet Wafic Said.

Saturday, 26 March

I go to see the kittens and they have disappeared. Later in the morning I hear some little squeaks, coming from the wash house at the back of the garden. The mother has eaten the meat I left and taken refuge under a sink. It is less exposed. Stella thinks she may have been caught short and gave birth prematurely.

We go to Bloudan for a picnic. We go up to Abu Zad, the café by the waterfall and walk along the track that leads ultimately to Helbun. Snow on the hills has melted and the path is muddy. We reach a rocky outcrop that looks down on the villages of Ain Hur and Shaghaya and almost as far as the Biqa' valley. In little patches of soil flowers are pushing out – a kind of crocus and heartsease. The soil is damp and the snow can only have melted in the last few days.

We return and drive to Shaghaya and eat our picnic there. The village is full of tractors. We are near the Lebanese frontier and the tractors are used for smuggling. They can use the mountain tracks avoiding the customs.

Sunday, 27 March

Ghaith al-Azm calls. His aunt, Amat al-Latif, died last night aged 96.

At seven I call on the Azms. The chief mourner is Shakir al-Azm. He is flanked by Ghaith and a son of Nazih al-Azm. Women call between *al-asr* (afternoon prayers) and al-maghrab (sunset prayers). Men call after *al-maghrab*. The announcement of the death mentions only male relations – and there are plenty of them. The family have hired a Koran reciter and I am reminded of the opening scenes of *Sabriya*.

Monday, 28 March

We go to the Meridien Hotel for a farewell party for Jane and Andrew Green. I talk to Abdul Majid Sheikh Husain, Rector of the Ba'th University in Homs. I tell him that "they" have refused the idea of an office in Aleppo. "They" got in his way a year or so ago when he was offered an Eisenhower Award to go to the United States. He went to Bulgaria instead.

Wednesday, 30 March

In the evening Bouchra calls with Nadia al-Ghazzi. It is one of the first times Nadia has come out since she was widowed.

At Easter 1994 Gabriel and Nathaniel joined their parents, and Peter and Theresa took a brief holiday in southern Turkey. They were returning to places – Antakya, Samanda , Iskenderun they had been to together in 1963.

Monday, 4 April

Returning to Damascus, we leave Arsuz. This corner of Turkey – it was part of Syria until 1939 – is utterly delightful and I fantasise about retiring to Antioch! It has history. It is a most interesting frontier town, between Turks and Arabs, with echoes of Romans and Byzantines thrown in. The mountains are superb. I would love to live here and explore the place. Flats can be rented, I hear, for US$1,000 a year.

We skirt Iskenderun and climb up the Belen Pass, observing traces of older roads. Each of us separately recalls journeys over this pass 30 plus years ago. I remember the sense of excitement and anticipation I had when I was on my way to thrilling places about which I knew very little, but about which there was an allure – Aleppo, Palmyra, Damascus, Petra. I am now much more familiar with these magical places, but the magic is still there.

Wednesday, 6 April

In the late afternoon I take the boys to Helbun. This is only half an hour away but it is a world away from Damascus. You get to this dusty village through a gorge. We leave the car and walk among some orchards, with lofty hills at the back of a broad, flat valley.

Thursday, 7 April

I have more crazy forms to fill in – the evaluation of effectiveness. It is so easy to massage figures, statistics, the results.

> They use the snaffle and the curb all right,
> But where's the bloody horse?

I have to say how many press reviews, how many of them were favourable and so on. Are our target groups satisfied, very satisfied, dissatisfied? How do you get a fair sample? I give it all minimum attention. It will all be fed into a computer with totally nonsensical conclusions emerging.

Friday, 8 April

We drive south to Dera'a, an unlovely town. It has a statue, unnamed and relatively modern, of Sultan Pasha al-Atrash who led the Druze revolt against the French in the 1920s and lived to a hundred, dying in the 1980s. Mustachioed with bandolier and rifle. I wonder who put it up.

We look at the ruined Roman amphitheatre and shoot off west to Tell Shihab, past the village to a waterfall. A score or so busses and vehicles are parked nearby. We pick our way down to a pool below the falls. We walk along the valley to a surviving railway bridge – the line used to go to Haifa. Back to the car – the whole place is packed with visitors. We go on to Mazarib Lake – another crowded picnic spot. People are boating on the lake. Tents have been erected for families who have come for a few days. We see families with brass trays, primus stoves, food, fruit and vegetables, transporting domestic conveniences to the fields. We do likewise and have our picnic in an olive orchard.

Saturday, 9 April

I attend a conference on language teaching at the University of Aleppo. About 30 attend. Before the conference gets under way the important folk walk in: the secretary of the University branch of the Ba'th party and the Rector. We stand for one minute (or less) in memory of Basil al-Assad. Then speeches. My contribution is a plug for the British Council teaching operation. Then papers from others. Many illustrate the need for practical guidance. Syrians have been encouraged to write theses on the decline of the semicolon or whatever. I talk about translation, basing what I say on notes I cobbled together in the car right up to the last minute. But I am sure of my ground and talk with authority, get some laughs and plenty of questions.

Sunday, 10 April

I battle with files, chasing my own tail. More interesting are three visitors. The first, Muhammad Jum'a, is a former Minister, a doctor trained in France. He heard my BBC broadcast on the Arabic service of the BBC and brings me a copy of his memoirs to read, perhaps to translate. The second would like me to give a lecture in Arabic on Marmaduke Pickthall: that would be a challenge. The third is a young man in search of a job.

I translate more of Ulfat's novel and write a 300-word piece on Abdul Salam al-Ujaili for an encyclopaedia being edited by Paul Starkey[3].

Wednesday, 13 April

As I work away at tiresome matters I have a phone call from Patrick Seale. "I've heard a lot about you," he says. "Your name is not totally unknown to me," I reply. We agree to have lunch together. We sit in the garden at the house and then go to the Marouch Restaurant. He was not born in Damascus, but first came at the age of six months. He describes himself as "The Hagiographer in Chief" and says lots of interesting things. "We shall never get to the bottom of it," he says more than once about the Hindawi affair that led to the break in diplomatic relations between Britain and Syria in 1986. He thinks the Ba'th Party is weakening. Assad is, he says, "both smug and worried." Patrick clearly has an excellent personal relationship with the President and talks to him frankly about Syria's lousy public relations. Assad hates any change and the loos at the palace are in an awful state. It is no one's job to look after them. Patrick's wife, Rana Kabbani, took him to see Ulfat Idilbi whose daughter, Laila, is married to the lawyer of the late Akram al-Ijja who has made "hundreds of millions" in arms deals. Akram married as his third wife a daughter of the long-serving Syrian Minister of Defence, Mustafa Tlas.

I call on the Minister of Culture about the forthcoming visit of the New Shakespeare Company who are putting on *The Taming of*

3 Julie Scott Meisami and Paul Starkey (eds), *Encyclopedia of Arabic Literature* (2 vols), Routledge, London and New York, 1998.

the Shrew in Damascus. We have secured some commercial sponsorship to cover costs of the visit. But this goes against the Ba'thist grain and we are not allowed to advertise.

Peter went to Jordan to meet the New Shakespeare Company and to escort them into Syria. After a brief break in Damascus they all went on to Aleppo, arriving late at night. Peter took his sons – on holiday from boarding school in England – with him.

Sunday, 17 April

The actors are invited to dinner at the Aleppo Club, guest of Dr Houriyeh, the Rector of the University. We are greeted there by him and also Ghias Barakat of the Department of English (and the Ba'th Party) and Tony and Alexander Akhras. Tony is the hereditary honorary British Consul. I introduce the guests, getting most of the names right. An engagement party is being celebrated in another part of the vast dining room. The Club is a most ornate former private house belong to the Aswad and Azali families. I am harangued by Dr Houriyeh and Ghias about who should be sitting in the front row.

Monday, 18 April

I meet Daniel Farson in the Baron Hotel. He is an ageing journalist/writer who is writing an article on the hotel. A few years ago he wrote on the Pera Palas in Istanbul for its centenary.

I take the boys to the theatre and meet Joseph Nashif who translates from Turkish to Arabic. I ask him what language he dreams in. "German," he tells me. For the performance, the right people are in the front row. I greet representatives of the great families of Aleppo – Mudarris, Kawakabi, Yaziji – and Sally Mazloumian and Armen. The play is splendidly acted. Funny, fast-moving, a bright contribution to Aleppo life. Bianca is a spoilt whinger. Kate is just high-spirited. There is immense appreciation – a receptive audience and a full house.

Tuesday, 19 April

Motaz and I call on the Governor of Aleppo. I invite him to the second performance of the play this evening. I raise the idea of the opening of a British Council branch in Aleppo. He talks about our working with the Arab Cultural Centre: that is obviously the party line.

Peter returned to Damascus.

Wednesday, 20 April

All went well at Aleppo last night. The Governor's wife attended, the Governor sending a big bouquet. There was a packed house and some scuffles outside. The group were pleased.

Thursday, 21 April

I go to the Azm Palace where the New Shakespeare Company will be performing this evening. Things are being prepared while there are plenty of tourists – European and Iranian – pottering around. The Iranians, I am told, are intensely curious and poke around everywhere. A door marked "Entry Forbidden" is always a challenge.

Theresa and I go to the performance. The Umayyad mosque's minaret of Isa shines, illuminated, over the Azm palace. The whole setting is romantic, gorgeous. The Minister of Culture arrives early bringing Talib Ibrahimi, a former Algerian Minister for Foreign Affairs. The United States Ambassador, Christopher Ross, and his wife, Carole, arrive, along with five hundred Syrians. The production is superb as usual.

Friday, 22 April

The final performance takes place in the afternoon at the Azm

Palace. Daniel Farson turns up for it. The place soon gets filled, though there are fewer VIPs. As the show proceeds I wander on to the rooftops of the Palace and take some photographs.

The Company's tour has been a huge success. It has established the British Council in Syria as purveyors of a quality product. Shakespeare never fails. The audiences are enthusiastic. People linger on to see the cast, get their autographs, and to be photographed with them.

We return home to prepare for the farewell party to the Company. The Minister's secretary phones to say the Minister will arrive at five past eight. I phone Brian Stewart – Chargé d'Affaires – telling him he should be here when the Minister arrives. She does not often come to foreign private houses and certainly not to the house of someone below Ambassador rank. She stays for half an hour and presents the company with a box of filigree goblets. After she leaves food and then dancing to the music of Didi and the Beatles.

Sunday, 24 April

The Minister's dragonian secretary is ill so I arrange for some flowers to be sent to her "from her friends at the British Council".

Warqa Barmada calls. There is a new Rector at the University of Damascus. He is Dr Abdul Mughni al-Ma' al-Barid, an Alawite pharmacist with an (East) German wife. I must call on him.

In the afternoon we take the car to Ain Khadra and walk along the railway line to the second station and back. The river Barada is in flood. The snows are still melting and splendidly sited restaurants bestride the river. We encounter friendliness everywhere – *tafaddal*, come in, be our guest.

Bill Badley calls. He talks about Daniel Farson. They were both at the same school – Wellington. Daniel was totally plastered at our party. When he is stone-cold sober, Bill says, he is boring. When he is drunk he is impossible. But there is an intermediate stage, a delicate balance, when he is interesting and interested. But that stage does not last long.

Tuesday, 26 April

I call on Ulfat Idilbi, discuss the contract for the translation and stay on and chat for an hour. She has travelled in China, Japan and much of Syria. She likes Paris, especially for the shopping.

Wednesday, 27 April

Rana Saadeh, a professional interpreter, calls and we go over 60 pages of Ulfat Idilbi's book. There are many words for different rooms of a house and for articles of women's clothing. Rana helps me sort out the difference between *dalia* and *arisha*; and between *malaya, hijab, mandil* and *baralin*.

Thursday, 28 April

I send to my headquarters a report on the New Shakespeare Company visit, saying that in dealing with the Ministry of Culture I grovel at the top, nag the middle ranks and "offer incentives" to those lower down.

Saturday, 30 April

We go out for a couple of hours, driving north almost to Saidnaya and on to Mar Elias, another church on a cliff overlooking a huge plain to the east and the town of Adra. Then back through pretty villages that, apart from a tarred road and a new mosque, have not changed much for years.

The British Council headquarters sent out an exhibition about British crime writers. One of the panels was about Joan Smith. Peter had been a fan of Joan Smith's journalism for several years, having read her book, Misogynies *soon after it was published in 1989. So he invited her to Syria to give some talks at universities.*

Theresa and I go to the airport to meet Joan Smith. On the runway is a United States of America plane. The American Secretary of State, Warren Christopher, has been expected and there are hopes that a deal may be imminent, with Israel returning the Golan Heights to Syria.

Joan arrives and I see her through immigration and customs. She is pleasant. She is going through a divorce from Francs Wheen: the absolute will be on Tuesday next. People, she tells me, are surprised that she is venturing to Syria. There is a very negative view of the country.

Sunday, 1 May

We take Joan to Palmyra. The place is crowded for we arrive on the last day of the Second Desert Festival. As we are at the Temple of Bel – or Temple of Bill, as one tour guide describes it, sirens and motorcades announce the arrival of Warren Christopher, the United States Secretary of State, and we meet his party as we emerge from the ruins. We see them race around the site, before being whisked off to the small airport. We hear two planes depart and silence returns to Palmyra.

We go on to the "races" and watch horses ridden bareback round a 1,400 metre course.

In the early evening we go to the theatre, the Roman theatre. It is packed, all seats taken, with extra chairs brought in for army and civilian officials, including the French Ambassador. I lay my hands on three for ourselves. There is an atmosphere of good-natured chaos. A show starts on the stage – music and mediocre dancing. The Minister of Tourism arrives with an entourage. The chairs are reshuffled to make room for him. Was this how the theatre was used two thousand years ago? – packed with music and dance.

Monday, 2 May

Joan's divorce absolute comes through tomorrow. She is calm but it clearly preoccupies her. The murderer in her novel, *A Masculine*

Ending, is based on her ex-husband. Back in Damascus, I hear that last night there were sirens and escorted convoys moving around the western residential part of the city. Was there some political tension? It was suggested – and it makes complete sense – that there was an Israeli delegation here negotiating the Golan Heights. All very interesting.

Wednesday, 4 May

We do not have permission for Joan to meet and talk to university students. However, we do go and meet the staff of the Department of English. The head of department is very nervous and we chat for a while. Some students are keen to meet Joan and are waiting in a nearby room. We go to the room and bolt the door from the inside. Joan talks to them and some staff go on about their theses in a boring way. The students are allowed to put in a word or two.

Thursday, 5 May

I take Joan to call on the Minister of Culture. Joan presents her with a copy of *Misogynies*.

We have arranged a creative writing competition among the students. The first prize goes to a Palestinian, Islam Dabar, born in Kuwait. He is an ambitious medical student and dreams of going to Canada. He decided to write his story at the last minute and scribbled it out in the kitchen.

Saturday, 7 May

We take Joan to Suwaida and have lunch with Hamza al-Atrash. He and his brother talk about Druze revolts against the Turks. There used to be three religious Druze families – the Hajaris, the Derbos and the Hinawis. It was Sultan Pasha al-Atrash who first entered Damascus in 1918 and Hasan Tarabai raised the Sherifian flag. The British should have extended patronage to the Druze as the French did to the Catholic Maronites and the Russians to the Orthodox. An interesting Druze slant on history.

Monday, 9 May

I am exhausted. The office is a majlis and people drop in. I am happy about that but when people drop in for *two hours*, then that is two hours I do not have spare.

Allen Hibbard, who is about to leave, writes a very nice letter of appreciation to the whole office, recognition of a team spirit in all the work of dealing with theatre, music and literature.

Friday, 13 May

I hear some gossip. Bushra, the daughter of the President, heard of Basil's death before her father. It was Mustafa Tlas and another general who told Hafez about the death. His first reaction was, "Was the body disfigured?" It was Bushra who accompanied her father to the University Hospital where Basil's body was taken. She could not stay in the morgue for more than a few minutes. He was alone with the corpse for an hour.

I also hear that a Syrian Minister's official salary is 9,000 Syrian pounds a month – that is about £1,300.

Saturday, 14 May

I type up about 2,000 words of an article about Freya Stark I have written for *Asian Affairs*[4]. I concentrate on the Syrian side and it casts an unfamiliar light on her and on a generation.

After lunch we go to the largely Christian village of Qal'at al-Jandar on the slopes of Mount Hermon, in a fairly militarised area. We climb up to the topmost tower. There are roads that we want to

---

4 "The Future of Freya Stark: The View from Damascus", *Asian Affairs*, 1994, reprinted in Peter Clark, *Coffeehouse Footnotes*, Diss, 2010, 26-31.

follow into the folds of the hills. From the curiosity of the villagers I infer that they do not have many visitors.

We return via the site of Paul's blinding-light conversion. An unappealing 1965 chapel has been erected, but we are on the brow of a hill looking down on the Plain of Damascus with the city nestling in the green of the Ghouta.

Monday, 16 May

A number of green and yellow bins have appeared outside the city, an attempt to encourage a litter awareness.

I notice that an increasing number of young men are sporting Basil al-Assad beards.

Tuesday, 17 May

There is a reception for "Europe Day". I talk to all sorts of folk and see Mustafa Tlas surrounded by six or seven people, all nodding at his words.

Wednesday, 18 May

In the evening we go to a concert at the Assad Library. Solhi al-Wadi has trained his string ensemble to near perfection. We start with the Bach double violin concerto, and after an interval Libana Qantar sings "Dido's Lament". She is wearing a fine evening dress, is nervous, her hands firmly at her side; she is lovely. Then some unknown Rossini and tedious Respighi. At the end Solhi has a warm reception and in the applause brings on a hesitating Libana, now wearing jeans. There are appreciative smiles and applause. Solhi has insisted. Her voice is more important than her clothes.

Thursday, 19 May

It is the Eid and we have a few days' holiday. We want to see the north-east of the country and drive up to Aleppo for the night.

Friday, 20 May

Bab, Membij, Jerablus, al-Raqqa, Rusafa. This last is an amazing place – a Byzantine fortress-city that was a pilgrimage site. The walls are two kilometres long and much of the city is in an excellent condition – the north gate, the cisterns, the two churches. What strikes us is the scale on which it was constructed and the remoteness. We see nobody about at all: we have the whole place to ourselves.

We return to al-Raqqa and have a drink by the bridge over the Euphrates until forced to move by mosquitoes.

Saturday, 21 May

We drive north, spacious, full of vast cornfields and sheep. Flocks are herded across the road. Others wander around, apparently lost. Have they escaped the slaughter of this Eid, to be sacrificed next year? The village houses have one storey and there are no breeze blocks.

We see the site of Tell Halaf. The main town is across the border – in Turkey. The railway line is the frontier, with watchtowers every 100 metres or so. There are sulphur springs. Tangy water seeps out of the earth into a pool that is deep and clear. Some youths are swimming in it, floating along, borne by a gentle current.

We go on to Qamishli and check into the Semiramis Hotel, run by a couple of elderly Assyrians. The town is built on a grid plan and was a kind of extended refugee camp, with Armenians, Kurds and Assyrians from Turkey and Iraq. It has also a small Jewish community with a Souk al-Yahud, a Jewish market. An Armenian taxi-driver, who has lived in Abu Dhabi and deals in car spare parts from Germany and Britain, takes us to the Zohrabian Restaurant. This has an extraordinary design, with galleries somehow like a theatre. The place is spotless with discreet lighting and air-conditioning. Nothing gaudy or makeshift. It has been going for eight months, and everything works. The beer is smuggled in from Turkey – the famous Efes beer.

Sunday, 22 May

We drive on east to Mulkiya – the Kurdish Deirik – and call at the police station to get a permit to see the Roman bridge on the river Tigris. The paint of a stencilled portrait on the station wall has dripped making it appear that the President has a runny nose. The police shout for a driver, Ahmad, who turns up with a battered 1957 Toyota. For 300 Syrian pounds, Ahmad takes us to Ain Dawar police station overlooking the Tigris and we collect a police escort. Then we descend a rough track through the tributaries of the river. We splash through reeds, and luxuriant plants tower over our heads. The Roman bridge is over a dry watercourse and springs from the only rock we can see. Gertrude Bell came here in about 1911 but we know nobody personally who has been here. There are Turkish border posts nearby and we are, I am sure, being carefully watched. (Why?) We turn back and stop at a spring where an old man is busily hacking away at the undergrowth.

We pick up our car again and head towards Hasake, stopping at the huge mounds of Tell Brak, excavated by Max Mallowan with the support of his wife, Agatha Christie, in the 1930s. We look at the excavated palace and the display of fragments of pottery laid out trustingly on the ground, waiting for the next season. On to Hasake, not a beautiful town.

On the road to Deir ez-Zor we see heavy clouds of sand seeping, tearing across the road. Visibility is reduced to zero. We stop. I open the car door and a raging gust seizes Theresa's hat, throwing it into the road. We check in, reluctantly, at the Cham Hotel.

I am very thirsty. The minibar in our room is locked and I phone for a key. I wait. I want a bottle of cold water. I have to wait for that. At dinner, the chef's speciality is off. A half-bottle of wine is listed at 175 Syrian pounds, but the only wine available is at 900 Syrian pounds a bottle. Theresa orders a cold gazpacho and is served a hot tomato soup. The swimming pool is closed: it is only open during working hours.

Monday, 23 May

We set off early and drive on to Halabiya, like Rusafa, a huge Byzantine fortress-city, but in a more engaging position, overlooking the perfectly still waters of the Euphrates. Then to Palmyra and home to Damascus.

Wednesday, 25 May

Peter takes three months' leave, mostly in Britain. Theresa joins him after a week or so. They take possession of their house in Brighton and, after the school has broken up, take their two sons for a magnificent holiday in the western states of America. He returns to Damascus in August.

Wednesday, 24 August

I go to a "prayer meeting" at the Embassy, the first with the new Ambassador, Adrian Sindall. It is a more relaxed occasion. I raise the matter of the British Council auditors wanting to close the Amman account, and relying solely on the official exchange rate for our local cash requirements. A ripple of shock horror goes round the room as the implications are quickly considered: a rise in allowances (hurrah!); a sharp rise in the costs of the Embassy with possible reduction of local staff and of performance; questions about the cost-effectiveness of the operation; a rise in rents and all local costs.

Thursday, 25 August

I meet Maggie and David Wolton at the airport. We immediately go for dinner at the Ambassador's Residence. Among the other guests are Cynthia and Solhi al-Wadi, and Lyse Doucet, a BBC correspondent, French Irish Canadian, a lovely girl.

Friday, 26 August

I go into the office and revise 1,900 words of translation. I can forget all about time when I am doing this. After lunch I take my guests, David and Maggie, to Abel's tomb. It is a Shi'ite shrine, looked after by Druze, but there are all sorts of visitors – 50 or 60. It is in a military restricted area and public access is permitted only on Fridays.

Sunday, 28 August

I go to the opening of the International Trade Fair. I am there early as the place fills up. Ambassadors (including mine), diplomats, officials. There are two speeches and texts are distributed to us 20 minutes after they have started. The second speech is by the Minister of Finance, Dr Muhammad al-Imadi, and is a comprehensive survey of the present political position. After that there are some dances and a show from dervishes – bowing to the sheikh, hands over the breast. One man whirls for several minutes, his long shirt out making him look like a cone. He whirls at the rate of one revolution per second.

Tuesday, 30 August

I have a visit from a teacher of English and Arabic. He is studying Aramaic and wants a scholarship to meet other scholars in Britain. Why go to Britain, I ask, when it is here that Aramaic is spoken?

Thursday, 1 September

The Ambassador has a "wheeze", which, on reflection is an unrealistic non-starter. The President's brother, Rifaat al-Assad, has a luxury house and adjacent office which he wants to sell. The whole complex is perhaps too big for the Embassy. What about the British Council joining in? Rifaat may be short of ready cash. His starting price is 16 million US dollars. The Ambassador would like to get it down to £2.5 million. I cannot see the Foreign Office agreeing. Nor can I see the British Council agreeing either to our buying premises, and anyway the rent would be too much. However, I go along with his notion and go to inspect the house in Mezze. The place has inlaid marble and is full of luxury and beautiful paintings. The third floor has a large majlis area with fine settees, but off to one side is a little love nest, a bedroom with a circular bed on a dais beneath a mirrored ceiling. Nearby is a luxurious bathroom with a large round bath. On the lower ground floor are ordinary family rooms, splendid but sober.

I take Maggie and David to Safita. At the hotel is a message from Kamal Abu Deeb, Professor of Arabic at the School for Oriental and African Studies and born in Safita. We are invited "for a drink". He lives in Lower Safita. The family are wonderful: mother, whose Arabic I find incomprehensible, lively sons and daughters. We chat and sip beer and araq till nearly midnight. Kamal fits in superbly, like a patriarch, but without any airs.

Friday, 2 September

We head for al-Kahf, through windy roads and ravined and terraced landscape. We have to ask the way repeatedly before getting there. We crawl along the path, through the gateway with the Mamluk relief inscription and up to the level of the citadel. It was razed in 1816 after having been an Ottoman prison. Our silent contemplation is interrupted by a minibus that turns up and a besuited elderly gentleman picks his way through the scrub and undergrowth and rocks to join us.

Saturday, 3 September

At Lattakia we eat at Spiro's. Ahmad al-Isa joins us. I arranged for him to spend some time at the University of Lancaster. He is intelligent, idealistic, energetic. There is a vacancy for the post of Party Secretary in the University. Is he a candidate? I wonder.

We go on to Jabala to look at the Roman theatre (which was a Crusader fortification for a while). Then back to Safita and Damascus.

I have two parties to go to, both at the Meridien Hotel. The first is to celebrate Qatari National Day. I look in, sip an orange juice and chat to a young diplomat from Ras al-Khaimah. Then in another part of the hotel I attend a farewell party for the Belgian Ambassador. There we drink champagne. I talk with Mahir al-Hamdi, the Palestinian representative. Mahir was a student at Cairo with Yasir Abdu Rabbu and appears in the stories of Yasir's wife, Liana Badr. He tells me that Yasir Abdu Rabbu is pressing for an entente with Jordan, dragging Arafat along with him.

In the following year Peter was preoccupied with the coordination of Syria's first opera. Solhi al-Wadi, Director of the Higher Institute of Music and Drama, had built up an orchestra and a ballet school. An Iraqi, he had been at Victoria College, Alexandria, a contemporary of King Hussein of Jordan, and studied music in London under Lennox Berkeley. He had been put in charge of developing western classical music in Syria and had received personal support from President Hafez al-Assad. If you are in need of anything, Assad had told Solhi, feel free to get in touch.

Solhi had said to Peter,

"I'd like to put on an opera: Dido and Aeneas, *by Purcell."*

"Well," said Peter, "let's see what we can do. Next year is the three hundredth anniversary of Purcell's death. We can get the British Council involved."

"I remember taking part in it at Victoria College," said Solhi. "It is a pan-Arab opera. Dido came from Tyre in the Lebanon and the action takes place in Carthage in Tunisia."

Peter thought that the opera would fit in with Ba'thist ideology, especially as it could be argued without too much distortion that Dido was betrayed by the European, the Greek Aeneas, an anticipation of later betrayals.

Solhi had been in London earlier in the year and the idea had been discussed by British Council Music Department. They would give their support.

Solhi and Peter had the idea of putting the opera on at Roman theatres in Syria and at the Crusader castle, Krak des Chevaliers.

Sunday, 4 September

At 10 Solhi and I go to call on the Minister. The Minister bubbles with excitement at the opera project. She does not support the idea of putting it on at Krak des Chevaliers. There are political/historical objections to exploiting a Crusader site. I say that we will need support from the private sector – that means commercial sponsorship. She reluctantly agrees to this.

Monday, 5 September

I take David Wolton, who has been the Chairman of Medical Aid for Palestine, to call on Dr George Habash. Mahir al-Hamdi takes us to the Damascus office of the Popular Front for the Liberation of Palestine. Habash was the big bogey of a quarter of a century ago. We sit in his office under a tapestry of Lenin looking into the future. On one wall is a picture of Che Guevara. We are in a time warp. George Habash is in his mid- to late-sixties and is friendly enough. He declines to talk English and has an interpreter, Abu Khalil. He is partially paralysed and seems to have a painful right arm. The wrist is swollen and he raises it slowly up and down, bringing it gently down on the arm of the chair. He and David talk of charitable works, "leaving the political questions aside". The office is not well-furnished.

Thursday, 8 September

I go to the Assad Library for a meeting of the Women's National Union. It is to celebrate the Elimination of Illiteracy Day. The lecture hall is packed with women.

Saturday, 10 September

Theresa returns. I go to the airport, getting there an hour and a half
before the plane is due. I have a beer, a coffee and a toasted cheese
sandwich, and read the proofs of a section of my translation. I am
happy to be reunited and fulfilled. I feel as if I have been married to
Theresa all my adult life.

Sunday, 11 September

I should finish the translation in three months. I want to have time
to read it all through, erase inconsistencies and establish some
stylistic coherence. Only a translator examines the construction and
detail of a text. I note some problems of the Arabic text – Ulfat is
sometimes confused about the month the narrative is in. I suspect
she wrote it at speed.

Monday, 12 September

I have a visit from Malcolm Abaza. I knew his father, John Abaza,
very well in Khartoum in the 1970s. Malcolm was a few months
older than my son, Paul, and as infants they were great friends. John's
father, Salah al-Din, was a Circassian who repudiated modern Egypt.
He had studied at the American University of Beirut and was a
chiropodist in Alexandria. Salah al-Din hated Abdul Nasser so much
that he had photographs of Isma'ilia bombed by the British in his
clinic. He married an Ulster girl and John was brought up as an
English Christian gentleman and went to Victoria College,
Alexandria and Trinity College, Cambridge. John knew only
"kitchen Arabic" – his father used to say that Arabic was "the
language of peasants and donkeys" – and has been stuck in
Khartoum as a Lecturer in English at the University since the 1960s.
His conditions have gradually deteriorated: no pension, no UK base.
He has an OBE, but that does not bring in any money. He is now
63 and faces utter poverty. Malcolm realises he will have to look after

his father in his old age, though a millionaire Welsh lady is interested in him; but John has a fierce integrity and will not be bought. His idea of wealth is having a car and a house with more than one storey. Malcolm was given that name after the king in Macbeth whose job was to clear up the previous mess: symbolic of the chaos of modern Egypt. John's marriage to Malcolm's mother broke up. She married (and divorced) again, but was able to send Malcolm to Winchester.

Malcolm just remembers his grandfather who died on a visit to Khartoum. Indeed, I now learn, he committed suicide. I helped John carry the old man who was comatose (dead?) downstairs in their house to a taxi to take him to hospital. I attended the funeral at a Muslim cemetery. It was (for Khartoum) a chilly day. Western mourners stood in a group on one side of the coffin. John's Sudanese colleagues, Muslims, stood in another group. John stood alone, belonging at that moment neither to one group or another. I have never seen a man so isolated.

But Malcolm is returning to his roots. He is studying Arabic at Edinburgh and has recently been travelling in Abkhazia and western Georgia where the Abazas came from.

Wednesday, 14 September

I call on the new President of the University of Damascus – Dr Abdul Mughni Ma' al-Barid. He is an Alawite whose family came from Antioch and migrated to Aleppo after the annexation by Turkey of the sanjak of Alexandretta in 1939. His subject is Pharmacy and he was the teacher of the President's daughter, Bushra, whose Damascus degree was in that subject. He is affable and wants to open doors and windows.

Thursday, 15 September

We go to a farewell dinner for Christa Salamandra, an American sociologist. There is a very pleasant collection of people there. A young Syrian tells me he has translated a long story by Aldous Huxley and had it published at his own expense – 30,000 Syrian pounds (about £400).

Friday, 16 September
After only four hours' sleep we are up and collect Sulaiman, the Hardy specialist, and drive to Tartus.

Sulaiman is one of 12 children, an Alawite from a village above Tartus. All the children are achievers. Father did "odd jobs" until the children came along. Then he educated himself and got the intermediate school certificate and became an elementary school teacher and librarian. Mother had no education.

Sulaiman and his wife, Sa'da, have a flat in Tartus near a bread kiosk. Their daughter is a pretty, quiet, scholarly girl who is set to do a PhD at Cambridge.

We have lunch and potter around Tartus. Sa'da is off to do an MA at the University of Warwick. She too came from a village – she is a first cousin once removed of Sulaiman – and went to intermediate school in Tartus, living by herself from the age of 12 until she was joined by her younger sister two years later.

We drive out to call on some Christian friends, Vaygan (named after the French General Weygand) and Susan, but better known as Abu and Umm Butrus, father and mother of Butrus/Peter. They were teachers but were unable to make ends meet on their joint salaries. They inherited some land and have a wonderful and profitable smallholding. As a peasant Vaygan is known as Abu Butrus, but when he puts on a suit he becomes Ustaz ("Professor") Vaygan.

Saturday, 17 September
Sa'da is off to Warwick next week. She is facing some resistance from her mother and grandmother. "Your place is with your children." But she is determined to get her PhD.

Back in Damascus the muezzin calls people to sunset prayer at 5.45 but then a power cut reduces him to silence. Thirty years ago when I first travelled in Syria the call to prayer was by voice alone – as it had been for the previous 1,300 years.

Sunday, 18 September

I go to the wedding ceremony of one of Motaz's relations. It is an all-male affair. Chairs are arranged in a large square. I shake hands with the groom, the father of the groom, Motaz and the father of the bride – and take my place. There is not much opportunity for talking to people. One guest is Ilyas As'ad, the Palestinian speech-writer to the President. A group of chanters recite sections of the Koran in quite a musical way: it is almost like rap. Then one man comes forward to make a speech, or rather deliver a sermon. I am reminded of Ian Paisley; it is full of smug self-congratulation about the Arab-Islamic nation. He preaches against birth control which is against Islam. The aim is to produce children, to produce more Muslims. The west is afraid of this. After that there is a kind of chant and response with everybody standing up. We are each served with a bottle of water, then some lovely juice, ice cream, cakes and a present of a little packet of sweets.

Theresa goes to the women's reception. Some women are not enthusiastic about the bride that has been chosen.

"She's late," says one.

"Perhaps she won't come at all."

"I hope so."

Monday, 19 September

Bouchra phones. She is packing for Ala al-Din who is going to Volgograd for seven years tomorrow to study medicine – one year of Russian-language study and six years of medicine. That is a great development. He is the brightest of Bouchra's three sons.

I am reading a book on Arab women by Bouthaina Shaaban who is now the President's regular interpreter, replacing Tawfiq Bujairami, a Palestinian who was educated in Iraq and, as a friend observed, gave up thinking when he completed a PhD on Wilfrid Scawen Blunt in 1970. He was always bitter about the Americans and the British. Bouthaina presents a more attractive face. An Alawite, she also has a good relationship with Bushra, the President's daughter.

We go to the Chilean National Day party. The Saudi Ambassador comments on the recent hot weather to Theresa, "The weather is Saudi. Perhaps there will be lots of oil here as well."

Tuesday, 20 September
We go to the American Center to the opening of an exhibition of paintings by Hala al-Faisal. They are of a lot of idle nude women doing all sorts of things to each other. It is too crowded to talk to people but Riad Ismat introduces me to the novelist (and daughter of a previous President) Colette Khoury.

Wednesday, 21 September
Motaz has been to the Ministry of Culture. We have received some KLM tickets for a forthcoming cultural event and it is suggested that the KLM logo should not be larger than that of the British Council. A small subtle but unmistakeable shift towards accepting commercial sponsorship for the arts!

Thursday, 22 September
To Aleppo. After a call on the Rector of the University and Dr Ghias Barakat, who runs the English Language Centre, we head north passing the monument on the Azaz road that commemorates the last battle in the Great War, between the retreating Turks and an Indian cavalry regiment. We drive to Cyrrhus. The first building we see is a Roman tower-tomb which, since medieval times, has been a

Muslim saint's resting place, with an added mosque and courtyard. We drive on to Selinfe, along the perimeter of north-west Syria, hugging the Turkish frontier all the time: Afrin, Ain Dara, St Simeon, Deir al-Azza, Darkush, crossing the Orontes and on to Jisr al-Shughur and then up into the hills.

We are joined at the Grand Hotel by Ghias Barakat and Ahmad al-Qutb, who has returned from six years in the United Arab Emirates, and their wives. Ghias and Ahlam lost a child and we can still feel the tenseness of the tragedy. He was found by Ghias, floating, dead, in the swimming pool at their home. It chills the blood. Ahmad is a Damascene and tells me of his father, Bashir, one of the founders of – and he points to Ghias – "*his* party". I am realising that Ghias has a major Ba'th Party role in the University of Aleppo.

Friday, 23 September
We sleep well and join Ghias and Ahlam for breakfast. Ahlam cannot enjoy the mountain air. She cannot enjoy anything.

We leave Selinfe and drive through hills of unsurpassed beauty, little villages clinging to the olive-strewn hillside, tiny outcrops of rock, views sweeping down over vast, broad bosky valleys. We find our way – after asking repeatedly – to Mehelbe castle. On the way is the tomb of a *wal* – a local holy man. We are in the heart of Alawite country and there is a noted absence of mosques.

We reach Qardaha, the birthplace of the President. It has a luxurious-looking hospital and a grand hotel. A lot of modern buildings has made Qardaha a privileged place. We go to the tomb of Basil al-Assad. It is in a small building within a large enclosure. The tomb is in a temporary smoked-glass structure covered with a green cloth decorated with quotations from the Koran and is guarded by soldiers. Some of Basil's personal possessions are on display – suits, a pistol, an AK-47. Incense dominates the smells within the tomb area and in the enclosure. Nearby is a bizarre mural painting portraying Basil aloft in the skies with the President looking up in distress, surrounded by midgets – the Syrian people. Another mural has Basil with horse and computer.

We drink some coffee and watch other … pilgrims (?) and leave to go into the hills again.

Sunday, 25 September

We are to have the film *My Left Foot* for the European Film Festival in December. There will be some European *cinéastes* as they are called. I decide to invite Theresa's sister, Mary Alleguen, who was the Production Manager for that film. So I phone her in Dublin. She is ready and able to come.

In the evening we go to a party for the new "Fulbrighters" – that is the term used. They are, as usual, a bright bunch. I also consolidate older friendships – George Jabbour, Sadiq al-Azm and the Palestinian historian Khairiyya al-Qasimi who is shortly to take up a teaching post in Saudi Arabia.

Monday, 26 September

I speak to my boss in London. I clear the fact that I am inviting my sister-in-law to Damascus. Then he tells me that the Director General wants me to go to Saudi Arabia on promotion. We have a laugh – I have never expressed any wish to go there. I also declined going there in 1991. I promise to think about it for 24 hours and give him an answer. I discuss the offer with Theresa.

Tuesday, 27 September

As soon as I am in the office I draft a reply saying No categorically. The post should go to a volunteer. Having sent that off I feel enormously relieved.

Wednesday, 28 September

My boss in London phones again. Edmund Marsden is ready to fly me to London to twist my arm. Saudi Arabia is a most important country from Britain's point of view, because of commercial interests, especially the sale of arms. This is exactly what horrifies me. I do not want my professional raison d'être to be a pillar, however small, of enriching arms manufacturers. The sale of arms to Gulf states was totally useless in 1990. I prefer to be part of the Peace Process.

Sadiq al-Azm phones to tell me that Ni'mat al-Azm, Freya Stark's friend from the 1920s, has died. In the evening Theresa and I go along to the Azm house. Theresa is ushered to the balcony where the Azm women are. I join the men in solemn silence, the Koran being recited on a tape. After a few minutes I am invited to join the family. Muna, Lisa, Hassana and their mother are there and there are peels of laughter as they recall their wonderful aunt. "Freya has summoned her," says Hassana. Their aunt, Amat al-Latif, was the pious one. She never married, reluctant to be subordinate to any man. Ni'mat was the adventurous one. She was a painter, married a Lebanese and admired King Farouk. Both sisters had been active in the Revolt against the French in the 1920s, smuggling ammunition under their clothes. I mention Ulfat Idilbi's novel I am translating which covers the Revolt. This sparks an outburst. "It was wrong of Ulfat to make a character in her novel shoot down a French plane. It was Uncle Nazih. Only one plane was brought down. By Nazih." (I wonder whether Ulfat was trying to humble the Azms by making her character, Adil, the son of a baker, the man who brought down the plane. Incidentally, Ulfat's husband and the father of Muna, Lisa and Hassana were the only two radiologists in Damascus between the wars. Was there also some professional tension?) Sadiq joins us, and also a son of Nazih, Yahya, who was given his name at the request of the Imam of Yemen. "If God were a woman," observes Yahya, "she would answer my prayers. I know how to talk to a woman."

Friday, 30 September

We go to lunch in Bloudan, guests of Hanna and Jenny Khoury. I am saddened to see that the old Ottoman Consulate building is being demolished. Wood's building. Burton's home. It is being pulled down, unmourned and without ceremony.

Saturday, 1 October

I hear a rumour that the Minister of Culture, Najah al-Attar, is to be Syria's Ambassador in Paris. Interesting but improbable. The United States Ambassador is Mrs Harriman who was a Digby and so a distant cousin of Lady Jane Digby who ended her days in Damascus!

Sunday, 2 October

I call on the Director of Antiquities, Dr Sultan Mheisin, a prehistorian who comes from Al-Tall. Michael Macdonald wants to work on Safaitic inscriptions. He applied for permission. It was granted and then withheld. I try to figure out why. The world of pre-Islamic epigraphy is minute and the dozen or so people involved in that world must be very competitive. I remember asking Michael about Father Albert Jamme whom I knew in Yemen. He was "mad" and his work useless. I suspect that someone has put in an unflattering word about Michael.

We go to the Ambassador's Residence for dinner with Douglas Hogg, a listener and a questioner, a nice man. He does not know about the Hama massacres of 1982, but nor does the Ambassador know which is Hogg's constituency.

Tuesday, 4 October

I go to the University where Douglas Hogg is to make a presentation of books to the English for Special Purposes Unit. Amiable confusion reigns. I have written the Minister's speech and am due to interpret it spontaneously on live television. But Hogg deviates from the text and talks about politics and expresses his confidence in a peace agreement between Syria and Israel. I am suddenly aware of a huge responsibility in getting it right. Millions of Syrians will be watching this on the news. Help!

The Embassy Club, known as the Pig and Whistle, should, it is suggested, be renamed the Hogg and Whistle.

Wednesday, 5 October

I have an interesting talk with Dr Samir al-Taqi, one of the heart surgeons we sent to Harefield. He has recently been elected MP for Aleppo. I ask him about the elections. He says the elections have been a turning point in Syria's history. There are new classes emerging. The recent easing of political tension has allowed other areas of political interest to assert themselves. He mentions in particular merchants and Kurds. The Kurds are in touch with Kurds outside Syria. Of 250 MPs 25 are traditional tribal leaders. Twenty-four MPs are women. Parliament is not allowed to discuss foreign affairs or defence but strong views are expressed on banking laws.

Thursday, 6 October

I have a phone call from my Director General, John Hanson, asking me to think carefully of Saudi Arabia. The British Council is ready to offer a package, an enhanced salary just for me and Saudi Arabia. I think he is expecting the answer No and apologises for offering me a bribe. He will be in Amman next week, and I offer to see him there. He accepts.

We have dinner with George Jabbour. His mother is there, a lively old lady, totally deaf, a graduate of an English medium school in Tripoli in 1926. The framed certificate is on the wall.

Friday, 7 October

We drive south of Shaqqa and are invited into a house which is like the portal of a khan, with bits of Greek writing and classical symbols on the wall. I suspect the building has served several functions in the last thousand years or so.

Saturday, 8 October

We drive east of Jabal Druze to Salkhad and Malha – which everyone calls Malah. This is where Wilfred Thesiger spent time in the Second World War. I have not bothered to look up his old contacts. Are there any memories of him?

Saturday, 15 October

I go to a reception for the Committee for Middle Eastern Trade, led by John Hill. He and Nabil Sukkar give talks on banking liberalisation. Syria needs to attract expatriate capital for investment in the country. Perhaps there is twenty billion dollars of such capital in Syrian hands. Ten years ago Egypt wooed back its own migrant capital, which amounted to 150% of Egypt's GDP. The price for Syria to pay is to allow more participation and freedom of expression.

Sunday, 16 October

I take the train to Amman from the Hijaz railway station, the handsome building put up in 1917. The whole railway service is run-down, scuffy, uncared for. The first-class fare to Amman is 160 Syrian pounds (about £2.40). We set off more or less on time and the hooter screeches away as we go through the rush hour souk in Midan. Then slowly into the dusty hills. Dera'a and the frontier.

The train takes ten hours. I take a taxi from the station. The Palestinian driver comes from Jenin and wants to be an accountant in Canada.

Monday, 17 October

I go to John Hanson's hotel and talk through the reasons I do not want to go to Saudi Arabia. He accepts – "No more pressure will be put on you."

This is the third time I have declined promotion.

Tuesday, 18 October

We have a drink with Brigid and Alan Waddams and meet their house guest, William Dalrymple, who is writing a book on this part of the world[5]. He is following the steps of a Greek monk who travelled extensively in the Middle East on the eve of Islam. He is looking at the fate and role of Christian communities. They are badly off in Turkey and Israel.

Wednesday, 19 October

I go to Homs with a specialist from London in English for Academic Purposes. We have lunch with the Rector of the University, Abdul Majid Sheikh Hussein. He is off to Argentina shortly. His father migrated there years ago and returned to Syria. He will be stopping in Britain on the way. He did a PhD at Bristol and has been in touch ever since with the lady who served food at the University canteen. He is going to see her for the celebration of her golden wedding.

In Homs I hear of the death of Ibrahim Abdul Nur, my oldest Syrian friend – I first met him in 1962. He was 63 and went blind, had a heart attack and was diabetic. I go out to Fairouza and sit with the family. The eldest son, Bassam, and the daughter, Abeer, are both in California.

Thursday, 20 October

A visiting British opera singer has been to the Higher Institute for

5 William Dalrymple, *From the Holy Mountain*, HarperCollins, London, 1997.

Music and Drama and upset everyone. She dismissed Purcell as being boring, and took over a singing class, pushing the Syrian teacher aside. Solhi went to see the resident lutenist, Bill Badley (who tells me the story), and said, "Play me some Purcell." Bill and some students do so, and Solhi says, "That's better. My faith in the British is restored."

Monday, 24 October

I have an interesting visitor, Dr Abdulla Hanna, a Marxist historian from Deir Attiya. He studied in East Germany and has written books on the history of peasants and workers in Syria. He is off to the United States to talk to the Middle East Studies Association about the environment and the buildings of Deir Attiya.

Wednesday, 26 October

I call on the Director of the Damascus Chamber of Commerce, Dr Ratib Shallah. He is talking simultaneously into two phones. Damascus is getting ready for the visit of President Clinton. Streets are cleaned, railings painted, work on a bridge quickly completed. Streets are relatively deserted as all Syria watches the visit on television. As we do in the office. Clinton's plane arrives at the military airport near Mezze. The American President appears at the top of the steps, looks into the sky, pauses unsmiling and slowly descends to be greeted by President Assad. During the day there are talks and a joint press conference. Assad ends his statement with "Thank you" in English. The first question is put by an Israeli American journalist.

Thursday, 27 October

I call on the Minister of Higher Education, Dr Saliha Sanqar, and invite her to come to Britain. Her Deputy, Dr Muhiuddin Isa, should come as well.

With one of my British Council guests I have lunch as Ratib Shallah's guest at the Orient Club. All plates and cutlery and napkins have the letters TH on them. This refers to the Club's owner, Tawfiq Habubati. The Club provides the best service in the city, is attractive and very much the place for the Damascus elite.

Saturday, 29 October

We drive to the British military cemetery in Mezze, park and go for a walk into the Ghouta at the back. We are suddenly in a rural Syria unlike anything else near Damascus. The purple convolvulus abounds. The cultivation is rich, the land fertile, apple trees and black-olive bushes, cabbage fields. Ramshackle home-made ladders are propped up against trees. Paths end up among the fast-flowing irrigation canals. Untidy farms sprawl, so near to but culturally remote from the East-European-style villas and flats a quarter of a mile away. Village scenes are cheek by jowl with suburbia. The lofty cypress trees of the cemetery give us our bearings. We return refreshed.

Monday, 31 October

I am in Amman for a meeting with all my Middle Eastern colleagues. We have a briefing on the political scene from the British Ambassador in Amman, Peter Hinchcliffe. Apparently King Hussein and the Israeli Prime Minister, Itzhak Rabin, get on well together and talk about how awful Arafat is.

"Whenever I shake hands with him," Rabin says, "I feel awful."

"You're lucky," says Hussein. "You don't have to kiss him. I have a shower for an hour after being with him."

Wednesday, 9 November

I take my friends, Chris and Linda of Magna Carta, a folk music group, to the Assad Library for their concert. Every seat is taken. The show is superb. They present a variety of styles and moods.

Everyone is in a good mood. The audience is mostly young and impressionable.

I have a phone call from Uri Davis who is coming to Syria tomorrow. He is a pro-Palestinian Israeli (also with a British passport) and wants to see Sadiq al-Azm and George Jabbour.

Thursday, 10 November

I call on the General Manager of Syrian Arab Airlines, General Omar Rida. "How many people do you think we employ?" he asks. "Ten thousand," I blurt out, not having a clue. In fact it is 4,000. It is generally reckoned that the ratio of employees to aircraft should be 150 to 1. Syrian Arab Airlines has 15 planes, but they cannot talk of overmanning or redundancies.

I have been enormously busy in the last few months translating Ulfat Idilbi's novel but today I have a sense of triumphant exhaustion as I bash out the last word – "vain". All the hard work is over. Henceforth it is a few hours' proofreading, getting things consistent and polishing it up.

In the evening Uri Davis phones. I arranged to be away from a phone in the hour or so after his plane landed. The intelligence services are made up of people who are intelligent and people who are not. You never know who is going to be on duty. If the latter had been on duty when he arrived and knew he had Israeli nationality, he would have been refused entry – and he might have made contact with me. Fortunately the former were on duty and he has been able to enter Syria.

Uri's family were originally Polish Jews who migrated to Britain and then Palestine in 1940, not for ideological reasons but because Uri's father was a fugitive from justice.

Sunday, 13 November

I attend the Armistice commemoration at the military cemetery. Most of the neat gravestones have a cross and an inscription in

English. But some are in Greek. Jews have a Star of David. There are also Muslims buried here. Some bodies were unidentified and have the moving words, "Known unto God". A hundred people are present. A trumpet solo accompanies the hymns. Prayers are read by an imam and three priests, Catholic, Protestant and Orthodox. A bugler plays the last post and a bagpiper plays a medley of tunes, including, bizarrely, "Over the Sea to Skye".

At the reception at the British Ambassador's Residence afterwards I chat with the Armenian Ambassador. Our most effective common language is Arabic. He has a PhD in Koranic studies and was Professor of Arabic at the University of Yerevan before he came here.

Monday, 14 November
I meet Yasir Suleiman at the airport. He knows me as a translator of contemporary Arabic literature. Originally from Jerusalem, he was a student at the University of Jordan when I was in the British Council there. He went to St Andrews for 18 years before becoming Professor of Arabic at the University of Edinburgh.

We go to the American Center where Shafiq Fayyad gives a fascinating talk on Bernard Shaw and the Arab world. He pulls different strands together – from Denshawai to T E Lawrence. Shaw contemplated writing a play about the Prophet Muhammad but was dissuaded by the Turkish Ambassador. Instead he wrote *Saint Joan*. She too also had visions and was very like the Prophet. The talk is preceded by a film of GBS – very good. He would have made an outstanding television personality – "saint, sage and clown" as Churchill called him.

Tuesday, 15 November
I take Yasir to call on the Minister of Culture – whose PhD is from the University of Edinburgh. Her eyes glisten and she clutches at her handkerchief as she recalls her time there.

We host a dinner party, inviting Uri Davis who is a star. He is well known to many by reputation. Some Syrians who studied in Britain remember him giving talks to Arab Societies. Mahir al-Hamdi, the Palestinian representative, tells me his first wife was Jewish. I hear that Sa'dallah Wannous is very ill, unable to leave the house.

Thursday, 17 November

I go into town in search of more of Sa'dallah Wannous's work – and find them in Nuri's which is, I think, the best Arabic bookshop in Damascus.

The Oddsocks Theatre Company is here and presents *A Midwinter Night's Dream*, a camped-up version of Shakespeare with only five actors. They mingle in the audience and act with tremendous fun. Bottom and Flute have people in fits. Every word, every gesture is so funny. Bottom overacts, Flute underacts. The audience is in helpless laughter. I see the novelist Hanna Mina (who does not really know English) in the audience. He says "Brilliant" in English afterwards. Mahir al-Hamdi, the Palestinian representative is also there. The show is receiving its World Premiere in Damascus! Next week they are playing in Cumbria.

Friday, 18 November

Bouchra calls and Theresa and I go off with her for a few hours. In 1971 Bouchra took me to Raihan, a village outside Damascus, to a house, and I remember sitting with her on the balcony. In the house were lots of papers relating to Said al-Ghazzi, Prime Minister in 1954. We return to the house, a handsome villa, somehow Chekhovian, in its own enclosure. A caretaker, Abu Mahmud, greets us. On the floor in the house are piles and piles of olives. Both Ghazzis and Azms had property in Raihan and a grandson of Abu Mahmud takes us to find the Azm farm a mile away. It has seen grander times. A half-crazed man called Faris opens the place up for us. There used to be stables, chicken runs here and some farm produce is still inside the house. A wadi is facing the house. Was this where Freya Stark took a photograph of Ni'mat and Amat al-Latif in 1928?

We head back to Damascus, stopping off to call on Bouchra's maternal uncle, Subhi – who was a contemporary of and was brought up with Nadia al-Ghazzi. We sit in their garden, sip coffee and chat. Subhi's daughter, Lamma – head covered – collects national anthems of the world and copies of the Holy Koran in different languages. Can I get her one in Chinese?

Saturday, 19 November

We go for a meal at Motaz's house in furthest Qudsiyya. Their flat is European, the food Syrian. Karim is a bonny lad, the centre of attention. We watch the video of their wedding.

The British Council Cultural Officer, Souha, phones from Tartus where she is accompanying the Oddsocks Company. The theatre is in no state of preparedness. People have been unhelpful and the electrical system is lethal. I authorise the cancellation of the performance. A little later the Director of the theatre phones. His "face is black", as they say. He makes all sorts of statements that, according to Souha, are just not true. The company must be miserable.

I go by myself to the Omani National Day. The Syrian ex-Ambassador, Najib Jazzar says to me, "Half the people here have not been invited."

Sunday, 20 November

Yasir Suleiman and I call on the Minister of Higher Education and discuss the idea of her going to Britain.

Monday, 21 November

In today's newspaper there is a paragraph saying that theatre lovers in Tartus were disappointed by the cancellation by the British group of the play because of illness.

Wednesday, 23 November

I attend a "prayer meeting" at the Embassy. I talk about the Tartus disaster and the status of the British Council teachers. "We promote a policy of positive greyness," I say.

Thursday, 24 November

Geoffrey King is here. He is an archaeologist whom I knew in the United Arab Emirates when he was working at Julfa. I take him to call on the Director of Antiquities, Sultan Mheisin. Conversation is cool but warms up when they exchange offprints of articles they have both written for the same German journal. They talk of Islamic archaeology in Syria of which there is a relative dearth. Then suddenly Sultan offers Geoffrey the option of working on the citadel at Homs. "Take it," I mutter. Homs has been a site since classical times. It has been a military site since the Ottoman Empire and so is virgin sod. Sultan proposes a trip to Homs on Saturday and lunch on Monday.

In the afternoon we drive to Safita in heavy rain. But after we pass through the Homs gap, the mountains on the road to Tartus, clouds lift and it becomes fine. We are the guests of Helen Bachour in the fine house of one of her relations. The other guests are teachers from the American Center and some of the Bachour clan, different branches of whom occupy most of the western side of Safita.

I hear a grim story. Somebody had a friend who became a senior officer in one of the intelligence units. The officer said, "Come and call on me for old time's sake. I'll send a car to pick you up." The car came. The man went to the intelligence headquarters. At the reception he said, "The General sent for me." He was taken to the basement and beaten up. He was there for three days until the General wondered where his old friend was. He was brought up from the cellar. The General apologised. The man said, "I just want to go home." End of friendship.

Saturday, 26 November

We go for a walk beyond Safita with the Americans and Helen's daughter, Naila. We walk down to a grove with a ruined chapel. Naila says her grandmother remembers all-night parties there, people coming down there with their horses. Parties still take place at the spot, but now young people bring their music.

Monday, 28 November

I take Geoffrey King to the restaurant in the old city where we are the guests of the Department of Antiquities. I chat with Adnan Bunni who has been in the Department since 1948, after having been a village primary-school headmaster. He has known all the great archaeologists who have passed through Syria – Schlumberger, Mallowan, Grabar and Peter Parr.

The Ambassador has been to call on the Minister of Culture. "It's a pity the actors fell ill at Tartus and had to cancel the show," she said. The Ambassador then explained what had happened. She was furious and asked for a report. Well, that is interesting.

Monday, 5 December

I call on the Rector of the University in Homs, Abdul Majid. He has been in Argentina and gave a talk at the Homs Club in Buenos Aires. President Menem's family originally were from Yabrud – their name used to be Abdul Mun'im. Recently Menem had a dispute with his army Chief of Staff, a man of Lebanese origin – Izzeddin was his name. There are lots of Syrians in the country. "If a person is from this part of the world," Abdul Majid says, "and is poor, he'll be Turkish. If he is of moderate wealth, Lebanese. If he's really rich he'll be Syrian."

Tuesday, 6 December

I return to Damascus by bus. The service is excellent. Smoking is banned. We are given a sweet as we set off – bang on time – and water is available.

Wednesday, 7 December

I have to translate a Lebanese marriage certificate. In it you have to state whether the bride "has been married before or is a virgin". There are no other possibilities.

Friday, 9 December

We go for a walk at the back of the Sheraton Hotel by the railway. It is a potentially attractive but undeveloped part of the city. The land rises sharply above the river Barada. Sheep graze on a nearby meadow and some "early modern buildings" have distinctive character.

We go to have tea with Ulfat Idilbi in her flat in Muharjirin. I take her a British Council calendar and a big bouquet. She is rather lonely. I tell her the translation is finished and there should be a print run of 2-3,000. Maybe 5,000, I say hopefully. We must rally people like Rana Kabbani to write it up. We talk of her family and look at photographs of effendis of years past. Her brother – like Rashid in the novel – was injured in the Revolt of the mid-1920s and died in Amman, just before he could obtain a pardon, having been sentenced to death. He used to be head of the Geography Department at the University of Damascus. Ulfat went to Daghestan when she was 75.

Sunday, 11 December

A journalist from the BBC calls to interview me. I decline to talk about politics, but am ready to talk about Syrian culture, music, drama, films, eating, drinking, the successes so far of the British Council. She pushed me to talk of the reasons for censorship and I have to break it off. She goes on to talk to the Ambassador.

Wednesday, 14 December

I have a meeting with Mahmud Zughaiby, General, Doctor and Head of the Military Medical Services. This is an unbelievably chaotic meeting lasting one hour, during which I have his undivided attention for perhaps five minutes. Business friends, subordinates, clerks waving bits of paper to be signed, salesmen flogging ophthalmology equipment, soldiers and coffee servers are all vying with me for his attention, as he chain-smokes and also makes telephone calls on his two telephones.

Friday, 16 December

Theresa's sister, Mary, is with us.

Saturday, 17 December

We show a video of *My Left Foot* to a group of people involved in Syrian cinema – Rafiq al-Atasi, Salih Dehni, Firas Dehni, Nabil Malih, Riad Ismat, Ghasan Jabri and others. Mary talks about the genesis of the film. The director, Jim Sheridan, had never directed a film before. Daniel Day-Lewis was inspired and spent four months in a cerebral palsy clinic observing the patients. When he came to the (nine week) production he was carried in by his brothers who fed him and he did not let up for one minute. Discussion and questions are pertinent and practical.

Caroline Sharman arrives with her Mexican husband, Alonso. She will be the Artistic Director of *Dido and Aeneas*.

Monday, 19 December

I have a phone call from Abdul Salam al-Ujaili. He tells me that Hans Wehr and Jacques Berque were interested in his work. Hans Wehr actually translated one of his stories. Two people – one in France, one in Azerbaijan – are writing doctoral theses on his work.

The weather is awful – and beautiful. Snow lightly mantles Jabal Kasiyun. One of our teachers observes, "I like the snow. It means there will be no water shortages and the peaches will be nice and juicy."

Wednesday, 21 December

I take sister-in-law Mary and Paul Need, an opera technician, to Aleppo. We go to the old city, to Antakya Gate and walk along the spinal cord or road through the souk. It is truly impressive and I get the same thrill that I had when I first saw it 32 years ago. We emerge after a kilometre of gloom on to the road with the massive mound of the citadel looming before us in the sunlight. Wow!

We stay at the Baron Hotel. Although dinner is advertised it seems they order food in from a nearby restaurant. There is a power cut and we are provided with dim lighting. Our rooms are small, the bed sheets are damp and the plumbing gives us a whole symphony. The furniture is too large for the rooms and the door to the lavatory scrapes noisily on the floor. It is the full Baron experience.

Thursday, 22 December

The actor, Jamal Sulaiman, invites us to the shooting of a film in Khan Gumruk. The producer is Hamid Ma'ari from Abu Kamal, a 1969 graduate of the University of Baghdad and a former Deputy Minister of Planning. He and his partner produce television series for sale to the Gulf. The story of the film is based in Aleppo in the 1950s and is about a young man who returns from studies in Italy with lots of new ideas. The director is Haitham Haqqi who is married to Layali Badr, sister of Liana Badr, the Palestinian writer whose work I have translated[6]. The khan is largely a wholesale store and at nine in the morning is still quiet.

We return to Damascus stopping at Jarrada, a Dead City, by a living village. Sheep and turkeys wander round a tower which has what is left of classical latrines on the third floor.

When we get home I find a message from the Embassy Spook to say that the Ambassador is to present his credentials to the President shortly and wishes me to accompany him.

Friday, 23 December
The call for the Ambassador to present his credentials may be tomorrow. I see in the newspaper that he received the Ambassadors of Saudi Arabia and Tunisia yesterday. "Stand by from 9.30," I am instructed. "It might be at 11." What fun! Just as well we have not gone away for the weekend.

Saturday, 24 December
At 11 the Embassy Spook calls. "We're on. Be at the Embassy at 12." Five of us are to accompany Adrian: the Defence Attaché Dick Clarke, the Management Officer, the Commercial Attaché, the Spook and myself. Dick is looking splendid in his Welch Regimental dress, with a sword at his side.

Three cars turn up from the Presidential Office including a vast one for the Ambassador and the Head of Protocol. I go with the Spook and Dick in a second car. Dick is told he cannot carry his sword into the presence of the President. "Only Her Majesty the Queen is permitted to tell me to remove the sword," he answers – and gets away with it. The front car has Syrian and British flags on

6 Liana Badr, *A Balcony over the Fakihani*, translated by Peter Clark and
   Christopher Tingley, Interlink Books, New York, 1993.

it and motorcycle outriders with (gentle) sirens. We go along the Beirut road and sweep up a wide road to the marble palace on the hill. A 50-man guard of chocolate soldiers is inspected by the Ambassador. A band plays the National Anthem (ours) and we proceed into the building, with great views over the city. Then into another large room. President Hafez al-Assad stands on a red carpet facing us. The Ambassador stops before him, flanked by Dick and the Spook, the rest of us neatly bringing up the rear. The Ambassador reads his speech in Arabic (prepared with the help of Iman Abdul Rahim). Assad has cold grey eyes that penetrate and suggest ruthlessness. He stands unmoving, Faruq Sharra', the Foreign Minister at one side, and two other bald men on the other: an all-male occasion. The Ambassador steps forward and introduces each of us. Assad has a very strong handshake. President and Ambassador withdraw to chat.

"Have you read a book by a dissident Israeli intelligence officer who says the Hindawi affair that led to the break in relations between our two countries was hatched up by Mossad?" says Assad. "We were both duped."

"I want to think of the future of our relations," replies the Ambassador tactfully.

Meanwhile, the five of us go to another room for a sweet and fruit juice. After half an hour we return to the audience chamber, are photographed with the President, shake hands again and depart. On the way down we pass by the medieval castle of Mezze that is a high-grade political prison, a reminder to all who go up to the Palace of the fragility of politics in the country.

We end up at the Ambassador's Residence and drink a bottle or two of champagne. The Spook and I both have the same observation about the President's eyes. They seem to be able to look into your soul.

Tuesday, 27 December

I have a phone call from Ma'mun Abu Zaid. It is strange that I cannot escape from the Sudan which I left almost 18 years ago. Ma'mun was one of Numairy's band of men who took over the country in 1969 and became Minister of the Interior. He was always the most cerebral of the Revolutionary Command Council.

The Jazz Caravan planned for next month has been cancelled because the country will be mourning the first anniversary of Basil al-Assad's death.

Wednesday, 28 December

During the morning I have a visit from two salesfolk from the Meridien Hotel, soliciting custom. I take pleasure in telling them what a lousy hotel it is. When does the swimming pool open? I ask. "Between 9 and 5." "Why is it open only when people cannot use it? It should be open from 7." "It is, people are cleaning it. It has to be cleaned." "And what about the reception desk. Twice I have been misled because they did not know who was staying there. And if the Duke of Wellington wants a glass of water before dinner he should not be told he cannot have it. In a five-star hotel services should be available all the time. If I ask for a glass of dragon's blood with coke, the response should be, 'Yes, Sir. Here you are.'" I feel good after that rant.

Thursday, 29 December

I have lunch with Ma'mun Abu Zaid. He is in Damascus as the guest of the Ba'th Party who provide him with a driver (minder?). The Party is also paying for his hotel. We go to the old city. He tells me that after the fall of Numairy in 1985 all the members of the Revolutionary Command Council of 1969 were put into Kober Prison for three years. Conditions were not too bad. He was able to read, write, study and receive friends.

"How are things in Khartoum now?" I ask.

"There are no amputations. Only lashings for being drunk in public, and for trading in liquor. You can drink in private."

"How do you get booze if it is illegal to trade?"

"It's smuggled in from Eritrea and Ethiopia. A year ago a bottle of whisky cost US$20."

At another table in the restaurant a young Kuwaiti gets up and dances in front of the musicians, his belly awobble. He is joined by a girl who dances most erotically, with rhythmic pelvic thrusts, her hair long and loose, her body bending right back so her breasts are the uppermost part of her.

Friday, 30 December
Jilly and Dick Clarke take us to the Golan Heights.

There are three belts of territory between Damascus and Israel: a Limitation Area where UNDOF checks on the volume of Syrian military activity: a Separation Zone, narrower and also patrolled by UN troops from Austria and Poland: and then the Israeli occupation, some of which has been annexed. It is not called a border but a "cross-over point". As we drive in the increasing mist Dick stops every now and then to give us a briefing. Note the massive tank ditches designed to thwart advancing Israeli tanks. We stop at the gutted hospital in Qunaytra, which, according to a statement, "the Zionists" used as a rifle range. The walls are pockmarked. A few families live on in Qunaytra but otherwise the place is devastated. Cinema, bank, houses, all left as monuments. We wander back to the gentler slopes of Mount Hermon and eat mince pies and Christmas cake standing up in the cold.

DAMASCUS DIARIES

Spontaneous demonstrations of grief after the death of Basil al-Assad.

Armictice Day.

Haitham al-Kawakabi.

1995

Thursday, 5 January 1995

I have a visit from the novelist, Hani al-Rahib, who tells me he is writing an Arab *Satanic Verses*. Would I translate it? I remind him of the murder of the Italian and Japanese translators of Salman Rushdie's *Satanic Verses*, and decline.

Monday, 9 January

I brief the Ambassador on the forthcoming visit of a senior British Council colleague, who has developed the growth of English-language teaching in the last few years. He is, I explain, "an accountant, one of the top two or three in the British Council, a couple of years short of retirement."

"He sounds a bundle of fun," observes the Ambassador.

Wednesday, 11 January

I have breakfast with the Lebanese pianist, Wissam Boustani, and Amira Fuad, a Glasgow-born Syrian pianist who is in Damascus in search of her roots.

Sunday, 15 January

In Aleppo I call on the Dean of the Faculty of Medicine at the University of Aleppo, Dr Munzir Barakat. He has a Turkish mother and started his medical work in the Altounyan Hospital run by the

Armenian family that befriended T E Lawrence. I used to know two granddaughters of the founder of the dynasty, Ernest Altounyan. Taqui Altounyan wrote two lovely memoirs of the family, and married Robert Stephens, the Observer foreign correspondent. Bridget married a diplomat, John Saunders, who became Ambassador in Beirut. Their father married a sister of R G Collingwood, the historian, and as little girls in the 1920s they spent summer holidays in the Lake District. There, they and their brothers got to know Arthur Ransome who immortalised them as the children in *Swallows and Amazons*.

Dr Barakat takes us to the Aleppo Club where all Aleppo seems to be having their Sunday lunch.

Tuesday, 17 January

Cornelia Khaled, who lectures in English at the University in Homs, calls at the office and introduces me to her colleague, Marwa al-Shalabi, smart and attractive, wearing a headdress. She did a PhD at Bangor and talks about wearing the headdress. "I am not fanatical. I started wearing it at Bangor after my father died. It makes me feel closer to God. They found it strange there, especially as I was working on 17th-century erotic poetry." Her mother and sisters do not like her wearing it and she is occasionally mocked at the University in Homs.

The Embassy Spook tells me of the awfulness of Greville Janner MP who has recently been in Damascus. Ignorant and uncouth, he seemed determined to pick a quarrel with the Syrian government and the Embassy.

One of our female teachers has been harassed by a member of the security forces. I report the matter to the Embassy.

Wednesday, 18 January

I call on Dr Saliha Sanqar, the Minister of Higher Education. She would like to accept our invitation to go to the UK. She has obtained permission from the Prime Minister and would like to go in late February or March. She invites me to a lunch at the Orient Club for a visiting delegation from Armenia headed by their Minister of Higher Education. I talk to the Armenian Deputy Minister of Culture, a composer. The Armenians are not in favour of the Chechens.

Thursday, 19 January

The Embassy Spook has seen a senior general about the harassing of our teacher. The general took immediate action. He sent someone to Ian, Director of the Teaching Centre, and passed on the good wishes of the President. The security guard has been taken off duty. "The offence is as if he has raped his sister," says the officer. There is speculation about his fate – a beating, bastinado, or as Ayoub says, "He goes behind the sun" – that is, has his eyes taken out. I am glad certain principles have been affirmed, but unhappy about the overkill. But that is the context within which we live and work.

There is another potential crisis that could become a real one. Two British Council teachers, one in Cairo and the other in Yemen have been sacked for "bringing the British Council into disrepute": they were part of an international paedophile network cited in some major police investigations. One of our teachers, Neville, knew the two teachers and proclaims their innocence. He has a photo of the Yemen teacher on display in his kitchen here. Neville is openly gay, makes remarks about male students that, if it were said of female students, would get him into trouble. He told Ian that he would not go to Cairo because he could face arrest.

I finish the Glossary to *Sabriya*. It is now ready for the publisher.

Friday, 20 January

We go to Kiswe, a little-visited scruffy town 15 or so kilometres south of Damascus. I am curious about it for it was the first stage on the hajj route to Mecca. Is there a khan? We walk around the town. There is indeed a khan, converted into some rough modern use. There are houses with wattle and daub walls and a few splendid old doorways and window frames.

Saturday, 21 January

With *Sabriya* finished I am suffering from literary post-natal depression.

We go to a Filipino wedding at the Anglican church. It is fairly chaotic with photographers wandering all over the place, with cords getting entangled with bride and groom. Afterwards there is a reception at a dirty and scruffy club. There is food but there is an argument between the organisers of the party and the management of the club about the payment of the rent and we are all thrown out.

Sunday, 22 January

I call on Ulfat Idilbi. Her central heating has been cut off and she is shivering in an overcoat. She has had an invitation from the Russian Cultural Centre for a two-day celebration in her honour. Much of her work has been translated into Russian, but she finds the attention at this time embarrassing, with the raging of the Chechen crisis. Ulfat is giving a lecture in April at the Assad Library on Islamic feminism; she plans to develop some of the ideas of Fatima Mernissi.

I read a play by Sa'dallah Wannous, *al-Ightisab* (*The Usurpation*). It is compulsive reading and portrays Israelis and the divide in their society with an emphasis on the good Israeli, the good Jew. The last scene is imaginative, with a dialogue between the Israeli doctor and … Sa'dallah Wannous.

Monday, 23 January

I receive my annual Performance Assessment. There are six categories and I am in the second – "Excellent". (The top category is "Outstanding".) My boss has done a very good personal appraisal.

Wednesday, 25 January
At a rambling Embassy "prayer meeting", we talk about the Assad family. At a ceremony at Qardaha to mark the anniversary of the death of Basil al-Assad, the next son Bashar was given some prominence. He lacks personality, and is a bit of a Prince Edward. It is his sister, Bushra, who has the personality. She, I suggest, is the Princess Anne of the outfit.

Thursday, 26 January
Solhi al-Wadi and I discuss the opera project. It will involve a lot of planning. The BBC World Service mentioned our plans today. I make a bid for financial support from British Council Music Department.

Brigid Waddams gives me a paper in Spanish[1] about the architect, Fernando de Aranda (1878-1969) who designed many of the finest modern buildings in Damascus – the Hijaz railway station, the Ministry of the Interior and private houses. He also designed the Zenobia Hotel and the Museum at Palmyra. And the huge Italianate palazzo building – the Abed Building – facing Martyrs' Square in central Damascus which I have always admired.

Friday, 27 January
We walk into the city centre. I am thrilled at the whole idea of Aranda and we pause to examine the Abed Building. He was never a qualified architect and yet he did these splendid buildings when in his twenties and thirties. We go on, past the Mamluk fountain in

1 Eugenio Garcia Gascón, "El Arquitecto Fernando de Aranda (1878-1969) en Damasco", *Awraq*, Instituto Hispano-Arabe de Cultura, Madrid, 1988, 67-100.

the Street Called Straight, and potter around Maktab Anbar, the house of a Jewish merchant built in 1867.

I am reading *The Porcupine* by Julian Barnes. It raises the intriguing question of the benefits of the fall of Communism. Are the people of Bosnia and Chechnya better off? Inflation, crime, insecurity, privileges for the few, enormous disparities of wealth: these are the definite consequences. What has changed? I apply the argument to Syria. There are portents and precepts. There is relatively little crime, and less begging than in Britain. There are disparities but there is a basic provision for all. And although universities are a joke, they do provide a ladder for the able and ambitious.

Saturday, 28 January
The Management Officer at the Embassy has, it seems, had a nervous breakdown and has been medically evacuated.

Monday, 30 January
I hear that Bouchra has bought a car which her son Husam drives. Ahmed has gone to Volgograd to see their son Ala al-Din who is studying medicine there. He may also do some business. His most successful venture is as an agent for renting out houses in Jobar: this is far more profitable than his shop in the souk near Bab al-Barid, selling ladies' underwear.

Peter goes to Britain for three weeks, training, consultation and reporting to his headquarters. He attends a training session in Stoke-on-Trent and escapes one evening to see Stoke City play Liverpool.

Thursday, 9 February
"What are the benefits of a performance review?" our trainer asks. I give a list and the trainer asks me to put them into verse. Over the coffee break I come up with:

We keep an eye on what's going on.
Where you're weak and where you're strong.
Let's look at the targets we set last year.
Is there anything in them that needs a steer?
We avoid disasters and likewise some gloating.
We hand out praise and shun scapegoating.
We share responsibility: it's horses for courses,
So we identify gaps in skills and resources.

Saturday, 11 March

We drive to Daraya, which used to be one of the major market towns of the Ghouta – along with Doumar. Today it is a sprawling dormitory town with veiled women and unprepossessing architecture. We drive along a country lane through fields of lettuce, olive and fruit trees, with distant views of snowy Mount Hermon and arrive at a village – Jidaidat, we are told. It is unselfconsciously attractive with a stream running along the main street. We run a gauntlet of invitations to visit homes. Many of the houses have extensive courtyards and the village has both church and mosque.

Tuesday, 14 March

I interview candidates for Karim Rida Said Foundation scholarships. One candidate already has a PhD from Cuba but this is not recognised by the Syrian authorities. Another is a homespun coffee-house philosopher whom we cannot stop talking. He is entertaining but woolly. Another has applied to do a Master's degree in translation. "Literature," he explains, "is my cup of tea." "And translation is your bread and butter," I refrain from saying.

I learn that the poet, Adonis, has been thrown out of the Syrian Writers' Union for urging (or practising) communication with Israeli writers. He thinks Arab civilisation is strong enough to stand up by itself.

Wednesday, 15 March

I have dinner with Catherine Roe of the Karim Rida Said Foundation with one of their new Trustees, Dr Abdullah Khawi. He is about 70, an international lawyer and a lover of music, an AUB graduate and very good company. He dashes around the world on legal business.

Friday, 17 March

We drive up to Jabal Kasiyun and walk eastwards. The little coffee stalls that used to be here have all been pulled down on the orders of the government. The city below us is in a bit of a haze but it is possible to pick out many features. On the mountainside to the east is the green domed shrine of something – Abraham or Cain, I cannot remember which. We walk on, hoping to reach it but the road swings round to the north and we lose sight of it completely. The road actually circles the top of the mountain. To the north and west visibility is clear and we can make out Abel's tomb and the Barada valley, and the new city suburbs of Doumar and Qudsiya, with the poorer Kurdish settlements below.

There is a fax in from Zelfa, the commissioning editor at Quartet of *Sabriya*. She is not happy with the subtitle of *A Damascus Story*: she thinks it is too weak. I then think up *Damascus Bitter Sweet*. The original Arabic is *Dimashq, Ya Basmat al-Huzn*, which, literally, means *Damascus, O Smile of Sadness*, which is rubbish in English. But if we have *Bitter Sweet*, the bitter reflects the sorrow and he sweet reflects the smile. I think it also sums up the meaning of the novel.

Saturday, 18 March

We walk to the shrine we saw yesterday. We go through Muhajirin and through the area at the back, and burst out of the ribbon development that is creeping up the rocky mountain. The shrine which can only be reached by a path here is in an enclosed garden and is entered by a low doorway. A custodian, Yusuf Khadim al-Arba'in, greets us with a gentle beatific smile. He prepares some tea for us as we gaze at the view of seething Damascus below. He conducts us round the shrine – the *mihrab* in the mosque of the Damascus notables and the cave of blood, where Cain killed Abel. The roof of the cave oozes moisture – the mountain weeps for the first murder. In the rock are marks left by the Angel Gabriel. And the word Allah can be traced in the rock. A few pilgrims are at prayer. Yusuf lives in Muhajirin and comes up here each day. He does not have many visitors – perhaps 40 or 50 on a Friday. "This is where Abraham prayed," he points out. "And also Khidr, whom people in the west call St George."

Sunday, 19 March

We go to a recital at Holy Cross Church with music ranging from madrigals to spirituals. The Ambassador turns up, casually dressed, and is seated next to the Patriarch of Antioch and All the East in his very glad rags and pastoral staff. I meet a European lady afterwards who was involved in what she calls "PWD". "Public Works Department?" I ask, puzzled. "No, Petroleum Wives of Damascus."

Monday, 20 March

I call on Solhi al-Wadi at the Music Institute and ask if he knows Abdul Rahman Munif, whose *Cities of Salt* I have been reading. Munif spent time working in Baghdad, didn't he? Yes, he did. Solhi tells me that after his father died in 1971 he was presented with a bill from the Iraqi Ministry of Finance for 200,000 Iraqi dinars death duty. He was prepared to pay, but was unable to do so in one lump sum. Abdul Rahman Munif said he knew someone who might help and arranged for Solhi to see Saddam Hussein who was a young Vice-President at the time. Saddam sent a note to the Ministry, and the payment was made in instalments, as Solhi had wanted.

I have a call from Bouthaina Shaaban. We have both been longing to meet each other and we tumble over each other with ideas. We talk about Arab women writers. Ulfat has shown her my text and she is enthusiastic. (I am amused at the way Ulfat is getting second, third and fourth opinions.)

Tuesday, 21 March
We go to an evening of Tex-Mex music at the house of Christopher Ross, the United States Ambassador. He speaks flawless Arabic, congratulating women on 'Id al-Umm, Mothers' Day, taking care with all the Arabic feminine plurals. It is interesting to note which Syrians turn up: Sadiq al-Azm, Ali Qayyim, Riad Ismat, Mamduh Udwan, Ratib Shallah, Rafiq Atassi.

Wednesday, 22 March
At the Embassy "prayers" I learn that Mark Lennox-Boyd MP will be here at the end of May. He is a godson of Freya Stark and accompanied her on the trip down the Euphrates when the old lady was in her late eighties. I suggest we take Mark to Jerablus.

Riad Ismat calls. He has a new play being performed next month and gives me a copy of the script to read in advance.

Friday, 24 March
At the Baron Hotel in Aleppo the plumbing is noisier and less efficient even than normal.

We drive south to al-Bara, the site of an extensive Dead City, scattered among olive groves. We walk through the orchards to an Arab fort from which to survey the whole area. Triangular tombs with empty sarcophagi, a church. It is amazing to contemplate so many ruins in an untended state. There is nothing here of the "heritage industry". Ruins are used as stables and warehouses. We go on to Sirjilla, a small compact site. A 13-year-old girl serves us a Pepsi with an open sweet smile. Two coachloads of Germans are picnicking in the ruins as well as a Syrian family on a Friday outing.

Saturday, 25 March

I go to the French Cultural Centre, where students, studying Arabic, put on the play, *al-Fil Ya Malik al-Zaman*, (*The Elephant, Oh King of Ages*) by Sa'dallah Wannous. It is superbly produced. The producer points out that you can improvise with Sa'dallah's work. Most of the performers are women so it is a *malika* ("queen") not a *malik* ("king"). And the leader of the delegation is a woman, Aysha, not Zakaria. The students are American, Swedish, German and French. There is a full house, the audience mostly Syrian.

Monday, 27 March

Our son, Nat, is with us and is ill. We have a Dr Cachecho in to see him. An interesting name – he is an Assyrian Christian and the name is cognate with the Arab, *qassis*, meaning priest.

I read some stories by David Malouf. I am not swept away by him, as I am by the work of Sa'dallah Wannous, whose inventiveness, resourcefulness and imaginative strength I hugely admire. The interval in the play I am currently reading allows the *hakawati*, the storyteller, to have a coffee break.

Tuesday, 28 March

I am the guest of Ibrahim Othman, a Circassian from near Hama, who is Director of the Atomic Energy Commission, at a dinner at the Umayyad Palace Restaurant, a cavernous place on the site of the palace of the Umayyad Caliph, Mu'awiyya. The other guests are two lecturers in Physics from the University of Surrey. One is an Alexandrian Greek and was at Victoria College, Alexandria. He remembers John Abaza as an inspiring teacher, "Johnny". In 1969

John advertised in *The Times*, proposing an Old Victorian Association and had 5,000 replies.

The restaurant has a display of "whirling dervishes" who provide local colour. I examine how they whirl. The head is held erect and slightly tilting backwards. The left foot hardly leaves the ground but shuffles one third of a revolution at a time. The right foot seems to hop at speed. The arms are folded upwards at the breast and then one hand is raised and the head inclines against it.

Wednesday, 29 March

We go to the glass factory of Abu Ahmad at Bab Touma. We watch molten glass from the kiln being blown into familiar shapes of bowls and dishes. There seems to be no awareness of safety. Do accidents happen?

Thursday, 30 March

I have a letter from Iraq, from a girl called Sajida, a fourth-year student at the University of Basra who heard me on the BBC Arabic service. She writes two pages, asking me how to learn English and requesting that she be my daughter. The script is unclear and her Arabic not always grammatical. What risks does a student in Iraq take in writing to a foreigner, an official, in Syria? What is her home life like, her aspirations, her expectations? I am quite moved by it all.

A daughter of Badr Khan al-Barazi calls. She tells me about hunting with saluki dogs. The Barazis of Hama are quite feudal and still "own" villages. The family go into the desert in cars and the dogs work in pairs, stalk and pursue rabbits which they kill but do not eat. "Do you hunt?" I ask the girl who wears a headscarf. "Oh yes, my father insisted that his daughters swim, hunt, drive a car and do all the things boys do."

At a party, a Syrian girl who works at the British Embassy tells me of her disappointed love life. "There was a man," she says, "but he was a Shi'ite and I am Sunni."

Saturday, 1 April

Alan Waddams, the European Ambassador, tells me of his call on the President. Assad wondered why the Europeans did not have just one Ambassador for all the countries.

"What do you think of that idea?" he asks.

"A lot of Ambassadors would not be happy," replied Alan.

The President found that very funny, and then went on to compare European and Arab processes of unification, and the relative success of the former. "The trouble is us Arabs," he observes sadly.

I go on to the opening of the Algerian Cultural Week. There are speeches from the Syrian Minister and from the Algerian Minister of Culture. I network energetically and meet the writer Sihem Terguman, who wants me to translate some of her work. The place is full and I wonder what the attraction is. Perhaps it is because the Algerian struggle for independence occurred at a time of pan-Arab feeling. Both Syrians and Algerians resisted the French. There may also be some Syrian sympathy for the Algerian government in their present plight of confronting the Islamists.

Sunday, 2 April

The music critic John Amis is here, guest of the Ambassador. It is not long before he is talking of "my cousin Kingsley" and "my cousin Martin", whom he has not seen since Martin was 14. I take him to the Music Institute and we hear Solhi conducting some *Dido and Aeneas*. Later, John says, "Solhi makes Purcell sound like Brahms," whereupon Bill Badley, the lutenist, says, "Solhi makes everything sound like Brahms."

Wednesday, 5 April

I take John Amis to the Music Institute where he gives a talk to the students, translated by Solhi, on the work of Walton, Britten and

Tippett. He talks of Walton's first symphony, full of storm reflecting a love affair at the time. The affair ended and he never wrote a final movement; an example of musical coitus interruptus, he says. "Mustn't say that," he adds and slaps himself on the wrist. "I'll have difficulty translating it", says Solhi.

Sunday, 9 April

We go to a recital given by Solhi's daughter, Hamsa. I am introduced to Rana Kabbani who is with her mother and her two children. Ulfat has spoken to her of me and Rana would like to review *Sabriya* when it comes out.

Wednesday, 12 April

I am asked at short notice to give a talk in English to the students of the Tourism and Hotel Training Centre. I decide to talk about youth hostels in Britain. Seventy or 80 smartly dressed future waiters and chefs listen attentively as I talk about cheap accommodation, the countryside, walking and cycling. There are questions for half an hour and I have to tear myself away.

Thursday, 13 April

The Cham Hotel in Lattakia must be the worst in the world. The dining room is empty but every place is laid. We go to one table but are ushered away. "That is reserved," we are told. Then I ask for a tea and a coffee. "We don't have any; would you like some water?" And the door to the beach is locked.

Friday, 14 April

We go to Marqab castle and I have a tiresome row with the custodian who wants to charge us each 200 Syrian pounds. Last time it was 10 Syrian pounds. They are charging the higher amount for foreigners and I try to argue that we are residents.

We go on to al-Kahf, the Isma'ili castle. Perfect peace. Nobody else around. No noise. No pollution. Distant views.

We drive on to Hama and eat at the Sultan Restaurant, in a kind of cave. We have a Hama speciality – *batrush*, mincemeat in an aubergine dip.

Saturday, 15 April

We wander round the centre of Hama and see the Ba'th Party headquarters, occupying the As'ad Pasha Khan, a vast 18th-century caravanserai. It is heavily guarded and of course is a challenge to Hama – as if there were a huge Conservative Party office in the middle of Ebbw Vale. We go in search of bread and are invited into the bakery of Hajj Abu Faruq. We see the dough being made into cakes and flattened and baked in an amazing Heath Robinson contraption.

The owner of the Cairo Hotel, Anas, which is becoming a good-value backpackers' hotel, takes us to lunch at the Family Club. "Islam is the final revelation," he says. "If you want anything that is up to date, whether it is medicine or computers, you find out what is the latest revelation. So it is with religion."

Sunday, 16 April

We drive on to Qasr Ibn al-Wardan, a Byzantine garrison and church in the desert to the east of Hama – I came here in 1971. With its brickwork and bands of basalt it is as if it were designed by the Victorian architect Butterfield. We return to Damascus stopping for a picnic at Tell Nebi Mand, south of Homs, the site of the great battle of Kadesh between Ramses II and the Hittites, portrayed on the walls of the temple of Abu Simbel in Upper Egypt.

Carmen Callil and David Malouf were on a visit to Syria. Both are writers with a shared Australian-Lebanese background. Carmen's family originally came from Bsharre in the north of Lebanon. The Callil is a corruption of Khalil and there is a family connection with the writer Khalil Gibran whose first name was idiosyncratically spelt in English Kahlil.

Tuesday, 18 April

Carmen Callil and David Malouf are in town. I phone Carmen at their hotel. She is flat out with an upset tummy and I take some flowers and arrange for a doctor to call. David is a gentle, curious and interested man. His family migrated to Australia from Lebanon after the First World War. They were Melkites and the nearest denominational school he could go to was the local Catholic one, run by Irish nuns, so "culturally," he says, "I am more bog Irish than Arab". It is only in the last few years that he has been seen as an Arab-Lebanese writer.

David received a Commonwealth Award and had an hour with the Queen.

"Tell me," she said, "about your book. I may not get round to reading it; I only read books I can read in bed."

David told her that it was about Australians who shared grim memories of the war but were unable to communicate about their experiences to others.

"That's interesting," said the Queen. "I was brought up on the Sandringham estate and thought I knew everything about the families. But the other day Edward came and told me that a battalion had been raised of Sandringham families in the First World War, and that they had all been wiped out. When I was a girl nobody ever told me about that."

She asked if David used word processors.

"No, I write everything in long hand first and then put it on to the computer."

"Philip is mad about computers."

"Antonia Byatt got some awful disease from a computer."

"Really, what was that?"

David told her and the Queen got out pen and paper, noted the scientific name and said, "I must tell Philip about that."

Wednesday, 19 April

We host a party for Carmen and David. The Australian and British Ambassadors, Syrian writers – Ulfat Idilbi, Sihem Terguman, Nadia al-Ghazzi, Riad Ismat, Mamduh Udwan, Usama Isbar and a dozen others. I sense Carmen is out of her element. She is a radical, forceful personality, at home in an environment that appreciates her and responds to her. But she is with creative intelligent people who have to operate in very different circumstances. David, by contrast, is equable and is at home everywhere.

Thursday, 20 April

I take Carmen and David to the airport to see them off. Departing passengers go through two or three barriers and at one, manned by one of the security services, David is stopped. His name has popped up on some screen. He is seen as Lebanese and not Australian. Perhaps there has been some David George Malouf who has offended Syrian authorities in Lebanon. I do not leave his side for a second. "What is your mother's name?" David is asked.

"Wilhelmina."

"Amina?"

David knows no Arabic, and is courteous but bewildered. Our patience and assumption that all will be well succeeds and David is allowed to go through to the Departure Lounge. Carmen is still under the weather and for this I am grateful. Had she been in the best of health she is unlikely to have dealt with the situation calmly.

One of our guests of last night sends a note of thanks. "Much more stimulating than a Trade Mission," she writes.

Friday, 21 April

Theresa and I walk into the hills beyond Ashrafiya in the Barada valley. I come upon a dung beetle pushing a ball of mud up the path with steady determination. Occasionally the ball slips back and down a foot. He clings on to it and ball and beetle both roll down. Then, Sisyphus-like, he works at it again. His manner of propulsion is strange. He digs his rear feet into the ball and propels himself backwards using his front feet. Where is he taking it? And why? What treasures does the ball of mud have for him? Eventually the ball slips from his (or her) grasp and rolls back a yard. She (or he) looks around but it is out of sight. What is the memory span of a dung beetle?

Sunday, 23 April

Today is the Eastern Easter and a public holiday. In the afternoon we again walk in the Barada valley, along the railway track, by streams and through woods. Youths are out swimming in the river and playing football. Families are picnicking. Near an old mill, a bearded character called Ali invites us for tea and we stop and chat.

Tuesday, 25 April

"My father was one of the founders of the Ba'th Party," Rana Saadeh tells me. "It was the worst thing he ever did. He was in prison twice after being a Minister. He was first in the Citadel. I used to see him there when I was a little girl, in the governor's office. He was with Abdullah Qadura and Tariq Aziz. I used to sit on Tariq Aziz's lap. Then in 1966 he was in one of the Palmyra prisons. There he was behind bars. I was brought up to think that only wicked people were put behind bars and wouldn't talk to him. He was released during the June 1967 war – so we have something to thank the Israelis for."

I call on the Minister of Culture. I would like her to support a committee that will deal with the nuts and bolts of the opera, and to authorise expenditure on costumes. She agrees, and wishes no expense to be spared.

"It has to be successful," she says.

"Could the opera be under the patronage of the President?" I ask.

"Why not? Put a proposal with dates to me."

Thursday, 27 April

We go to an open day at the International Centre for Agricultural Research in Dry Areas (ICARDA) just south of Aleppo. There is an international cast of researchers and staff. The Director is an Egyptian, Dr Ahmad Baltaji.

We go with some of the staff into the fields. The land was purchased by the Syrian government and leased to ICARDA at a low rent. During negotiations villagers started to put up buildings in order to get more compensation money. The men of the two nearby villages were at first suspicious of ICARDA, but then sent their womenfolk to work there, but watched them carefully in case they were raped by foreigners. Attitudes changed when money came in. The villagers prospered and to display this new wealth the men took second wives from the earnings from their first wives.

We have lunch on a tell and I chat to the village *mukhtar* – how many wives does he have, I wonder.

We drive on to al-Raqqa for the night.

Friday, 28 April

We walk around al-Raqqa. It is hot and dusty and we keep to the shade where we can. (Sun and shade have different connotations in English – a sunny disposition, a shady character, and so on.) The building materials are quite different here. We look at the Great Mosque that dates back to AD 772, but was reconstructed by good old Nureddin.

We go on to Qal'at Ja'bar, a popular destination for picnicking families from Thawra and al-Raqqa. The Ayubid castle is perched on a rock overlooking the turquoise blue of the artificial Lake Assad. We look at the dam, built "in defiance of imperialism and Zionism", as a plaque says, a graceful curve and not as solid as the Egyptian Aswan Dam. The town of Thawra represents all that is worst in East European architecture – hideous grey-brown blocks of flats, designed for a very different climate.

Saturday, 29 April

We drive along a road on the northern bank of the Euphrates, through villages that remind me of Nilotic villages in Sudan – single-storey structures made of local material – no breeze blocks. We stop at Zalabiya, a Byzantine fort, twin to Halabiya on the other side of the river. We avoid dogs that anyway seem too exhausted by the sun to want to trouble us.

Sunday, 30 April

Motaz and I call on Mr Sanadiki, the agent for British Airways, to ask for some sponsorship for the opera. Our timing is excellent. The agent and his colleagues are in the best of humour for British Airways landed last night for the first passenger flight to Damascus for 13 years. Sanadiki has the exclusive agency. We are offered discounts, and invited to a celebratory lunch. They agree to undertake all the costs of the programme we will produce for the opera.

Monday, 1 May

Solhi al-Wadi seems to have disappeared. I meet the Artistic Director of the opera project, Caroline Sharman, at the airport and we discuss some of the details. I am filled with apprehension and depression about the whole project. Should I cut losses? Can I disengage?

Tuesday, 2 May

Solhi turns up. There had been some friction between him and the Minister, but all is well, and we have a very good meeting with Caroline and others about the opera. The citadel at Aleppo is not suitable for a venue. Someone suggests the Sports City at Lattakia. The Roman theatre at Jabala is dangerous. I suggest the hotel at Qardaha! This has been built for visiting heads of state and there must be a ballroom.

I hear that Bishop Kenneth Cragg will be in Damascus in August and proposes a lecture on 20th-century Arab literature. Would the British Council be interested in organising a venue? I have been a great admirer of the Bishop since I heard him lecture in Lebanon in 1971. I immediately write to him.

Wednesday, 3 May

One of Caroline's British team, Paul, has been trying for three days to get access to the Ebla Cham Hotel, the proposed venue for the opera. But there have been obstacles because of "security". And Solhi has disappeared again. I am frantic.

By the end of the day, I am exhausted, I read a lot of Arabic – most consoling.

Thursday, 4 May

After a heavy sleep my mind is clear. I must press on with the opera project. Nothing on the British side must be subject to challenge or criticism. I have a long and fruitful meeting with Caroline on costs. Paul gains access to the Ebla Cham and Solhi reappears.

In the evening I go to the Assad Library where Ulfat Idilbi gives a talk on Women and Leadership in Islam. Her chairman is Nabil Sukkar and he mentions my translation. Ulfat is marvellous. A little old lady – she is 83 this year – she sits down, unfolds the text of her speech, takes out a big pair of glasses from her handbag, slowly puts them on and reads in a clear lovely voice, taking no notice of the obtrusive lights and cameras. The audience is composed mostly of women, middle-aged and middle class.

Saturday, 6 May

I have breakfast at the Marouch with Robert Tewdwr Moss, 33-years-old, who is writing a travel book on Syria[2]. We chat for three hours. He was in Syria last year, met Daniel Farson and nearly got into a fight with him. He is staying at the Haramain Hotel for 165 Syrian pounds (£2.30) a night. It is not in the guidebooks. You get to know it, he tells me, on the *on dit* network.

Monday, 8 May

Solhi and Caroline arrange for a recital, consisting of excerpts from *Dido and Aeneas*, for the Minister. She arrives with the Heads of each of the sections in the Ministry. A hundred musicians perform superbly. Wafa, in a headscarf, sings "Dido's Lament". We have a meeting with the Minister afterwards. Caroline, Motaz and Solhi emphasise the costs – costumes, the set and so on. We get agreement to everything and feel very pleased with things.

Later in the day I am told the Ministry has no money for costumes. But this money is needed at once. I see Caroline and we are both in despair. I try to see Solhi. He is not at home. Everyone at the Ministry has gone home. I find Solhi's wife, Cynthia, and she is reassuring. "The left hand does not know what the right hand is doing."

Wednesday, 10 May

I collect Caroline at the hotel and we walk along to Solhi's office for a final meeting before she goes back to London. Solhi has been in his office since 6.30 in the morning, translating poetry of e e

2 Robert Tewdwr Moss, *Cleopatra's Wedding Present*, Duckworth, London, 1997.

cummings into Arabic for his own amusement. We have a fruitful meeting. Things seem to be on course with budget committees set up and other machinery for implementation in place.

Sunday, 14 May

Blake Morrison has been with us for a few days. He has spoken to students at Homs and gives a talk at the Assad Library. He is sensitive and eloquently decent. His talk is beautifully prepared. It opens minds and is as I would wish. Cornelia Khaled is staying the night and we all stay up till 1 drinking araq in our garden. Then at 1 I take Blake to the airport, driving through the Street Called Straight. He catches a plane to Istanbul. Tomorrow he is reading poetry in Brighton.

Tuesday, 16 May

I have two crises before 9 am.

There has been a BBC team in the region producing a television programme on railways. I have discussed ideas with them. I get a phone call from them in Amman. They were on the Hijaz railway returning to Syria but not allowed back into Syria. They were frog-marched at gunpoint off the train at Dera'a, and had to walk back to the Jordan frontier. A Bedu gave them a lift, sympathetically thinking they were Romanian refugees.

And then, one of our teachers, the British wife of a Kurdish Syrian, has been badly beaten up by her husband, arbitrarily divorced and provided with a single air ticket out of the country.

Thursday, 1 June

After two weeks away the work has piled up.

At 9 we host some British MPs in the office. We have arranged for the Marouch Restaurant to bring food in. The group is led by Sir Mark Lennox-Boyd who accompanied Freya Stark, his godmother, on the Euphrates trip in 1977. Apparently she was already "going off the air". The other Conservative is Roy Thomason, besuited, who looks like the Bournemouth solicitor he is. One of the Labour MPs is a university contemporary of my colleague here, the Director of Studies, Ian. There is one peer, "Rupert" Redesdale who is presumably a great-nephew of Nancy, Unity, the Duchess of Devonshire and Lady Mosley. I meet them all later in the office of the Minister of Culture. They speak highly of me. I have already spoken highly of her to them.

Friday, 2 June

There is Syrian opposition to the opera project. Are there cheaper ways of doing things? Could it be postponed? I anticipate four months of intense stress. But some students at the Institute of Music call on Solhi to wish him well.

We have a critical meeting about the opera at the Ministry. All goes well. The Ebla Cham Hotel rather than the citadel is the preferred venue in Damascus.

Monday, 5 June

Catherine Roe of the Karim Rida Said Foundation calls. Ulfat's son, Ziad, who is in his fifties, is in a hospital in Houston fighting a losing battle against lung cancer. He has always been extremely fit, regularly taking exercise. His family do not know how serious it is. And what about his mother?

Wednesday, 7 June

A British student of Armenian origin who has been studying Arabic here has had an awful experience with the *mukhabarat*. He was detained for an hour. I see the Deputy Minister of Higher Education and complain. It is not easy for him. Syrians cannot discuss these matters formally and foreigners shy away from discussing it. I tell the Deputy Minister that Syria has a bad name and such incidents confirm negative images. I say it, I say, not as confrontation, but "as a Syrian".

Stan Tracey and his band have arrived. I looked after them in Yemen in 1981. They are due to play at the Azm Palace and I am expected to make a little speech. I decide to do so in Arabic. There is a problem. The evening call to prayer from the minarets of the Umayyad mosque nearby is due. We do not want jazz to be played during the call. I have to ask Stan to play by himself for 15 minutes and then, after the call to prayer, to be joined by the rest of the band.

Thursday, 8 June
My office is like a majlis all day.

A month or so ago the poet Adonis was expelled from the Syrian Arab Writers' Union for having met Israeli writers and declared in favour of normalisation of relations. This has caused a lot of alarm among many Syrians who go to international conferences. Yasir Suleiman is organising an international conference on identity in the Middle East and has invited the Damascus political scientist, George Jabbour. George fears he would be manipulated by an agenda over which he had no control. I have arranged for Riad Ismat and Mamduh Udwan to go to the British Council Literature Conference in Cambridge. Riad is worried about Israelis attending. I tell him that the chance of him being exploited is minimal. He would be like someone at the theatre who finds himself in the audience sitting next to an Israeli. And Rana Saadeh has been invited to be an interpreter at a conference in Jordan. There may be an Israeli delegation. If the Syrians walk out what would her position be? I tell her that she was simply a functionary. Dilemmas, dilemmas. I later learn that it is a Palestinian, not an Israeli, delegation attending the Jordan event.

Marwa al-Shalabi who teaches English at Homs University tells me she is translating some of Blake Morrison's poetry and will be teaching it next year. Eighty per cent of the university English literature curriculum is fixed. Teachers can choose 20 per cent of the syllabus. Usually they teach their own PhD subjects. I have been urging people to consider contemporary writing. I cannot bring Shakespeare or Dickens to Syria, but I might be able to bring contemporary writers.

Rana Saadeh tells me that my speech last night was grammatically imperfect but politically correct, especially when I referred to the Minister's support for international cultural activity.

Friday, 9 June
Motaz, who accompanied Stan Tracey's quartet to Aleppo, phones to say there was nearly a punch-up between two of the players.

Saturday, 10 June
We drive to Zahle in Lebanon for lunch. The town is at the end of a valley with a pedestrian precinct and restaurants overlooking the fast-flowing stream. There are still two or three old hotels. The Hotel d'Amerique is dated 1906 and is US$20 a night. Zahle is fiercely Christian: women wear shorts and open sleeves; plenty of French on the shops including *Le Look pour les hommes*.

Monday, 12 June
One of our teachers, a quiet and thoughtful man called Richard Boggs, is a talented photographer and I have arranged to have an exhibition of his photos of Sudan. I feel pleased with the venture. It is an echo of pan-Arabism and also promotes local talent. Just before the Minister of Culture arrives to open the exhibition a man comes up the hill to the office on a bicycle, carrying a *kamara*, a wooden frame of flowers, an elaborate bouquet from the Minister. The British, European and Sudanese ambassadors are present. The Minister does her bit, as professional as ever, and the Sudanese

Ambassador and Richard point particularly Sudanese things out to her. Many suggest the exhibition should be turned into a book[3].

Rana Saadeh tells me that I am the Minister's favourite Cultural Attaché.

Tuesday, 13 June

I work in the office to midday, and then go to the bus station and take a bus to Aleppo. The service is excellent. Smoking is forbidden and my neighbour fidgets with frustration, fingering a cigarette packet all the way. The bus is air-conditioned and I sleep on the way to Homs. Across the aisle is a man with a gun. Most passengers doze. We stop on the Homs bypass for a *shawarma* and reach Aleppo just over four hours from Damascus: all for 150 Syrian pounds – just over £2.

My comfortable journey is in contrast to that of the Ambassador who comes in the office Jaguar. The air-conditioning in the car breaks down. The Jag does not go very fast and, for security reasons, the car windows cannot be opened.

We are in Aleppo for the Queen's Birthday Party in the garden of the Shahba Cham Hotel. The British community all arrive first. Then Syrian officials and a handful from the university – but not those on the guest list. It is exhausting to stand around waiting for the drunken Brits, unaware of what they are doing or saying, to take their leave.

Thursday, 15 June

The budget for the opera is beyond that of both the Institute for Music and the Ministry of Culture. A special case is being made to the Prime Minister's office. We need to bribe the manager of the Ebla Cham, a retired Alawite general, who is obstructing our plans.

---

3 It was, 18 years later: *Becoming Plural, A Tale of Two Sudans* by Richard Boggs, Garnet Publishing, Reading, 2013.

We are recruiting a new member of the British Council staff. We have received 114 applications, including a Shishakli, some of our students and relations of our and Embassy staff.

Friday, 16 June
I am reading a fascinating book on the Alawite region by a French officer, published during the Mandate[4]. He is excellent on the local sheikhs and the balance of power in the mountains.

Saturday, 17 June
Bouthaina Shaaban has asked me to read some chapters about a book she has written in English on Arab women's writing. I wonder for whom she is writing. There is an assumed "rightness" – international, feminist and progressive. I share such prejudices but they reinforce a point of view, rather than convince the sceptic or convert the dissident.

Tuesday, 20 June
I book Geoffrey King and some visiting archaeologists into the Haramain Hotel, which is in a leafy land off Souk Sarouja. It was built as a residence at the beginning of the 19th century and after the First World War was a police training centre. It became a hotel in the 1940s and today it is where backpackers and other budget Europeans hang out.

Wilfred Thesiger, aged 85, has been awarded a KBE in the Birthday Honours and I am asked to draft a letter of congratulation for the British Council Director General to send.

I have a call from Kurt Mendenhall from the University of Texas who is writing on the French Mandate, focussing on Alawite resistance to French rule in the 1920s.

---

4 Paul Jacquot, *L'Etat des Alaouites*, Imprimerie Catholique, Beirut, 1931.

Thursday, 22 June

We interview candidates for the new job. Three stand out, including the Shishakli, a granddaughter of the President in the 1950s. Fair-haired, relaxed and blue-eyed, she radiates personality. She is, as my colleague Souha says, *musayyifa*, carefree, as if it is permanently summer.

Sunday, 25 June

The Ministry of Culture does not understand sponsorship of the arts. "If we pay for it all," says the Minister, "we do not need Shell's money, do we?" I argue with the Minister that sponsorship enables us to do much more.

Monday, 26 June

The Embassy Spook and I drive to the south of the country, past Suwaida and east into the desert, a bleak and lonely landscape. Fifty kilometres from Rushaida is a wadi with two tents. A few kilometres further on is a solitary house around a well. There we meet Muna, a young Syrian archaeologist. She takes us over some boulders where we meet Michael Macdonald, the British scholar, an authority on Safaitic inscriptions. There are hundreds, thousands, of inscriptions – or graffiti – scratched on stones and they date from 100 BC to AD 300. Some are written boustrophedon, in a Semitic script. Other graffiti are in Nabatean or Greek. Many are contemporary with the Roman occupation of Basra. They are not very informative, giving just a name and a brief message, a kind of "Kilroy was here".

Michael originally read English at Oxford and then did a second degree in Arabic, Aramaic and Syriac, studying under Professor A F L ("Freddie") Beeston who taught himself Welsh in his old age.

We drive further east to a lake and, off the road, to a tell that was a Roman frontier camp. We walk on for a kilometre to a pile of stones, the tomb of the third-century-AD Arab poet, Imr al-Qais.

We leave Michael and his colleagues at about 7 and drive back to Damascus. As the sun is setting we see two hundred white camels slowly shuffling across the road.

Peter's concentration on Syria was broken by the news that his son, Gabriel, was expelled from Bedales for drug offences.

Wednesday, 28 June
I drive to Homs and meet up with Geoffrey King and his team, who are surveying the tell. It has until recently been a military site – at least from Ottoman times – and the Department of Antiquities want it to be surveyed and excavated. The Director of Antiquities, Sultan Mheisin, joins us and we spend an hour or two going over the site. The ruins are in a precarious state and rescue archaeology is urgently needed.

Thursday, 29 June
The news of Gabriel's expulsion has been devastating, comparable to the death of a parent or partner or the break-up of a marriage.

I drive to Lattakia and meet Marwa and her Palestinian husband, Muhammad. I stay with them at their smallholding in the hills above the city, at Murij, in a lovely rural setting. Muhammad teaches Linguistics at the University in Aleppo. His family is originally from Jaffa. His brothers work either on the farm or in government. Marwa writes poetry and translates poetry from English.

Friday, 30 June
We sit around for most of the day gossiping. We call on Jihad at the farm next door, watch animals at play and walk through his crops. It is all a little rural idyll, with extensive views over the sea and distantly to Lattakia.

In the evening we go to a café in Lattakia overlooking the sea. It is part of a large complex – a prime site – owned by Jamil al-Assad, brother of the President. The café is full of narghileh-sucking folk, families and children.

Saturday, 1 July
I leave Marwa and Muhammad early and have breakfast with Kurt Mendenhall, who teaches Politics at the University of Texas.

We drive through Lattakia to Qardaha. The mausoleum to Basil al-Assad has been inlaid with marble. We drive into the hills to Jobat Burghal, Upper and Lower. Lower is an attractive village in the hollow of the hills that cannot have changed much for a century. Upper looks down on Lower. At Upper we locate the large house of Salman, or Sulaiman, Murshid, who led a chiliastic revolt against the French in the 1920s, was the leader of a spiritual Alawi movement for the next 20 years and was hanged – still wearing a tarbush – after independence. Kurt knows the son, Saji, who is apolitical but supports the President and claims to have 80,000 followers. We see three tombs in the garden. The road from the coast was built by forced labour in the 1920s.

Tuesday, 4 July
I have the proofs of *Sabriya* to go through. I am deeply impressed by the story – it is moving and well constructed. In the middle there were inconsistencies about timing and I cleared those up. But the power of the story sweeps the reader along.

Wednesday, 5 July
The opera project is gathering momentum. Two months ago I thought it was four steps forward, three steps back. Now it is four steps forward, two steps back.

I talk to a deep-voiced Gabriel. After expulsion from Bedales, he has been accepted at Ardingly. The conditions are a regular urine test and sessions with the chaplain. There is school uniform, weekly chapel and pressure to conform. A contrast to Bedales.

I start reading a novel by the Algerian Ahlam Mustaghanimi[5] which Bouthaina has recommended.

Thursday, 6 July

I have lunch at a smart restaurant. Since June, when the manager went on pilgrimage, they no longer serve alcohol. So the place is half-empty, though non-alcoholic beer is available.

Friday, 7 July

Last night I was sitting in the garden reading. I heard a rustle of leaves and then plonk. A kitten dropped from the wall. I kept quiet. A mother cat was prowling around. Then I go to the kitten, its eyes glazed or barely open. I stroke it. It is alive, awake but quiet and passive. A little later I hear the mother slithering down a tree to inspect the kitten. I try to entice it to drink some milk, and leave a saucerful out all night.

This morning I inspect the garden. The milk has been drunk and there are now two kittens. Mum appears on the wall and glowers at me.

I go to Bloudan during the day, leaving a saucer of milk out. When I get back the saucer is empty.

Saturday, 8 July

There are now three little kittens in the undergrowth. Mum greets me with a suspicious glare. During the day I hear the cheep of another kitten on the wall above. I leave out some more milk and some food. It is consumed.

5 It was translated into English: *Memory in the Flesh*, translated by Baria Ahmar Sreih and Peter Clark, American University in Cairo Press, 2003; Arabia Books, London, 2008.

I go into the old city and call at the tomb of Nureddin. A young couple are praying outside it. For a child?

Sunday, 9 July

I hear a kitten mewing on the wall and bring it down to join the others. There are now four sweet kittens cuddling together.

I have a visit from Amal al-Jaza'iri, a descendant of Emir Abdul Qadir, the Algerian leader of resistance against the French in the 1840s, who was exiled to Damascus. She is married to Jawad Hawwash, from a feudal Alawite family whose castle Kurt and I were looking for the other day.

We are moving to a new flat and I am introduced to my new landlord, Georges Ladhkani. He is a sprightly old gentleman of 97. He studied law at the American University of Beirut in 1916, returned to Damascus and was recruited into the Ottoman Turkish army in 1917. He served in Masyaf as a medical orderly and after the war resumed his studies, and practised law from 1924. We have a beer and chat away merrily.

Monday, 10 July

The novelist, Hani al-Rahib, calls. He is in trouble. He has been strongly criticised in the Damascus and Beirut press for having met Israelis abroad and fears arrest. We talk about Muhammad Shahrur, whose book *Al-Kitab w'al-Qur'an*, I have been reading. He is "a Luther", Hani says.

Tuesday, 11 July

Motaz and I call on the mad general in charge of the Ebla Cham Hotel and conference centre which is under the direct control of the President's office. The hotel, he says, cannot be used for the opera. He is an Alawite as are all the people who work there.

I spend time trying to coax the mother cat to talk to me. She wants to. She sees me putting out some milk. Like cats the world over, she makes eye contact and then sits down. The kittens are getting bigger, their eyes either open or half-open.

Wednesday, 12 July

Motaz and I call on Dr Ghasan al-Aida, nephew of Osman, head of the Sham/Cham chain of hotels. We are asking for free accommodation for the opera people at Cham Hotels. He is a bit cautious but we then talk about Sudan. He is in the process of buying the Grand Hotel, Khartoum (for ten million dollars). His lawyer there is Daf'a Allah al-Hajj Yusuf, whom I used to know in the 1970s when he was Minister of Education. Another mutual acquaintance is Bona Malwal, a former Minister of Information, whom I helped to get to Oxford in 1977. Ghasan's attitude changes and he agrees to our demands.

Thursday, 13 July

Warqa Barmada of the University drops in and we gossip about Syrian universities and their heads. Houriyeh at Aleppo is part of a faction associated with the Minister of Defence, Mustafa Tlas. Both are married to sisters of an old Aleppo Sunni family. Abdul Majid at Homs is on excellent terms with Wahib Tannous, the Ba'th Party official overseeing the universities. Hallaj at Lattakia is thick with the merchants of that city, including the President's brother. And Maa al-Barid of Damascus, former Dean of the Faculty of Pharmacy, was the teacher of Bushra, the daughter of the President.

Friday, 14 July

I call on Solhi. He assures me that the mad general at the Ebla Cham will be sat upon. He has been told to take things easier – and obviously to drink less. "I will not give up my whisky," he tells me. "It keeps me going."

My neighbour Ghasan al-Umari, from an old and distinguished family, has died. He had been a hotelier and had worked in Aden. Known as Gus he was only 60. I call on the family and meet his brother, known as Rocky. He is in real estate in Virginia and has a Peruvian wife. Before he migrated to the United States, Rocky was a sportsman and played in the Syrian national basketball team.

Peter took a month off – Brighton and a fortnight in France.

Wednesday, 16 August

Several of Caroline's team are in Damascus working on the opera project. Many manage with the uncertainty, but Paul comes to my office; his equanimity has exploded. "I am at the end of my tether," he says. "I've had it up to here … I've been here for three weeks…" I tell him I've been here three years and Motaz for three decades.

Hani al-Rahib calls. He has been expelled from the Writers' Union.

"*Mabrouk*, congratulations," I say.

"You're the fiftieth person to say that. Hisham Dajani has also been expelled, and Hanna Mina, Sa'dallah Wannous and Kamal Abu Deeb have resigned."

I am invited to a party at our new landlord's house. I meet prosperous middle-class Christians. One is an elderly Palestinian polymath who watches the stars every night. He expresses a Christian solidarity with the Serbians. "The Muslims should not be in Europe."

Thursday, 17 August

I hear there has been a stand-up row between the mad general at the Ebla Cham and the Minister of Culture, the latter supported by the Minister for Presidential Affairs. The mad general has been told to cooperate.

I drive to Lebanon, to Bikfaya, and meet Marie-Reine and her family – she was my Lebanese secretary in Abu Dhabi. There are thousands of Syrians working in Lebanon, earning US$12-18 a day. They sleep on the site on labouring jobs the Lebanese are reluctant to do. They try to get jobs in the Gulf.

Saturday, 19 August

I have breakfast in Broumana with Cornelia Khaled of Homs University. We then drive into Beirut and call on the historian Nicola Ziadeh who lives behind Hariri's palace. Nicola was born in the Midan area of Damascus in December 1907. His family are Christians from Nazareth, and his father was working as an accountant on the construction of the Hijaz railway. He is a wonderful old man, witty, with a pipe in one hand, a glass of beer in the other and a twinkle in his eye. He published two volumes of autobiography on his 85th birthday and plans a third for his ninetieth. He still writes for the papers and has broadcast for the BBC since 1939 when he was recruited by Stewart Perowne, Freya Stark's one-time husband.

I drive back to Syria via Hama.

Sunday, 20 August

I spend some hours with the Faculty of Agriculture at the University of Aleppo. The Dean and his heads of department are wooden-headed party hacks, graduates mostly of Eastern European universities. I am asked to consider a workshop on salinity in the Euphrates valley. I ask if the people of the Euphrates dam are involved. Or the oil companies. They would be familiar with the geology of the valley and have much to contribute. I ask about their relations with the Ministry of Agriculture.

"Weak," I am told.

I challenge this.

"We have tried, but they don't want to know."

"Try again."

"It's against our dignity. What should we do?"

"Market yourselves."

I do not think my remarks are welcome, especially as I tell them the story of Robert the Bruce and the spider.

Monday, 21 August

I have undertaken to write an article on Muhammad Shahrur, the Islamic philosopher and Professor of Engineering at the University of Damascus. His book has been the talk of the Arab chattering classes. Nicola Ziadeh had a copy on his table.

Tuesday, 22 August

The opera saga continues. Things promised fail to turn up. The British team spend much time hanging about. But I get the impression that all sorts of people up to the Minister of Culture herself are experiencing similar frustrations. There is also the problem of the Ministry's cash flow.

I go to call on Bouchra. Her son Ala al-Din is back after one year in Volgograd where he was studying Russian in a class of six, preparatory to six years medical studies. Another son, Husam, is a problem. He has no job and should be helping his father but does not work well with him. The youngest son, Zafir, is fine, and will be a hairdresser. The two little girls romp around like kittens, smiling at me from afar.

Wednesday, 23 August

I do not know whether the opera will be a great success or a monumental failure. Caroline drives the British team along. All agree that the performers are superb, and the Minister appreciates what we are doing. Today there are interviews about the opera with

Caroline and Solhi in the local press. The opera is seen as a joint venture and on a pan-Arab theme: Lebanon and Tunisia. The Minister would like to invite my Director General for the opening.

Wa'il Barazi calls. He wants to translate Blake Morrison's *And When Did You Last See Your Father?*

Saturday, 26 August

I prepare a stand at the Meridien Hotel for "British Week", an extraordinary display of naffery. There is a polystyrene telephone kiosk, some replicas of the Crown Jewels and cardboard cut-outs of beefeaters and uniformed bobbies. Guinness will be on sale.

Sunday, 27 August

The paint has not yet dried on the opera set. Wages have not been paid to the workmen. I want to maintain the momentum of activity.

I have lunch with Bishop Kenneth Cragg. His first words are, "What's the Test match score from the Oval?"

After lunch I take him to see the Mufti, Ahmad Kaftaru, at his house at Jaramana. He is about the same age as Kenneth Cragg – early eighties – and totters into the majlis and collapses on to cushions. "I bid welcome to the children of Sayyidna Isa" (our Lord Jesus), he says. He talks of tolerance and interfaith relations. He recently had a 60-minute meeting with the Pope who told him that he read the Koran each day. "And I read the *injil* (the Gospels) every day." The Bishop and the Mufti are soon talking warmly together. The Mufti has his own interpreter but Kenneth replies in Arabic. We leave after an hour, the Bishop helping the Mufti to his feet. They walk hand in hand to the door. The Mufti's wife is present throughout, a severe-looking lady in her forties, tape-recording it all. The Mufti, a widower, married her last year.

Monday, 28 August

I have a call from Ali Mahmud from the secret police. I believe he is the colonel who is in charge of my file. He has dropped in for an amicable chat before making a request. His wife is doing an external PhD at the American University of Beirut on health care and needs to improve her English. I arrange for her to have free lessons at the British Council.

Bishop Kenneth Cragg gives a lecture at the Assad Library, with Rana Saadeh interpreting. He talks of aspects of modern Arab literature. He is comprehensive and refers to Michel Aflaq and to the Hourani brothers, meaning Cecil and Albert. Rana omits the reference to Michel Aflaq who is persona non grata here. And people might think Kenneth is referring to Akram Hourani who fell out with Hafez al-Assad and is also a name not to be mentioned in public.

Thursday, 31 August

I have a meeting with Hisa, sister of the Saudi novelist, Abdul Rahman Munif. She is on the lookout for English novels to translate into Arabic. I suggest *Eight Months on Ghazzah Street* by Hilary Mantel. "I wouldn't touch that. I have a Saudi passport and I could be made stateless." (As her brother was until he was taken up by Saddam Hussein.)

Another visitor is Wa'il Barazi who is translating Blake Morrison's book. I tell him if it can be completed and published before the end of next year I would arrange for Blake to come out again.

The main event of the day is another opera crisis. Paul phones urgently and we talk it out. Paul is fairly rough but I have to support him, and defer to his expertise. That is why he is here. The point gets through and we reluctantly decide to postpone the opening by one week.

Friday, 1 September

I realise I ought to inform the Ambassador about the postponement, I cannot get through to him on the phone. I drive to his Residence. He is asleep. I get through to him eventually on the phone from the office. He goes through the roof and is really quite unpleasant. He sees a scandal, a waste of £100,000 of the taxpayers' money on a ridiculous venture. Hafez al-Assad has been brought into it as Patron and the British name is mud. He wants to see the Minister tomorrow morning and withdraw the British team. Whew! It depresses me for the rest of the day. Yesterday I had to cope with some delicate negotiation and face home truths. I do not want an unhinged Ambassador identifying me as a scapegoat for some major disaster.

I go to the office and escape into the world of 18th-century Sudan, writing a review of a book on popular religion in the Nile valley.

Saturday, 2 September

I speak to the Ambassador again. He is a little more temperate and invites me to dinner tomorrow.

Sunday, 3 September

I keep crises at bay though I feel tense with anxiety.

More agreeably, I have lunch with Riad Ismat. I arranged for Riad and Mamduh Udwan to go to the British Council Literature Seminar at Cambridge. They were very impressed by Marina Warner and Lavinia Greenlaw. He and Mamduh, playwrights both, cornered Arnold Wesker and had a merry conversation with him, who awkwardly said, "You do know that I am Jewish … but I have disagreed with Israeli policies." They talk about translating his work into Arabic and putting it on in Damascus.

At dinner with the Ambassador, he sort of apologises and

comments on how calmly I took his tirade. We gossip about Jordan and how Petra is not what it used to be.

Tuesday, 5 September

Nagging doubts about the opera project persist. Today is another rollercoaster of a day. Solhi and Caroline ask me to go with them to the Ebla Cham. The mad general refuses to allow the set to be erected because the stage may not take the weight. He wants an independent engineer to do a report. Solhi knows it can take 200 tons, and the weight of the set and people amount to 40 tons. I call on the mad general but will have to resign matters to the Ministers of Culture and of Presidential Affairs. I hang around while workmen turn up late.

I am restless all day with anxiety. I also wonder whether Najah al-Attar's job is on the line. Nu'man, the set designer, tells me if things go wrong he could be in prison. Would I be asked to take early retirement?

Wednesday, 6 September

I am awake, restless, all night. The best thing would be to have a massive heart attack. I wake up repeatedly thinking, "I am still alive."

I see the Ambassador who is no longer aggressive and takes points I make about the postponement.

Edmund Marsden, senior colleague at British Council headquarters, phones. He has been invited to the opening of the opera.

"How are you?" he asks.

"Hot and harassed," I say.

I explain the opera dramas and he asks,

"Will I be in the way? Answer as friend to friend."

"Yes," I say.

But he is kind and supportive.

I spend a couple of hours with a Syrian friend who lives in the United States, wandering around the coffee houses of Souk Sarouja, which used to be called Little Istanbul. We meet some of his friends and exchange subversive jokes about the regime. My favourite is the Lebanese word for contraceptive – *hafiz al-'air*. This can mean "protector of the penis" but could also be read as "Hafez [al-Assad] the prick".

Thursday, 7 September
Things with the opera improve and the day ends more hopefully than any in the last few weeks. One fear I have is that Solhi wants the opera to go ahead and Caroline and Paul think things are not ready. Confrontation. It would be my disagreeable task to support the professionals recruited. But today Paul says the set is ready.

Friday, 8 September
Caroline phones. The dressmaker is refusing to release the costumes she has made until she has been paid. But otherwise all seems to be under control and I am moderately confident.

I attend a party in the old house and school, Maktab Anbar, hosted by Fuad Tabla in honour of Wafic Said and his friends. (True Damascenes call him Wafi', turning the c into a glottal stop.) Everything is luxurious – folklore dances, a guard of honour, wreaths of jasmine, flowers . . . homage to a billionaire. Ulfat is one of the first to arrive. Wafic Said has brought out a number of friends to show them Syria, accompanied by John Carswell the art historian as guide. He worked with Kathleen Kenyon in Jerusalem in the 1950s. They arrived in Wafic's private jet, with two luxurious seats in the front, a circular lounge and rows of seats behind. There is also a bedroom and a bathroom. Among those with Wafic are Lord and Lady Palumbo – she is Lebanese and I chat to her in Arabic; the dashing Carla Powell; and Lord Hesketh.

Monday, 11 September

I go to the Ebla Cham for the first rehearsal on the set. The introduction, incidental music with a *hakawati*, a coffee-house story-teller, tells the story of Dido and Aeneas in Arabic. Foreigners may wonder whether they have come to the right performance. The chorus is ragged and reedy, but they may be nervous. The set needs to be painted and there are still ladders around. There is much polishing required and only five days to go. At this stage I feel I can do nothing. There is a momentum that I hope will be maintained. All our input – the training, the soloists, the technical support, the public relations – has been excellent. There is another article in today's paper saying that the project reflects the virtues of Hafez al-Assad.

Tuesday, 12 September

I have a meeting with all staff and teachers. It is like a State of the Union Address, I spell out my own philosophy of management, the importance of personal development and the need to enjoy ourselves. Work is fun, an adventure. There are no questions. I silence – or bore – them all.

Opera tickets are going fast. There are no crises today.

I get a request from the Ministry of Culture, strange but flattering. The Minister is going to a conference at Palmyra later this month and wants me to translate the speech she is giving into English. I will need to adapt her eloquence to appropriate English.

The local media is full of the opera: a television programme last night and high coverage in the newspapers.

Wednesday, 13 September

Solhi phones early. He has had an accident and has injured his foot and is in some pain. He will be hobbling to the rostrum. Like Klemperer, we both say. But otherwise all seems to be in order.

I attend a seminar given by Muhammad Shahrur. There is a discussion on Islam. Muhammad is about 50, quiet, a Dublin graduate. When he talks he is animated and forceful.

"There are only two tenets for being a Muslim," he says. "Belief in the oneness of God and belief in the afterlife. Abraham was a Muslim. Moses was a Muslim. Jesus was a Muslim."

"What about fasting, the pilgrimage, alms?" he is asked.

"Those are pillars of faith."

I take no part in the discussion but it is clear that I have read more of Shahrur's work than some who do.

Thursday, 14 September

Solhi phones again early. Last night's rehearsal was wonderful. It seems he broke down with emotion at one point. Certainly he was, I hear, in tears later.

There are three crises today. The Minister objects to the sponsors' names in the programme, though she had already given the OK. Secondly, I hear that cables and bulbs have been stolen from the Ebla Cham. And thirdly, the mad general is not allowing a final rehearsal tomorrow evening. By the end of the day the last seems to be resolved.

We go to one of the final rehearsals. It is good. The set, the colours, the movement are all magnificent. The little girls dancing in their costumes. Susannah Self as the almost camp sorceress. Hyacinth with her final "When I am laid..." and the sailors, cupids ... all a fantastic spectacle.

We go to Zabadani to a party hosted by Nabil Khurdaji, a top dentist. Local peasants are roped in to cook bread in a traditional way. They themselves probably prefer sliced bread in packets.

Friday, 15 September

We go to the Ebla Cham for the final rehearsal. There are perhaps

500 in the audience, friends and relations of the performers. It is magnificent. There has been so much progress in the last few days. In May I said to Caroline, "It's going to be great – either a great triumph or a great catastrophe." In the corridors, backstage performers are excited, tearful, embracing each other. I gaze on, thrilled.

Saturday, 16 September

I polish off the translation of the Minister's speech and take it to her. I read it aloud to her. She makes one correction.

We get to the Ebla Cham early and people pour into the theatre, a capacity audience. I try to allocate VIP seats for the Shell people – who have given sponsorship money – but the ushers have let in the general public. Najah al-Attar gives a speech. She has not taken my advice and mentioned sponsors – it conflicts with Ba'thist ideology. She lauds Solhi – whose applause decibel rating is higher than that of the President. There are nine Syrian Ministers and the Chief of Staff, General Hikmat Shihabi, present, as well as the Lebanese Minister of Culture. There is a sense of awe in the audience. We are presenting excellence, colour, movement, singing, and most of the performers are Syrian!

Sunday, 17 September

All are aglow with the production. During the day the Ambassador sends a cordial letter of appreciation – a great day for Syria and a great boost for UK-Syrian relations.

I have lunch with Burhan Qassab-Hassan, a former soldier. He offers a party at his restaurant to celebrate the publication of *Sabriya*. He sees himself as a liberal, loathes fundamentalism and was a keen opera lover when he was at Sandhurst.

We go to the second performance. Again it is a packed house. The authorities lock us all in during the performance – an alarming situation. There are police in the grounds. Mrs Khaddam, wife of the Vice-President, attends. I am able to present Caroline to her afterwards. Again the performance is a stunning success. The Syrian performers mature each time. And Dido takes off her outer robe in the most seductive manner imaginable. She trips around the stage, flirtatious as a teenager in love for the first time. I continue to enjoy the plaudits but there are lurking crises with the transfer to Bosra.

Monday, 18 September

Congratulations continue to flow in. "I can't believe I am in Syria," says one person. People cannot credit the fact that Syrians have been able to excel like this. One Syrian friend says the opera should go to Lebanon. It would undo the damage of 20 years' occupation.

The Ambassador tells me that a senior Syrian said to him, "You have done so much for Syria with this opera." Only my German counterpart is unwilling to refer to it. I tell him that Solhi wants the Germans to help him put on *The Ring* next year.

We go to a party hosted by Jilly and Dick Clarke, the Defence Attaché. He turns to his service friends and says,

"What do we say when someone does well?"

There is then the chant – OGGI OGGI OGGI OY OY OY. I am strangely moved.

Wednesday, 20 September

Motaz, Souha and I go to Palmyra. We pass the Air Force headquarters. Here Hafez al-Assad lived before becoming Minister of Defence in the 1960s. The British Council driver, Bassam, tells me his grandmother lived in the nearby village. She was a midwife and helped to deliver Basil al-Assad. There is a social interconnectedness about Syrian society. At Palmyra we go to the Roman theatre. Workmen are toiling away. All seems to be well. At the hotel Paul is smiling: that augurs well. We call on the chief of police for the Palmyra region. He is affable. Motaz's father-in-law used to hold this post. The chief says that 50 policemen will be on opera duty, controlling crowds and monitoring traffic. Lorries will not be allowed to come near Palmyra. We leave the chief as he fumbles to put on a Syria-UK Friendship badge we have brought him.

Thursday, 21 September

There is a major opera crisis. The set has been transferred to Palmyra but a crane is needed to hoist it into the Roman theatre. But no crane has turned up. As Paul says, "No crane, no truss. No truss, no lighting. No lighting, no opera." Motaz and I go to see Solhi and a few phone calls are made. A Japanese company is doing some construction work at Homs, a hundred miles to the west of Palmyra. The Japanese Ambassador arranges with the local boss of the company for the crane and crew to go to Palmyra.

Friday, 22 September

We have tea and cakes with our new landlord, Georges. His wife, who is in her mid-eighties, is active in Orthodox charitable work and has been chairman of one charitable society for 30 years. They married in 1940. After serving in the Ottoman army in the First World War he had no wish to be a soldier again. When Faisal was king in Damascus after 1918 he was recruiting all young men under 22 for the new Arab army. Georges had a friend in the registration department, the *nufus* office, who agreed to give him an identity card stating his date of birth as 1895 instead of 1898, "but I am only 97 and a half," he explains. He was in Egypt in the 1930s "when they had a king" and has always been a keen ballroom dancer. He is still working two or three hours a day as the legal adviser of a company – he took on the job when he was 88 – but is planning to retire "to spend more time with my wife".

And to enjoy his satellite television, and to read two hours each day. He lends me a volume by the Moroccan feminist, Fatima Mernissi.

Saturday, 23 September

We drive to Palmyra for the performance of *Dido and Aeneas* at the Roman theatre. It quickly fills up to capacity and I sit next to the Governor of Homs. We hear noises outside. I learn later that people with tickets have come from Homs and Aleppo and are not being allowed in. The police have admitted the people of Palmyra without tickets. Stones are lobbed over the wall into the theatre until the police disperse the disappointed opera lovers. There is nothing I can do and I feel acutely embarrassed.

The performance starts on time, but the electricity fails during the overture and we are all plunged into darkness, but the orchestra plays on without the slightest hesitation. The wind whips up and I think I hear thunder. Orchestra scores are blown about. But all perform superbly.

We have dinner with the Governor and his stern-faced and headdress-wearing wife. The Chief of Police is also with us. They chain-smoke, before, between and during courses.

Sunday, 24 September

Three down, two to go. The first of two performances at the Roman theatre at Bosra on Saturday. It should be a gala performance with the Prime Minister and John Tod from British Council London. There is a problem erecting the set in the theatre. Cranes, forklift truck, helicopter, 100 workers, levers, pulleys. The resources of the state can be invoked.

Monday, 25 September

I have a visit from the Armenian Ambassador. He was formerly

Professor of Arabic at Yerevan University. We talk in Arabic though his English is quite good. (Better than my Armenian.) He gives me some books on the Armenian genocide and the final Syrian journey of the survivors.

We go to a reception at the house of the Indian Ambassador for visiting Islamic scholars. An American Islamic scholar, Bruce Lawrence, is present. He is researching the Sufi Ibn Arabi, who is buried in the Muhajirin quarter of Damascus. He tells me he was by the tomb, reading Ibn Arabi, and fell into conversation with the imam who tore himself away, saying, "I'm going to this fantastic play that is being performed." He meant the opera!

Wednesday, 27 September
I go to Bosra. There are delays in setting up the hoist which is called a *bilinkir*, presumably derived from the French for stretcher, *brancard*. Paul Griffin is in good humour and suggests a film should be made about the opera to be called *Carry on Regardless*. Hattie Jacques would play the part of the Minister.

I have a fax from Joan Smith who is writing a review of *Sabriya* for the *Financial Times*. I have not yet received a copy myself yet[6]!

Caroline phones from Bosra. The workmen are refusing to put up the set until they have been paid. I recklessly authorise payment, though do not know where the money will come from.

Thursday, 28 September
Riad Ismat calls. He has an idea of translating the work of a contemporary English playwright and producing it locally in Arabic. We would try to bring out the author: Pinter, Wesker, Edgar?

---

6 Ulfat Idilbi, *Sabriya: Damascus Bitter Sweet*, translated by Peter Clark, Quartet Books, London, 1995; Interlink Publishing, New York, 1997, 2003.

Saturday, 30 September

I take John Tod from British Council London to Bosra. He has brought out five copies of *Sabriya*. No Prime Minister. No Ministers, but plenty of Ambassadors. The Governor of Dera'a presides. The basalt rock and the theatre's massiveness are a fitting backcloth. The performance is the best yet. We join the players and musicians. Euphoria and hugs.

Sunday, 1 October

I dash up to Damascus from Bosra for a few hours and then back to the last night of the opera. It is estimated that between 6 and 9,000 fill up the seats. That makes over 20,000 who have seen the different performances. I hear someone behind me murmur, "Absolutely fantastic". There is applause at the end of the prologue and at several times during the performance.

The great adventure has turned into a tremendous success: a profound, widespread, and, I hope, lasting impact; and 180 Syrians have been trained in aspects of putting on an opera.

Monday, 2 October

I have a fax from Joan Smith. She had a piece in *The Independent on Sunday* yesterday about the opera, mentioning how nine Syrian Ministers attended the opening night. "Can you imagine nine British Cabinet Ministers attending the opera together?"

Tuesday, 3 October

Theresa and I host a party for the principal performers and those associated with the opera. About 60 turn up – including all ten British (of whom two have found Syrian partners). One star is Razan, the 15-year-old principal ballerina, self-assured and articulate in English. The Minister comes, bubbling with good humour, followed by her assistant with a pile of presents. I make a speech expressing appreciation. I first thank the President for his sponsorship and pause. True to convention, there is ritual applause at his name. I plug Solhi and the importance of dreams. I thank Paul for his patience and when I thank Caroline I am overcome with emotion, cannot speak and just go to her and give her a big hug. The Minister gives out goblets to the British team. "Can I kiss you?" Paul asks as he receives his. "No," smiles the Minister. Solhi's wife tells me that there has been no event like the opera since Najah al-Attar became Minister 20 years ago. And it is the first time Hafez al-Assad has given his sponsorship to an international non-Arab event. "You and Solhi just clicked," she says.

Wednesday, 4 October
The Ambassador sends a teleletter to my Director General and to the PUS of the Foreign Office, raving about the impact of the opera: "… talk of the town", "General Shihabi making a rare public appearance", the boost to Anglo-Syrian relations, the Minister of Culture over the moon.

Thursday, 5 October
Theresa and I go to Beirut, staying at the Mayflower Hotel. We walk into the city centre. One of the pleasures of being married is sharing an experience such as exploring a city together. We walk round the grounds of the American University, a prime location, with mature woodland and buildings, with views over the Mediterranean and to the hills to the north. Students mill around: apparently it is their first day back. A couple of self-important begowned academics head for some function: a sign of Beirut picking itself up after the ugly nightmares of the 1970s and 1980s. We walk on to the devastated area near the port and to the Borj, the old centre of downtown Beirut.

We have lunch with Hassana and Fuad Salam. It is a reminder of an older Beirut, not of the flashiness of today. We eat beneath a portrait of Fuad's father who was a member of the last Ottoman parliament.

Friday, 6 October

We drive up to Byblos. I want to drive through the mountains to the Biqa' valley but a garagiste tells me there are bandits who will extort money from us. If there is the slightest doubt I would not go. But could it be a Maronite canard about Baalbek Shi'ites?

As we return to Syria I see Bassam, the office driver, on the Lebanese side of the border driving the British Council car. He gives me a shifty look. I cannot remember authorising any such journey.

Saturday, 7 October

I ask about Bassam and the car. Apparently he went to Lebanon to buy some medicine. Unauthorised use of a diplomatic car is a criminal offence with severe penalties. I suspend him "pending enquiries". It is all very distressing. I have known Bassam since 1971 when he was eight and have been a friend of his family. I did him a favour by employing him, and in many respects he has been excellent. But he has thrown it all away.

Sunday, 8 October

The Syrian staff are concerned about Bassam. They acknowledge that he has acted with criminal stupidity, and I am ready to allow him to resign and for him to receive a month's salary in lieu.

My Line Manager arrives at the airport from London. He is depressed about working in London and looks unhealthy. Ferocious budget cuts are expected with offices in Tunisia, Morocco, Yemen and the Gulf threatened with closure.

Tuesday, 10 October

I take my Line Manager to inspect some potential new premises.

The first is in an excellent location. It has been vacated for a year and files and dust have gathered all over the place. On a dusty chair lies a newly dead cat. Another cat has been trapped in the building, panic-stricken.

At 8 we go out to a meal to celebrate the publication of *Sabriya*. The Line Manager joins us. The meal is hosted by Burhan Qassab-Hassan at his slightly seedy restaurant. Ulfat Idilbi brings several women from the Women's Union including the widow of a former Prime Minister. Other guests include Miriam Cooke and her husband, Bruce Lawrence, and Bouthaina Shaaban and her Iraqi husband, Khalil. I am called on to make a speech which I do in Arabic, telling the story of how I got involved with *Sabriya*. Then Ulfat makes a speech expressing her pleasure.

Wednesday, 11 October
Bassam's mother calls, pleading for him. He is at home, depressed, chain-smoking and constantly drinking coffee. I have to be polite but firm.

The office landlord calls to discuss a renewal of the lease. He wants an increase because of a rise in property values. We argue for a reduction because of a drop in rents.

Thursday, 12 October
Motaz tells me he spoke to my Line Manager who apparently did not believe in the value of cultural relations but was converted on seeing a video of the opera. It was all those smiling faces.

We go to the Spanish National Day party. Since the opera our profile has risen. We seem to have got on to new lists and are getting more invitations.

Saturday, 14 October
We walk to the village of Kafr Sousa, now submerged in the city. It

is just possible to make out fragments of the older village, amidst the dull breeze blocks – a small souk and overhanging trellises.

Tuesday, 17 October
I have a visit from Tim Llewellyn, a former BBC correspondent who is now freelance. He is planning a programme on Syria and we discuss the political situation.

Wednesday, 18 October
The Foreign Secretary, Malcolm Rifkind, is expected shortly to come to Damascus. Meetings with officials do not start before 10 and there are three possibilities for filling his time: a "power" breakfast with British businessmen; a walk round the old city (but not the Umayyad mosque, he instructs); or a British Council breakfast.

Cornelia Khaled of the University at Homs calls, asking for a reference for a Fulbright scholarship. I write about her with unqualified enthusiasm. The other referees are Nicola Ziadeh, Professor Staif of the University of Damascus and Allen Hibbard. "No one from Homs," Theresa observes. "No women," I observe.

Thursday, 19 October
At the airport I meet John France and Susan Edginton. I have arranged visits for them to Crusader castles. He is interested in Crusader routes. Susan is the world expert on Albert of Aix and is editing his history. She has been working on it for 20 years. It arose out of a PhD she did under Joan Hussey.

Friday, 20 October
I have breakfast at the Marouch Restaurant with John and Susan. He was at the University of Reading and was a colleague of Anne Pallister who beat me to a post in the History Department at the University of Leicester 30 years ago. John and Anne had been close

friends from schooldays – "We were never lovers," he makes clear. She committed suicide in 1986 when she was 44. Apparently she decided quite coldly to kill herself. She put food in the fridge for her husband, left him a note, took a massive overdose and went to bed. Her husband came home, did not see the note and went to bed only to discover the horror of a dead wife the next morning. After her work on Magna Carta she felt she could not go on.

The Defence Attaché does not get on well with the Ambassador. "Let me remind you," he told the Ambassador, "that my colonel appointed you."

"Who is your colonel?"

"The Queen."

Saturday, 21 October

Theresa and I go for a walk up the Barada valley. It is a tacky part of the city, rural Syria engulfed by urbanism. So much could be done to make it an attractive place – the river, the gentle hills and so on.

Sunday, 22 October

I go to the American Cultural Center. Miriam Cooke leads a discussion with Syrian women writers – all in Arabic[7]. The place is packed. The microphone breaks down. Ann of the US Embassy is too small to be seen. Riad Ismat and I stand at the back – men in a women's forum. Miriam kindly plugs my translation, and Ulfat Idilbi, though absent, overshadows all the discussion on the modern Syrian woman's novel.

7 The evening is described in Miriam Cooke, *Dissident Syria, Making Oppositional Arts Official*, Duke University Press, Durham and London, 2007, pp 60-64.

Thursday, 26 October

Sam Younger, who is Managing Director of the World Service of the BBC, is in Damascus, with Marmaduke Hussey, Chairman of the BBC and a member of the board of the British Council. I invite them to breakfast at the office. I used to know Sam 15 years ago when he was editor of *Middle East International* to which I occasionally contributed. Sam is a son of a Labour MP and a cousin of George Younger, who was in Margaret Thatcher's Cabinet. Hussey, "Dukie", is a big man, affable, a grandee, very supportive. His father used to be in the Sudan Political Service and went on to work for the British Council as Director Middle East. I ask about political balance on the BBC Board. He tells me the Vice-Chairman is a Labour MP "but I'm far more left-wing than he is". I brief them on the work of the British Council in Syria and they field questions from the staff.

Sunday, 29 October

I write a report on the opera: a string of superlatives. The opera reached all levels of Syrian society, up to the President, and by repeated transmissions on the television, millions of Syrians. As I write I realise that everything was over the top – the expense, the matching funds, the philosophy, the impact, doing such an operation in such a difficult country.

I have a call from Haidar Bouzo, the office landlord. He is an upper-class Kurd, a former Minister. He is very amiable although a cousin of his has just died – Adnan, a leading footballer. Haidar has just been to Libya for a conference on the Lockerbie bombing, as Syria's only representative.

In the evening we go to the party celebrating Turkey's National Day. We chat to Dr Karmo – he is Deputy Minister of Higher Education – and his wife; he has a PhD from Dublin from the late 1960s. After the Suez war of 1956 Syrians did not go to study in the

United Kingdom, but, as potential PhDs they had learned English, and so instead they went to Ireland. He tells me that Muhammad Shahrur, the Professor of Engineering, who has written the best-seller on the Koran, argues against the wearing of the veil though insists that his daughter wears one.

Monday, 30 October
The writer, Robert Tewdwr Moss, turns up. He tells me that a party of people – Lord Hesketh, Carla Powell, Alan Whicker, Bruce Anderson and others have been out as guests of the airline, British Mediterranean. They have been behaving like Hooray Henrys in a foreign land. Robert also tells me that Mary Lovell will be in touch. She wrote a book about Lady Jane Digby and will be writing a book about Sir Richard Burton. Apparently Burton's widow did not destroy all his papers, and Mary has come across some. She approaches a subject, she says, not believing anything you have heard.

Tuesday, 31 October
Haidar Bouzo calls. We explain to him that we want a canteen attached to the teaching centre in the premises we are renting from him. We are losing custom to the Americans because we do not have this facility. It will need structural alterations for which his permission is required. "People come to you for learning and culture," he argues, "not for distractions. People who go to a centre because there is a canteen are frivolous." He puts up obstacles. But when Ayoub, who seems to enjoy all these negotiations and does it very well, says we are looking for alternative premises, the obstacles vanish like the snow in springtime.

Thursday, 2 November
Miriam Cooke drops in. She was brought up in Tunbridge Wells

and her first degree is from Edinburgh where she studied under Pierre Cacchia (with whom she did not get on).

I call on Najib Shihabi of the Department of English who is from the Lebanese Shihabi clan. I talk of offering books on contemporary English literature to the university. He wants books on Applied Linguistics. Ugh! Most of the Department are Applied Linguisticians.

Friday, 3 November

I read the rest of Liana Badr's book, *The Eye of the Mirror*. It is an epic about Tall al-Za'tar, the Palestinian refugee camp in Lebanon. At times she is experimental, using the first person as a visiting journalist or as one of the principal characters. Three of her books have been published in English, but all by niche publishers, alas. And so she does not enter the mainstream. She writes harrowing descriptions of the siege and "evacuation". Women are the heroes, keeping homes and relationships together.

Sunday, 5 November

The Israeli Prime Minister, Itzhak Rabin, has been assassinated. What will that do to the Peace Process? One of the tiresome landlords I have to deal with hints that if Syria does sign a peace treaty there will be a big demand for property in Damascus.

Monday, 6 November

I have breakfast with the Ambassador. Malcolm Rifkind and John Major are going to Israel for Rabin's funeral. Rifkind's visit to Damascus is up in the air. He may come for six hours or for an overnight visit. If the former I will have five minutes with him. If the latter, half an hour.

A fax comes in with a cutting from the *Financial Times*. Joan Smith has written a splendid review of *Sabriya*.

Tuesday, 7 November

I sort out a list of Syrians who have been to Britain under British Council auspices. Seventy-seven altogether and increasingly a better spread of people: scientists, women, people outside Damascus.

The rains have started and winter is setting in.

Wednesday, 8 November

At noon I get a summons to go to the Embassy to meet Malcolm Rifkind (or Rifkunt as one of my Syrian colleagues calls him). I bump into a breezy, relaxed Andrew Green who is accompanying him. The Secretary of State is in the loo when I arrive. The top floor of the Embassy is transformed into a mobile office. One man is busy on the phone. Another is scanning faxed press cuttings. A girl is at a typewriter. Coffee pots, teapots and cartons of fruit juice are on a shelf. Malcolm Rifkind comes in, relieved. We stand talking for my allotted five minutes. He fires questions at me and seems well briefed. I tell him that we see our role as subversive, promoting the values of an open and plural society. He laughs encouragingly. He has heard of the success of the opera. (Bully for him!)

I go to the airport to meet Leila Abouzeid, the Moroccan writer. I have been told that she is quite a big woman. I accost all the larger women coming off the plane from Tunis and Algiers and get "old-fashioned looks". Eventually Leila accosts me. Actually she is quite petite in appearance, looking older than I expected. I take her to the house before the hotel. She is surprised at my interest in contemporary Arabic literature. I tell her I am an endangered species.

Thursday, 9 November

The meeting between Rifkind and Assad went well, I hear. Assad wants a breakthrough in the Peace Process. He thought Rabin's arguing about his hardline opposition was a negotiating tactic, but Rabin's assassination demonstrates the reality of the situation. And no head of state or government is keen on the concept of assassination or tyrannicide.

I take Leila to call on Ulfat Idilbi whose memory is failing. She cannot remember having met Leila in Morocco nor Joan Smith here. But she has heard of the *Financial Times* review!

Monday, 13 November

I arrange a meeting for Leila Abouzeid at the British Council. We have invited a lot of women writers. I chair, and everything is in Arabic. Leila talks for half an hour and then there is a discussion. Bouthaina Shaaban took Leila to the Syrian Writers' Union and berated them: "Why do you not bring in writers from other Arab countries. Why leave it to the British Council?" Leila tells a story about being in Cairo and being told, "You'd be a great writer if you were not Moroccan." There is a discussion about whether there is a specific women's literature. One person, reflecting – I think – Ba'thist ideology says No. But the sister of Abdul Rahman Munif talks about her brother's memoir about his childhood in Amman and says, "I read it and my experience in the same city in the same household was quite different."

Tuesday, 14 November

Processions celebrating 25 years of Assad in power cause the most unbelievable traffic congestion. I am half an hour driving round Umayyad Square, and then an hour to get home – a journey normally of five minutes or less.

Wednesday, 15 November

More celebrations. Theresa and I stroll among good-humoured but not vast crowds. Several things seem to be going on simultaneously: speeches being broadcast, dancing, a few picturesque horsemen, a badly playing band.

Hooky and Jane Walker call and we go to the Umayyad Palace Restaurant for dinner. He was the last British Ambassador in Baghdad. He has had to leave his posting prematurely three times: Cairo in 1967 (because of Rhodesian sanctions), Damascus in June 1967 (June war) and Baghdad in 1990.

Thursday, 16 November
We are the guests of British Airways at the dinner/dance of the British Women in Damascus. We eat (well), drink (lots) and dance (vigorously), staggering home at about 2 am.

Friday, 17 November
We pack sweaters and gloves and drive to Burqush. It does not get colder as we climb. Snow covers the top. The place is deserted. Visibility is poor. But the cobwebs are shaken away.

I am reading Muhammad Shahrur's book on the Koran. He writes about women's dress, legislation on human rights and so on, totally liberal on every issue.

Then to the Hamra theatre for a piano recital by an Armenian girl, Talan Haroutsian. She is shy and almost weepy. The programme is in English, Arabic and Armenian. We have a speech from a woman about the glorious Correctionist Movement and then the music – Bach, Schumann, Chopin and three 20th-century Armenian composers. After that the bishop comes in and blesses us all in his melodious but incomprehensible Armenian.

Sunday, 19 November
I call on Hayan Atassi, a neighbour of the Ambassador, who will sponsor Geoffrey King's next archaeological trip to Homs. He is an engineer from a well-known Homsi family, studied Engineering in Iowa in the 1950s, prospered and has a house in Orlando, Florida. To my amazement he hands over 400,000 Syrian pounds (about

£6,000) in cash to cover the costs of the trip. He has a project, the Jandar resort just outside Homs. I promise to visit it …

… and we do later in the day. The resort is in an area, 1.5 kilometres by 1.5 kilometres. 150 plots are planned and Hayan's son-in-law, Mahir Darkali, shows us round. Each plot is expected to cost 40 million Syrian pounds – US$800,000, but there are a lot of wealthy Homsis in the Syrian diaspora, especially in South America. The situation is delightful, open, with a gentle breeze coming off the snow-clad Lebanese mountains.

Monday, 20 November
At Aleppo I call on the feckless head of the Department of English, a graduate of the University of Leicester, who is negative whenever a bright idea is proposed.

We have afternoon tea with two teachers, Mustafa and Madeline. In the university there are girls wearing a black veil over their faces. They refuse to raise them during a lecture. Some lecturers will not teach them unless they do uncover their faces. One veiled girl explained to her that she must not talk to a strange man – and that includes university teachers: it is a sin for a man to hear her voice. It is as if the Muslim Brothers are spoiling for a fight.

Tuesday, 21 November
I spend two hours at the university in Lattakia. Munzer Muhammad is one of the few really good academics in Syria. He has been made Dean of the Faculty of Arts and is due to have a book out, published by Dar Tlas.

Wednesday, 22 November
The premises issue is not yet resolved. I have a call from one landlords, Wa'il Murabit – he lives in Cyprus. His father, still alive, was Syrian Ambassador in Saudi Arabia, and he has worked for

Adnan Khashoggi for whom he had to be lawyer, accountant, travel agent and banker. Khashoggi's mother came from Damascus and was a sister-in-law of Yusuf Yasin, Ibn Saud's Syrian adviser. The Murabits have family connections with the Bouzos.

Thursday, 23 November

Only two working days to going on leave. I write to two potential landlords – Bouzo (Yes) and Murabit (No). I accept a commission to write a piece on the Battle of Omdurman for a centenary volume[8]. Nancy Lindisfarne writes to congratulate me on *Sabriya* – she saw the *Financial Times* review. I am also in correspondence with Mary Lovell about Richard Burton.

Saturday, 25 November

We walk into the centre of the city. By the citadel a young couple ask us to take their photograph with their camera. I suggest they move 20 metres along so snow-capped Jabal Kasiyun is part of the background. They are students at the university. He is Moroccan, she is Palestinian.

Sunday, 26 November

We have lunch with Bruce Lawrence and Miriam Cooke. We get on well. I appreciate very much what she does. She is falling out with her "sisters". She and Margot Badran were hardly on speaking terms by the time they finished their great anthology of Arab women's writing, and the beautiful friendship with Bouthaina Shaaban seems under threat. She has been with Ulfat Idilbi who knows that her son has been very ill, but does not know how ill. Miriam and Bruce were

8 Peter Clark, "The Battle of Omdurman in the Context of Sudanese History", in Edward M Spiers (ed), *Sudan: The Reconquest Reconsidered*, Frank Cass, London and Portland, 1998.

in the Far East and met Yusuf Islam (Cat Stevens) who attributed his conversion to Islam to Marmaduke Pickthall's translation of the Koran.

Peter went off on leave for two months, catching up with family and friends, lots of cinema, some theatre and a meeting with his Middle East colleagues in Morocco. He returned to Damascus alone, Theresa following a week later.

Bishop Kenneth Cragg with the Syrian Mufti.

The Minister of Culture hosts a dinner for the participants in the opera.

Ulfat Idilbi.

1996

Monday, 15 January 1996

"You have been missed", is the cordial welcome I get from colleagues. I quickly settle in and it seems as if I have not been away.

Wednesday, 17 January

I have a meeting with a landlord to work out details of a contract for new premises. The owner is a woman who was married to an Atassi from Homs. I actually negotiate with her son who is doing a doctorate at the Sorbonne; his thesis is on space in Damascus. Conversation is all in French.

I have lunch with Bouchra and her family. Always so relaxing. The youngest son, Zahir, is now working at a porcelain factory. Husam is working with his father. Another guest is a relation, Dr Khalid Nasra, who has been a teacher in Belgrade for 30 years and has a Serbian wife.

Motaz collects me at the house and we go to a *ta'ziya*, a wake for Dr Adnan al-A'idi. He was the father of Ghassan who helped us with accommodation for the opera performers. Another son, Osman, receives the mourners. The place is packed. Motaz tells me that an accountant gave up working out how much the A'idis were worth, after reaching 800 million US dollars. My French and German counterparts are there, as is Burhan al-Abid and the economist, Nabil Sukkar.

Thursday, 18 January

It is the day of the Homs Road Show. The Ambassador has the idea that he and some of his senior staff go to a provincial city and call on leading figures – the Governor, the Party Secretariat, the University, the Chamber of Commerce.

The Governor is well informed about Homs. The man who serves coffee in his office looks as if he has just come off a building site. The Party Secretary is an elderly lawyer.

We go to a huge lunch hosted by Tarif Akhras[1], a merchant and engineer, who sells sugar to the government for 60 million dollars a year. I sit next to his father-in-law, a Qubaisi.

There is an evening reception at a hotel, hosted by the Ambassador. We have not invited the intellectuals of Homs. I talk with an architect, Safwan Asaf, and some vets. One of the guests is an Americanised Syrian hellfire preacher of the "Alliance church". He greets people with the invariable "Hi, how ya doin'?"

Friday, 19 January

I contemplate a cultural event this year. I would like to bring over Nadim Sawalha to do his one-man presentation of Usama bin Munqidh, the Syrian contemporary of the Crusaders, who wrote an interesting memoir[2]. Nadim is the father of Julia who plays Saffie in the television comedy series *Absolutely Fabulous*. It would be great to do it in the ruins of Shaizar where Usama came from. I mentioned the idea to Abdul Majid, head of the University at Homs. We could mobilise the Party and local authorities. All we would need is a few hundred chairs and some lighting. Nadim and his brother, Nabil, have been the pioneers of drama in Jordan, and are chums of the

---

1 His niece, Asma, later married Bashar al-Assad.

2 Usama Ibn-Munqidh, *An Arab-Syrian Gentleman and Warrior in the Period of the Crusades* (translated by Philip K Hitti), I B Tauris, London, 1987.

Ambassador who was active in amateur dramatics when he was posted to Amman.

Sunday, 21 January
I receive the fourth Arabic book in a week. Because I translate I suspect everybody thinks I am ready to turn anything into English. Someone from Lattakia brings me a volume of essays by Gabriel Saada: nice to have, especially as I am prepared to be a liaison for an Embassy Lattakia Road Show.

Wednesday, 24 January
I call on the Minister of Culture to discuss ideas for 1996, and raise the idea of Nadim Sawalha and Usama bin Munqidh. The problem is that brother Nabil has been doing a one-man satirical show on the West Bank and in Israel in which he guys Arab heads of state, including Hafez al-Assad. I explain that Nadim is not Nabil, but I am steered away from the idea. Too close for comfort. Nabil is a marked man. But she approves of other ideas I have. She gives me a silver filigree tea set. I do not know how much it is worth. I am supposed to declare to my employers any gift worth more than £50.

Thursday, 25 January
Our youngest son, Nat, becomes a teenager today. There seems to be something symbolic about this. Childhood is no longer one of our direct concerns. Responsibility moves down the generational line. We are shifting to the role of being spectators.

I call on the Minister of Higher Education, Dr Saliha Sanqar. I arranged for her son to get into one of our classes. She asks me to pay for her son to spend two months in London to study English. I decline.

Friday, 26 January

I am preparing an article on Muhammad Shahrur[3], and for background am reading a book by the more conservative Muhammad Hamidullah, originally from Hyderabad, whom I met when I was doing my Pickthall researches. He points out that the Sandwich Islands are the antipodes of Mecca, so a Muslim can face any direction when he prays – all are equidistant to Mecca. He also has a lovely passage about the Hyderabad of his youth, the final days of the Nizamate. It was the last surviving bit of the Moghul Empire.

Saturday, 27 January

We drive to Lebanon to do some shopping. As we return to the frontier, we meet a long stationary queue of 120 cars. I walk on and clear our passports and learn that President Hrawi of Lebanon is coming to Damascus for a Ramadan breakfast. There are dozens of official cars, motorcycle escort riders, vans with sirens. Concern for ordinary people has absolutely no place when a Big Man is on the move. We are lucky, and with my diplomatic car plates I am able to drive straight through. But an hour or so before sunset, the traffic behaviour is manic.

Sunday, 28 January

I call on our landlord, Georges, who will be 98 next week. He is recovering from a gallstones operation and proudly shows me the 30 stones preserved in a bottle. He has to have five meals a day, instead of three. But he looks well and is in a smart suit. In the First World War when he was in the Ottoman army he was the ADC to a

3 "The Shahrur Phenomenon: A Liberal Islamic Voice from Syria", *Islam and Christian-Muslim Relations*, 1996; reprinted in Peter Clark, *Coffeehouse Footnotes*, Twopenny Press, 2010.

medical officer in Masyaf and had to officiate at all births. Officers used to have their food sent in. The food of the troops was awful.

Thursday, 1 February
We have lunch with the British Council lawyer, Hanan (Bouchra's schoolmate) and her new Italian husband, Alfredo, in their new flat at Jaramana which is mainly a Druze suburb of Damascus but with a Christian enclave. The flat is on the fourth floor and overlooks the orchards of the Ghouta and beyond to the hills. Hanan wants us to pay her a regular retainer. "I have four children," she explains. "My masters would tell me," I say, "to find a lawyer with no children."

Alfredo drives us back and says I should stay on in Damascus and be a businessman, representing British companies in Syria.

We go to the house of Vanda Hamarneh and Nabil Batal for the evening. There are lots of Hamarnehs there. The family is Christian and comes from Madaba in Jordan and there is a connection with the other Christian Madaba family, the Sawalhas. I talk to Laila who translates subtitles for a video film company. She gets 500 Syrian pounds for a typescript of about 10,000 words. I tell her the commercial rate would be more like the equivalent of 3,500 Syrian pounds. Dancing starts at 11.30 after excellent food. It is Syria at its best. Why should we leave?

Saturday, 3 February
I take a card to our landlord, inscribed "To Georges, Ninety-Eight Years Young (not 101)".

Sunday, 4 February
I take Geoffrey King and his two colleagues, Christina and a restoration architect, to call on Sultan Mheisin, Director of Antiquities. All is chummy. Then on to Hayan Atassi who immediately asks if they have enough money. He is ready to pay for

further visits – in June and in subsequent years. He calls in Abu Mazin, a miskeen-looking man in an ill-fitting suit. He is actually a retired general and we are invited to regard him as a fixer up to the level of General Mustafa Tlas, Minister of Defence, who comes from Rastan just north of Homs. I thought he was an underpaid accountant. "I'm beginning to like Syria," observes the architect.

I take the archaeologists to Homs.

Monday, 5 February

The architect's work is mostly restoring the Welsh castles of the 12th and 13th centuries – English constructions planted in an alien environment by an army of occupation with a limited manpower, requiring fortifications similar to the Crusader castles, for the same logistic reasons. We go to the top of the citadel, recently vacated by the army. It has been a military area for centuries.

I take the archaeologists to call on Abdul Majid, the Rector of the University in Homs, an agreeable meeting. Abdul Majid has a copy of what must be one of the longest doctoral theses in the world, by a Greek, Papadopoulos, on Islamic art, presented to the Sorbonne. It is in six volumes with 1,000 plates and 1,000 pages of text. I ask Abdul Majid about the best bookshop in Homs. There is no doubt – the shop owned by Dr Munzir al-Haik, the historian of Homs. Abdul Majid's driver takes us there. We go upstairs above the shop, to a room that is like a majlis. Munzir is talking to one man, a Lecturer in French, and others drop in. Munzir has written a kind of Pevsner guide to the buildings of Homs, a fascinating well-produced volume. He has a lot to say about the citadel and its history. He seems very familiar with every aspect of it.

Wednesday, 7 February

Bouthaina calls. We are sending her to the Cambridge Literature Seminar in August. She is very much involved as interpreter in the peace talks, sitting next to the President in his negotiations with Warren Christopher. As a creative person she enjoys the work: the personal dynamics, the body language, the facial expressions.

"Do you keep a diary?" I ask.

"I wouldn't dare," she says.

"Keep one and when you go to Britain, deposit it in a bank. In 25 years' time it will be a valuable record, and will help provide for your old age!"

We have dinner with Brigid and Alan Waddams and slag off Ambassadors. They are the objects of flattery and deference. They have limited contacts. The advice on which British policy is based is potentially flawed. There should be far more interchange between business, diplomacy, journalism and academia. All can contribute to an understanding of how a country works.

Friday, 9 February

We go for a walk to Ain al-Fijja and then across the railway line and into the hills. It is a winter walk – we have done it before – not too hot. Up a valley and up the slopes of terraces to another road. A pall of mist hangs over it all, putting us both in mind of … Dovedale. A broad dale with steep hills that over geological time has thrown up some bizarre shapes. It is still Ramadan but we are greeted courteously, and cordially invited into homes.

I read the typescript of a book, *The Gates of Damascus*, that is to be published in April. William Dalrymple had it and passed it on to Brigid Waddams. It is about a woman who teaches at the university and whose husband has been a political prisoner for 11 years. It shows aspects of Syria that we conveniently overlook – the social tensions between Sunnis and Alawites and the seething hatred that does exist. There are also the problems of family life, individual aspirations, the corrupting nature of the regime, the police state and the lack of freedom of expression.

Saturday, 10 February

I take Geoffrey and his colleagues to call on Sultan Mheisin. He expresses reservations about commercial sponsorship of archaeological work.

"Why are they doing it? What's in it for them? Is the CIA or Mossad behind them?"

I make a vigorous counterargument. Osman A'idi is putting up money for excavations at Afamia.

"People say, he is putting in one pound to make five."

"But we are getting one pound, which we might not otherwise have had."

The underlying idea is that the state has a monopoly of the interests of the country, even though there is no money for what should be done.

The Ambassador hosts a dinner for the archaeologists, with Sultan Mheisin and Hayan and Mrs Atassi as guests. She is a Kayali from Hama. Her father was Military Attaché in Cairo in 1958, and she did an MA on the poet Nizar Kabbani who worked in the Embassy while her father was Ambassador. Sultan's reservations about commerce seem to disappear.

Thursday, 15 February

Theresa and I go to the University to hear Sadiq al-Azm give a talk on Taboo and Literature. He talks about Salman Rushdie. The outburst of hostility was from the non-Arab world. Rushdie was satirical about the religious establishment and not about the spirituality of Islam. Khomeini's fatwa was not a fatwa but a *hukm*, a sentence. The Saudis objected to it, arguing that you cannot have a sentence without the process of a trial. There are 30 people present and there is a good discussion, all sympathetic to Rushdie. The chair is Hassana Mardam-Bey whose family were the great political rivals of the Azms.

Sunday, 18 February
In Beirut

I am woken up at 3 by a *musahhir* who is walking around the area near the Mayflower Hotel, banging a drum to wake people up to take their last meal an hour before dawn, when the Ramadan fast starts. I am surprised to hear this in such a westernised part of the city.

Wednesday, 21 February.

Theresa, Gabriel and I drive by Homs, to Tell Kallakh; then through a beautiful valley to the Lebanese border to Tripoli.

Thursday, 22 February

We drive from Tripoli to the ski resort of Faraya. There is some tension in the country and we meet frequent checkpoints. Faraya is crowded. Car parks are filled to capacity. Traffic wardens guide us through. We end up at the Auberge Suisse. The resort is well organised. We pick our way carefully into this new world. Gabriel likes skiing and we are here for his sake. We hire skis, boots and batons for him and he joins a ski lift, known as "Baby-run". Different runs are assessed according to difficulty, and this is the simplest.

I reckon there are 4 to 5,000 people here, the vast majority Lebanese. It shows how the Lebanese can do things really well. Good organisation, available amenities, reasonably cheap, making skiing accessible to a large bulk of the middle classes, and not just the elite. It is the largest of the skiing resorts though others are being developed – at the Cedars, Laqluq and Zarour. And there are plans for floodlighting the slopes.

Monday, 26 February
Back in Damascus.

A neighbour has died and I make a condolence call. The flat is full of mourners, all men, sitting on chairs around the room. Six brothers – sons of the deceased – stand when anyone enters. There is not always shaking of hands. Instead host and guest face each other and give a mutual salute, each briefly placing the right hand on head and heart.

Tuesday, 27 February

I have a visit from Shadi Abdul Nur, son of Ibrahim whom I first met in 1962 at Palmyra. His sister Abeer is now in Santa Clarita, California, married to George, and has had a daughter, Linda. George would really like to come back to Syria. Shadi's brother, Bassam, is in California living 20 minutes away from his sister. Mum is well in Fairouza and Shadi, a bright lad, is in his second year at the Faculty of Medicine in the University of Damascus.

Wednesday, 28 February

The writer, Nadia Khost, calls and presents me with her huge new historical novel, the title of which translates as *Love in the Land of Syria*. She tells me the role of women has deteriorated during the last century. One hundred years ago women were able to go on pilgrimage to Mecca unaccompanied.

I have a chat with the Embassy Spook about contemporary Arab politics. The growing illegitimacy of Arab regimes is illustrated by migration and undermined by the information revolution. Corruption is also a manifestation of illegitimacy. People no longer give credit to the rationality of political or bureaucratic decisions. He has been asked to write a paper on the permanence and "stability" of regimes. We discuss how it might have been a different story if he had had to write the paper in 1960 or 1970.

Tuesday, 5 March

One of the teachers, Neville, phones with a crisis. He has had his car stolen. He had picked up a soldier in Martyrs' Square and taken him to his flat for the night. "We slept in separate rooms," he says, but only after he moved to the spare room to get away from the soldier's hacking cough. In the morning he found 600 US dollars, 5,000 Syrian pounds, his radio and his car missing. Neville comes in and we talk about reporting to the police, an edited version where the "rent boy" scene is irrelevant.

We have a breakfast party at the office for four visiting British MPs, led by Andrew Faulds. After we eat I say a few words and talk about the drawbacks of privatisation in Syria – how it has led to corruption and inefficiency. Andrew Faulds leans over to the two Conservative MPs. "Are you listening to this?" he says.

Wednesday, 6 March

I have a visit from Majida Bouzo, daughter of our office landlord, Haidar. She runs her own publishing house – one of two – in Lattakia. This is two more than Aleppo has, she tells me. Her husband, Ahmad, is a doctor who runs the Sufi Hospital. They know everybody in Lattakia and want to arrange a lunch for the Ambassador.

Thursday, 7 March

I have breakfast with Yasir Suleiman, Professor of Arabic at the University of Edinburgh, who is on his way to Homs for a week at the university. He tells me of Iraqi Jews in Israel who prefer to write in Arabic.

I brief the Ambassador on the Neville crisis. I did the right thing in reporting the matter to the police and being "economical with the truth". But if the Syrian authorities know of the gay aspects Neville could be expelled. If that happens, we have to be ready and accept it.

"What will you do if he gets through this crisis?" he asks.

"Give him a final warning."

"I don't agree. He should be told to leave. Not within 24 hours, but in a few days or weeks."

I point out the inconvenience. "We have a teaching operation to run."

"It's your management decision," he concludes.

Friday, 8 March

In Antakya (Antioch), Turkey, which was part of the French Mandate of Syria between 1920 and 1939.

We wander around the city, passing the Greek Orthodox church which has an inscription, dated 1900, recording in Arabic verse that the church was built under the patronage of Sultan Abdul Hamid II.

We drive up to the citadel. There is a welcome bar there and we chat to the barman, Kemal, a 65-year-old Korean war veteran, and admire the view through his binoculars over the city and the mountains of Musa Dagh beyond. We then walk along the walls to the ruins of the citadel.

This is Antioch, a famous name – where Christianity started, one of the great cities of the Mediterranean world, but the place is totally unsanitised. I like it. Antioch/Antakya is a frontier city, on the borderlands of Arabia and Turkey. It has a cultural ambiguity I am so fond of. There is also a touch of the 20-year French occupation – the avenues, the lycée, a certain style of buildings. There is no evidence of outrageous wealth cheek by jowl with poverty. And the countryside around is tranquil and unspoilt: villages constructed of local materials amid green mountains.

Sunday, 10 March

Back in Damascus.

The police have identified the stealer of Neville's car. It is only a matter of days before they apprehend him. He has taken ten days' leave from the army. What will he say when taken? Will the shit hit the fan and will we get egg on our face!

Monday, 11 March

I learn that Reem, the daughter of our lawyer, Hanan, was married at the age of 17 to a violent man who had been married before – Hanan did not know that. Like her predecessor, Reem has been beaten up. The husband has had an affair and a child with a former mistress and wants the child to be registered as his and Reem's! Reem has gone back to Hanan and is asking for a divorce. She is 20.

The Ambassador and I call on the Minister of Culture. There is a summit meeting at Sharm al-Shaikh that hopes to reactivate the peace process. The President is not going. The Ambassador expresses his regrets about this. Our Prime Minister, John Major, will be there. The Minister launches into a tirade – "who cared when the bones of our children were crushed?"

Just before I am about to set off for Lattakia, Ayoub tells me that the man who stole Neville's car had an accident at Nabk in the stolen car, killing himself.

I drive to Lattakia and meet Ahmad al-Sufi and his wife, Majida. He is much older, was trained in Egypt and Britain. They live in a sumptuous flat above the hospital. He is also a novelist and has been a member of the Ba'th Party from early days, but is critical, especially on issues of human rights.

Tuesday, 12 March

Jamie of the Embassy and I call on the secretary of the Ba'th Party in Lattakia, Dr Muhsin Khayer, to discuss the Ambassadorial Road Show. On the way we pause to look at the Casino, symbol of the Mandate years, recently restored as a hotel. The Party is very close to the Assad family here. In his office I count 11 telephones. Jamie talks of the Ambassador's wife planning to give a coffee party for the women of Lattakia.

"We are not fanatic here," he says. "Women and men are entertained together."

We go over the list of people who should come to the Ambassador's reception. "Do not forget the Mayor of Qardaha," he says.

We go on to the Joud industrial complex and meet Haitham Subhi Joud. The Jouds started their industries in 1933 when Haitham's grandfather opened a shop at the age of 24. They now control the distribution of soft drinks, make Pinguin refrigerators and many other things, and export to South America. Haitham and his uncle, Faruq, both speak excellent English. Haitham studied at the American University in Paris.

I have lunch at Spiro's with Nuhad Abdullah, whose father used to be the Assad family lawyer. He concentrates on his architectural practice but is also a Professor at the University. He is critical of the regime and thinks the Alawites – he is one himself – have advanced too fast. He fears a backlash after Assad's death. Many Alawites in Lattakia come from the "sanjak", the old area containing Antakya/Antioch and Iskenderun that was transferred to Turkey in 1939. The sanjakis have stressed the Arab element of the Ba'thist ideology.

He is illuminating on Lattakia. The Casino was built in 1925 by an Armenian architect, Limanjian. There are Greeks still in the city and there have been two synagogues. Some Jews have converted to Islam – Haddad and Misi are Jewish names. There is still an area that was known as the Jewish quarter – Harat al-Yahud. Nuhad is writing a book on the architecture of the Mediterranean coastline. He also designs hotels. We go to his house for coffee, passing his old family house that used to be the headquarters of British intelligence during the Second World War – where Evans-Pritchard served. He has a lot of aerial photographs of Mediterranean coastal landscapes. His father-in-law was the Minister of Labour in the first Ba'thist government of 1963.

Wednesday, 13 March

I drive back to Damascus. Neville has recovered his money from the pockets of the dead driver who had been unable to control the car which went into a spin, overturned and killed him.

Saturday, 16 March

We go to the new statue of Saladin by the citadel to meet Hussein Hinawi. We are early and spend the time people-watching. "Are you Russian?" people ask. I get into conversation with one old man who tells me he has six girls and six boys, all married.

"How many grandchildren?" I ask.

"*Ktir*" ("Lots"), he replies.

Hussein turns up, a smartly dressed Palestinian, whose family is originally from Acre, a tour guide with excellent English. He has been interested in Lady Jane Digby in Damascus and Mary Lovell has put us in touch. He takes us to the house in Aqsab, behind Bouchra's flat, where Lady Jane lived. We call on Abu Zubair Shallah, a 66-year-old, who lives in the restored ruins of the old house. The Shallah family bought the house a century ago when there were orchards and purling streams at the back. Some families have made homes in restored parts of the ruins. We go up rickety stairs and come across fine wallpaper of the last century and the relics of a turret, all an echo of a grand town house. Today Abu Zubair keeps pigeons on the roof.

Sunday, 17 March

The Neville drama continues. There is a visiting security consultant at the Embassy and I talk to him. If Neville had been on the Embassy staff he would have been out of the country immediately. He suggests that Neville could be in personal danger from the family of the man killed.

Yasir Suleiman comes to tea. We have also invited our landlord Georges. Yasir quizzes him about his service in the Ottoman army.

"Why don't you write your memoirs?"

"I don't have time."

Monday, 18 March

I tell Neville that when his contract ends in the summer I will not agree to its renewal.

"What about equal opportunities?" he asks.

"The renewal of a contract depends on mutual agreement." I say he has been guilty of extreme imprudence. It has nothing to do with the gay aspects of the case.

Personnel crises like this are exhausting.

Tuesday, 19 March

I am called in to see the Ambassador. He is with the security adviser. Both think Neville should leave the country.

"I do not have sufficient legal grounds for that," I explain. "He has an employment contract. The most I can do at present is not renew it."

"We are concerned about his physical safety," says the adviser.

"I calculate that the risk is slight."

"But suppose he is killed."

"Then I would have got it wrong."

The Ambassador thinks that the danger of a demand for blood money – and Neville's imprisonment until it is paid – is a greater risk.

"Have you seen the dead body?" the adviser asks me. "It has all the appearances of a classic case of entrapment. Neville could be a security risk. If he is approached to provide information he must report it to the Embassy."

I see our new Director of Studies, Sandra, later. The exterior of the car, I learn, was smashed up but the driver's seat was intact. Another twist is that a friend of Neville who was sacked as an Embassy driver has been arrested by the police and roughed up. All this could suggest entrapment. I am out of my depth in all this.

In the evening I go to a seminar at the Goethe Institute on the Peace Process. Sadiq al-Azm comments that the Peace Process is like a Renaissance political situation where a couple are forced into marriage though the couple hate each other. The great powers are like the parents.

"You don't have to go back to the Renaissance," I say. "What about the British royal family?"

Wednesday, 20 March

"You were on a hiding to nothing," observes the Ambassador. I think he means that whatever decision I took over the Neville case would, in some respects, be wrong. There is only one way of proving that he is at risk and that is when he is killed.

"I cannot summarily dismiss him without the probability of a 'wrongful dismissal' case against the British Council."

It is clear that the Ambassador would like me to sack him. It is as if he wants me to pick his chestnuts out of the fire.

Thursday, 21 March
Aleppo
We attend a film festival function at the Kindi cinema. An official makes a routine speech and when he mentions the name of the President, there is no spontaneous applause. I exchange silent but meaningful glances with a colleague.

Friday, 22 March

I drive to Lattakia, west along the road to Bab al-Hawa and Harim. The weather is stormy, with occasional thunder and lightning. The countryside is intensely green and when the clouds lift there are splendid extensive views. Then down (or up) the Orontes – warm green hills on the left, lush meadows on the right, to Quai, a Maronite village, isolated in a Muslim area, with very distinctive vernacular architecture. The village is off the main road and I divert and potter about. White paving stones sparkle from the recent rain. It is a compact village more like a southern French bastide town than a Syrian village. One road leads up to a monastery founded in 1878. I continue through the unsightly town of Jisr al-Shughur and divert to the village of Rabbia, set in wooded hills, and then through Turkoman villages to Lattakia where I check in at the hotel, occupying the former Casino.

Two pleasant academics call – Ibrahim Hallaq and his wife, Rima Himawi. Ibrahim is an Alawite from Lattakia but his father migrated from Antakya, not from any Arab solidarity but to escape Turkish military service. Lattakia and Aleppo are full of people originally from the former sanjak of Iskenderun, and in both cities they have a charitable organisation called Sons of the Province.

Saturday, 23 March

I call on Gabriel Saada, the leading literary figure and historian of the city. He is a short man, in his eighties. "My mind is French, my heart is Arabic," he says. He has been a tobacco merchant and he shows me his magnificent library – 14,000 volumes – and presents me with two of his books.

I walk up to what is left of the Crusader castle and absorb the feel of the city. The castle site looks down on the grid plan of the Roman city. A mosque and an Armenian church are close by.

I am taken to a packed Arab Cultural Club for a concert given by local musicians. A music teacher, Jacqueline Elias, conducts her pupils, mostly middle-class girls, in songs. The audience includes the Governor, the Party Secretary, Muhsin Khayer (and his wife, Marcelle) and the Chief of Police. Muhsin plays on the piano a piece of his own composition – *A Ma Mère*.

Sunday, 24 March

The Ambassador has arrived and we go in convoy to call on the Governor, Abdul Mun'im al-Hamwi, originally from the Hauran. He has been a Minister of Agriculture and Governor of Qunaytra. Then in a convoy, with a police escort, to the office of the Chief of Police. This is in the former headquarters of the French Alawite State.

Then we spend a few hours with the Jouds, first at their factory which is not overmanned and is highly automated. Then to lunch at the Siwar Restaurant owned by a son of Rifaat al-Assad. It overlooks a bay on the far side of which is a Palestinian refugee camp. Finally to the Joud house, extraordinarily sumptuous, like something out of *Dallas*.

The late Basil al-Assad wielded an irregular control over Lattakia with the support of his goons. It has been cleared up in the last two years.

In the evening I call on the historian, Hashim Uthman, who has – he tells me – a bigger library than Gabriel Saada – or Ustaz Gabi, as he calls him. As well as a vast collection of newspapers. He practises as a lawyer and has written several books.

Monday, 25 March

I accompany the Ambassador on a call on the Party Secretary. The Ambassador is very good at kissing leading Ba'th Party officials without embarrassment. He is also good at teasing out information. For example, we learn that the President has given up smoking, out of concern for his health.

We return to Damascus, stopping for lunch at Baniyas, at a restaurant that used to be the canteen of the Iraq Petroleum Company.

Thursday, 28 March

I go the American Cultural Center to hear Cornelia Khaled give a talk, in Arabic, on Alice Walker and female circumcision. Cornelia wears power clothes and puts on power spectacles. She speaks with fluency and authority. All her fans are present.

Sunday, 31 March

A British lady was in an accident yesterday. An Air Force officer was driving with a girlfriend at speed, went on to the pavement and knocked her over, breaking her leg. He stopped, said, "You'll be all right," and drove off.

Wednesday, 3 April

There is concern in the Embassy about the increasing numbers of tourists coming to Syria and the likely increase in Consular problems – deaths, arrests, serious illnesses and people who are just loopy.

Salma Khadra Jayyusi calls and I take her to lunch at the Sheraton Hotel. Allen Hibbard wrote a critical review of her work. "Why?" she exclaims. "Is he Arab?" She thinks all Arabs are jealous and backbiting. I agree to translate a favourite story by Nadia al-Ghazzi[4] and a play by the Jordanian, Jamal Abu Hamdan[5], for her next anthologies.

4 "The Man Who Saw His Own Funeral" was published in Salma Khadra Jayyusi (ed.), *Modern Arabic Fiction*, Columbia University Press, New York, 2004.

5 *Actress J's Burial Night* was published in Salma Khadra Jayyusi (ed), *Short Arabic Plays*, Interlink Books, New York, 2003.

Thursday, 4 April

Abdul Salam al-Ujaili calls. He spends most of his time in al-Raqqa or Aleppo or travelling. He was recently in Paris for Jacques Berque's memorial service. Abdul Salam is a little deaf and has an eye glass – not a monocle – which he keeps in a small leather case and takes out to examine small print.

After work we drive off to southern Turkey, passing the Ambassador, his wife and two single women colleagues in the Embassy. They are off to Cappadocia. I have the fantasy of telling the border officials that there's this white-haired weirdo with three birds in his pick-up pretending to be the British Ambassador.

Tuesday, 9 April

I go to Lattakia to take part in a university seminar on translation. At the opening the Rector of the University is present and so is the University's Party Secretary – who takes precedence. Shahada Khoury talks about Arabic in the world. Then a rant about how bad it is in Algeria that they prefer to use French. I talk in Arabic about practicalities of translation. We have lunch afterwards at the Zenobia Restaurant and Shahada Khoury gives me a copy of a volume of poems written by his 16-year-old grandson who lives and writes English poetry in Cleveland, Ohio. The grandfather has translated one of the poems into Arabic.

Wednesday, 10 April

I accompany Rosemary from the Embassy to the Lebanese border to meet visiting (British) MPs. We meet there Tawfiq Darwish, the Deputy Speaker of the Syrian parliament who represents Jabala and is from Lattakia. I go in a car with Derek Fatchett and Tawfiq (who has no English) and am having to interpret, dealing with heavy politics. The European position on the Middle East conflict is different from that of the Americans. Syria is aware that the Golan Heights has lost its military significance in this day and age. Much is dependent on the Israeli elections in May and American elections in November. We are all in fast cars with accompanying police cars sounding their sirens.

Thursday, 11 April
We have breakfast with the MPs in the office. First we eat and then I talk for ten minutes and we have a question-and-answer session. John Gunnell is fascinated by the opera. He is chairman of the House of Commons opera group.

We go to the University to see the students of the Department of English put on *Doctor Faustus*. It is the first time they have presented a play in English since 1960 when they put on *The Merchant of Venice* for Gamal Abdul Nasser!

Friday, 12 April
Theresa and I go to a recital at the Catholic church given by Abdullah Shehada on the kanun, Shauna Beesley on the harpsichord, Cynthia al-Wadi on the organ and Firas Zen al-Abdeen on the cello. The first part is marred by the television cameramen who get in the way, shining blazing lights on everyone. When the camera focusses on me I glare ferociously. But they leave and we are left to enjoy the music including Vivaldi's *Four Seasons* (or one of them).

The Minister has asked me to translate a speech she is due to give.

Sunday, 14 April
I have arranged for a mission statement to be printed out, framed and displayed in every room of the British Council: "The aim of the British Council in Syria is to serve the people of Syria and to make friends for Britain."

Tuesday, 16 April
The Israelis have been bombing Lebanon. I phone Ann, my opposite

number in Beirut and offer support and sympathy. Planes have been noisily circling over the city, electricity power has been cut off and tens of thousands in the south have been made homeless. We need to stand by in the event of an evacuation. Portillo has been in Israel making statements supportive of Israel's position: that does not help her.

Thursday, 18 April

The Ambassador calls at our office. He is less bouncy than usual. He was called in to see the Deputy Minister of Foreign Affairs. "I had far more sympathy with what he said than with what I was obliged to say."

Friday, 19 April

I am translating a story by Nadia al-Ghazzi. Her father was Prime Minister in 1954 and committed suicide after the June 1967 war with Israel. She was married to a senior lawyer and she herself was a lawyer, and her stories are derived from her legal experience.

We drive to Ain al-Fijja and walk along the railway line, Theresa's favourite walk. It is a fine spring day and all Damascus seems to have come out. Groups of young people are dancing under the trees, people are strumming guitars and beating drums. We get constant invitations to join them.

Saturday, 20 April

We go for another walk, taking a taxi to Rakhla, beyond Burqush and walk in the lower foothills of Mount Hermon. A group of soldiers walk up with us. "What do you think of Israel?" I am asked. In the distance, on the other side of Mount Hermon, we hear the steady boom boom of Israeli shells. We pick up a track and another group of soldiers stops us, but are satisfied with our identity and we get to the village of Qatana and find a bus, a "micro", that takes us back to Damascus.

In the evening I go to a party at the German Ambassador's in honour of their Deputy Minister for Foreign Affairs, Helmut Schafer, a big man who was a student and a teacher in Ohio. He travelled around the Arab world 24 years ago.

Sunday, 21 April

The Embassy calculates that the chances of Syria being involved in a war have increased in the last fortnight from one to five per cent. The odds are still 19 to 1 against but the risks have increased fivefold. I discuss contingencies. I need to know exactly where all the British Council family live and advise them of ensuring that they have stocks of food, water and cash in the house.

I give a talk on Translation and Culture at the University. I have an audience of 150 including Sadiq al-Azm, Nadia al-Ghazzi and colleagues. Questions go on for half an hour.

The British Council driver, Zahir, takes me to Palmyra and I check into the Nakhla Hotel. There are now ten hotels in Palmyra/Tadmor. Thirty years ago there was only one.

Monday, 22 April

I am up early and have to wake up the hotel staff to prepare breakfast. Zahir drives me on to Deir ez-Zor and I am put up, as the guest of the Ministry of Culture, at the Cham Firat Hotel. My room overlooks the Euphrates. We are all here for the opening of the museum that has been funded by the German government. I join a hundred or so guests, all with name tags, making people look like a personification of the bibliography of Ross Burns's *Monuments of Syria*: Balti, Sach, Tate and so on. I meet the British archaeologist David Oates who looks unwell, leans on a stick and is yellow-faced.

The Minister delivers her speech and my translation is distributed. It has been retyped although "exchange of covenants" has been changed to "exchange of convents". She hesitates on the more political parts, making the impact more dramatic. Being intensely familiar with the text I can feel the power of her oratory.

I talk to André Raymond, a youthful 70-year-old, who went as a teacher to Sadiqi College in Tunis in 1947. Then I talk to the man in charge of Ministry of Culture public relations, Hassan. He is a Turkoman who started in the Ministry as a member of a dance troupe.

Tuesday, 23 April

Back in Damascus I learn that Ulfat Idilbi is having difficulty with getting a visa to visit Britain. The cool, cerebral, efficient Consular official is unhappy about the fact she has not disclosed her medical plans. The official needs to see the deeds of Ulfat's Damascus house to ensure that she is not going to be an unwanted immigrant! It is extraordinary. Ulfat is 80. Her son, Ziad, is seriously ill in London. He is Wafic Said's best friend and banker. Does the Consular official imagine she is going to get a job at McDonald's and marry an Englishman? The official also wants to check on her son's bank balance. Of course he has never heard of Wafic Said, let alone Ulfat Idilbi. With embarrassment I phone Ziad (who lives in Portman Square) and explain what is required.

And David Oates has been taken ill at Deir ez-Zor and I arrange for him to come to Damascus and be admitted to the Shami Hospital.

Warren Christopher and Benazir Bhutto are both in Damascus.

Wednesday, 24 April

David Oates is now in the Shami Hospital. I go to see him. He looks dreadful. The Ministry is ready to arrange for him to be transferred to Britain but not on Syrian Arab Airlines.

One of our teachers, Simon, is the son of John Morrison who was Master of Wolfson College, Cambridge and worked for the British Council in Palestine in the 1940s. Simon's mother was the governess of King Faisal in Baghdad when he was an infant. He succeeded as king when he was a baby and used to be carried everywhere and did not learn to walk until he was four.

We have arranged for David Oates to be flown out tonight. He is suffering from gallstones but with complications. There is a heart murmur, he has jaundice and has had a stroke. He really is in a mess. He has been sedated and rambles a bit.

Thursday, 25 April

The driver, Zahir, took David Oates to the airport last night and was very helpful. I have told Zahir that he has to be more assertive – there is no word in Arabic – and when he is in the car he represents me, the British Council, the British Embassy, the British government right up to the Queen. When necessary he must exert that authority. Last night he did.

Friday, 3 May

Mamduh Udwan has asked me to translate one of his plays[6] and I work on it. I have also recently been translating a story by Nadia al-Ghazzi. Mamduh, I hear, has had a heart attack.

Sunday, 5 May

I work at polishing up my translation of Nadia's story. When I started I thought it was too difficult. There is in the style a mixture of the mock heroic and the mundane. I get this across by mixing registers: "Their tummies were replete."

For my headquarters I work out a list of "priority groups" and name 169 people. I know them all and can approach any of them at a cocktail party.

6 *The Mask* was published in Salma Khadra Jayyusi (ed), *Short Arabic Plays*, Interlink Books, New York, 2003.

The Minister of Foreign Affairs, Faruq Shara'a, is a graduate of English from the University of Damascus. He used to work for Syrian Arab Airlines in their London office.

Tuesday, 7 May

The very pro-Israel Labour MP, Greville Janner, was here recently. Sadiq al-Azm was asked to entertain him. Janner arrived and introduced himself – "I am a Labour Zionist". Sadiq said, "I'm an Arab nationalist." After that they got on quite well and afterwards he sent Sadiq a box of House of Commons chocolates.

Wednesday, 8 May

We go to see our landlord on his name day. A lot of well-dressed Christians also call. Georges does not need glasses and, apart from being just a little deaf, is as fit as anyone 40 years younger.

We have tea with Sulaiman Ahmed and his wife, Sa'da, and their daughter, Balsam. Mother and daughter are both doing PhDs in Britain. Although they are Alawites, Sa'da regularly goes to church in Britain, takes a close interest in the sermons and discusses them afterwards with the minister. What a wonderful breakdown of barriers and removal of stereotypes!

Thursday, 9 May

Muna in the office, who has helped me with my translations, has a grim personal life. Her husband is a bright lad from a poor family. One of his brothers died leaving two children. Another has been in an accident and is paralysed from the neck down. Muna and her husband have seven extra children to look after. Her husband spends his time consoling the brother. Muna has two or three jobs to keep the family going.

I go to Bouchra's for a party. There are about 40 people in the small flat. Bouchra dances. I dance. A lovely girl on whom Bouchra's son Zafir seems sweet dances. Fadi beats a drum while his father plays his guitar. Small children sit on laps and fall asleep. Others strut around. I stay and eat pizza, tabuleh and cake, and get home at midnight.

Friday, 10 May
I finish translating the play, *The Mask*, by Mamduh Udwan – at his request.

Saturday, 11 May
Theresa reads the play and is impressed. When I translate my critical faculties are limited – I am too close to the text. But I appreciate that the play has pace and the surprise at the end is well contrived.

Sunday, 12 May
I am asked by the Embassy Spook to see him. I am taken to a "secure" part of the Embassy and into a conference room, cut off from the rest of the Embassy. A member of the Syrian parliament whom I have met – he is a Communist but calls himself a "market Communist" – wants to see the spook on "neutral ground". Could they meet in our garden? I have no objection but draw the line at offering information on a scholarship candidate who has been a political prisoner and whose name has been mentioned by the Communist MP. Is there an active Communist Party network here?

I go to see Mamduh Udwan in hospital. The other visitor at the bedside is Abdul Rahman Munif.

I spend a couple of hours searching for the cemetery where Lady Jane Digby is buried. The grave is in the small Protestant cemetery. But this is firmly locked and I cannot find the keeper of the key. I then collect Rosemary and Michael Halsted from their hotel. He is a former British Council colleague. She is a great-great-niece of Lady Jane. I take the kitchen stepladder along and we go to the cemetery.

We put the ladder by the gate, but it is not big enough to climb over. A lad comes along with a big huge grin on his face carrying a builders' ladder. He lends it to us and we are able to use it to scale the gate. Michael stays in the road and Rosemary and I find the grave. Rosemary puts some flowers on it, I take a photograph and wander off to look at the grave of Henry Thomas Buckle the historian who died here in 1862. I came to both graves myself in 1971. Then home for a drink and a meal. Rosemary is thrilled by it all.

Monday, 13 May
We go to the Assad Library for a recital by a German string quartet. They play Beethoven's opus 95. Another violist joins them and they play a quintet by Zemlinsky, Schoenberg's brother-in-law, and finally the quintet by Bruckner, celebrating the centenary of his death.

Wednesday, 15 March
My Line Manager is here. The first thing he says when I meet him is, "God, I'm exhausted." He assesses me – "Excellent" – and asks for comments. All I can say is that I have tried to introduce the concept of "Syrian ownership" in everything we do. Atmosphere at British Council headquarters is poisonous. People struggling to survive. Senior colleagues shouting at each other. A sense of nervousness. One senior colleague called another "a fucking Scottish git" and then had to apologise.

Thursday, 16 May
I take my Line Manager to the Franciscan church. He is amazed to come off the busy street to hear Pergolesi's *Stabat Mater* being beautifully played. The National Orchestra are rehearsing. It is an eye-opener to see Muslims playing so wonderfully a Christian cantata in a church. Wafa is in the chorus. I remember her parents

objecting to Wafa being in the opera and not wearing a headscarf. Objections were overcome when she chose to wear a wig. Her hair was being covered in public. We move on to the Institute of Music and Drama and watch a sword fight – it is part of a final drama demonstration exam.

Friday, 17 May

We go to the Franciscan church for the concert. It is packed and we are seated in the front next to the Papal Legate – *al-Safir al-Babawi*: it sounds better in Arabic. The *Serenade for Strings* is followed by a pause for the Call to Prayer. Then Solhi conducts the Pergolesi. It is superb; hard to realise that most performers are Muslim. At the end there is a standing ovation led by al-Safir al-Babawi.

Peter is in England for a fortnight, calling at his headquarters and seeing his sons during their half-term, renting a flat in Hove.

Friday, 31 May

We get a takeaway from a Turkish kebabci in Brighton. One of the employees comes from Samanda , near Antakya. We talk first in Turkish and then in Arabic which is his mother tongue. But he hates Arabs. "Dogs," he calls them, "donkeys". I insist that we are all *bani Adam*, children of Adam.

Sunday, 2 June

Back in the office, I meet and greet my colleagues. Rumours abound. There have been bomb explosions in Lattakia and Aleppo and here in Martyrs' Square. Security measures have been stepped up and people have been detained for "economic crimes" including the former Minister of Tourism. I think Syria is in a fragile state. Rumours attribute troublemaking to the Turks.

Monday, 3 June

There are rumours of impending Cabinet changes. At a party a senior Syrian doctor tells me, "Only two people know what the new Cabinet will be: Assad and Allah." But he suggests confidently that Hani Murtadi will be Minister of the Environment. "He will be the token Shi'ite."

Tuesday, 4 June

We have dinner with Cynthia and Solhi al-Wadi. He tells me that elements of the Party are getting at him. He has failed some students.

"Do you have friends in high places in the Party?" I ask.

"No, I have never cultivated these."

"What about at the very top?"

"Yes," he says. "Assad has told me to get in touch with him if I need help. But I am unwilling to play that card."

He shows me his pride and joy, a 1930 gramophone which has to be wound up. He has played 78 rpm records on it all his life. When he was at Victoria College, Alexandria, to escape philistine contemporaries he used to take his gramophone to the deserted cricket pavilion and console himself with music. He plays for me a crackling *New World Symphony*.

Wednesday, 5 June

I call on Hayan Atassi who has been doing all sorts of things to help promote his sponsorship of the British dig at Homs. An article is to appear in *al-Ba'th* newspaper tomorrow. He has copied and circulated Geoffrey King's report to the Minister of the Environment and people in the Party, as well as leading professionals and merchants in Homs.

Tuesday, 11 June

I am invited to have coffee with the Minister of the Environment,

Abdul Hakim Munajjid. We talk Arabic all the time. He is a Homsi and studied palaeontology in Paris. We talk about the importance of taking exercise and the ageing process.

Wednesday, 12 June

I hear that a daughter of my friend, Mahmud Zughaiby, Head of the Army Medical Services, is married to a son of the Minister of Defence, Mustafa Tlas.

Thursday, 13 June

Bouthaina Shaaban has been accepted on the British Council Cambridge Literature seminar. Margaret Drabble, David Lodge, Arnold Wesker and all sorts of people will be there. Also Carmen Callil. I write to Bouthaina telling her to look out for Carmen, and to Carmen telling her what a precious person Bouthaina is.

We host a lunch in honour of a visiting jazz group. I have invited Robert Mulki and his wife. He is a successful lawyer, with a place just outside Zurich and a flat in London, but when there they always stay at the Cumberland Hotel which used to be £5 a night but is now £125 a night. We also invite three of the Syrian stars of the opera, one of whom has a place at the Royal College of Music and another at RADA.

Friday, 14 June

I see Theresa off for a break in Britain and drive south to the town of Nawa, not a place on the international tourist trail. It has a large mosque dedicated to Imam Nawawi, a famous collector of the sayings of the Prophet Muhammad, but it is locked and deserted. I wander around the town, built round one street nearly a mile long. All sorts of merchandise is on sale – fruit, spanners, little headscarves for girls who "return to religion". I ask a trader where the shrine, *maqam*, of Imam Nawawi is. I find it, in a courtyard round a tree of great antiquity. I am told there are visitors to the tomb, but there is no special day in the year for pilgrims.

Peter drives on for a couple of days in Jordan, where he worked between 1968 and 1970.

Saturday, 15 June

I drive by Kerak, Wadi Araba and back to Ma'an. The building that used to be the Petra Hotel – I stayed there in 1963 – is now a museum dedicated to the memory of Emir Abdullah, grandfather of King Hussein.

Sunday, 16 June

I call on the historian, Sulaiman Mousa, whom I used to know well during my time in Amman. On the way I have a puncture and get help – but I need a *miftah musallab*, a crossbow spanner. We find one at a nearby garage. Then I get the tyre repaired. Here the word for puncture is *banashir*, in Syria, *goma*.

A Jordanian newspaper reports that there has been an attempted coup in Syria.

Sulaiman has been reading *Sabriya*. He tells me I should not have translated *tha'ir* as "insurgent". That is how the French described them: an interesting translation point.

Tuesday, 18 June

It is the Queen's Birthday Party. I calculate that it is the 27th I have attended in eight different countries. I talk to Abdul Majid of Homs who has let his Damascus house to Yousef Jajati, head of the Jewish community in Syria. He tells me there are about 25 Jews in Qamishli and about the same number in Aleppo. I talk of Eric Rouleau and Claudia Roden, both descendants of Rabbi Doueik of Aleppo.

Thursday, 20 June

I am reading a book by Marie Seurat about her husband Michel who was killed when in the custody of the Syrian secret police[7]. She is a Memerbachi and her mother was a Dallal, a grand Christian family of Aleppo.

Saturday, 22 June

I join the Ambassador in Aleppo at the office of the Governor. I walk from the Baron Hotel, right through the souk from Antakya Gate to the citadel. In the early morning a shaft of light coming through the roof of the tunnel-like souk is like a diaphanous column.

After the Governor we call on the Chief of Police. How are things? All is well. No crime in Aleppo. Then to the Party Secretary whose office is the grandest of them all, with fine finished woodwork, 11 pictures of the President and eight of Basil.

Sunday, 23 June

I think of opening a branch of the British Council in Aleppo. (Or reopening, for there was an office here from the Second World War to 1956, the time of Suez.) We could start with a point for educational information, attached to an office for commercial information. We could thus open by stealth under the wing of the Honorary Consulate. I suspect that once started, there could be some momentum.

Wednesday, 26 June

Salma Khadra Jayyusi has asked me to translate a play by Sa'dallah Wannous. I go to see Sa'dallah at his house in Birza. He is pale, wears a woolly hat to conceal the effects of the chemotherapy

7 Marie Seurat, *Birds of Ill Omen*, translated by Dorothy S Blair, Quartet Books, London.

treatment he has been receiving. I tell him that Salma has asked me to translate his play, *Ahlam Shaqiya*. He shakes his head and I fear it might be the choice of the play. But it is Dr Salma he objects to. He has no objection to my translating any of his work, but not for Salma. Well, that's that. I stay on for an hour, sipping tea and meeting other callers including Faisal Darraj, the Palestinian writer. When I leave Sa'dallah is apologetic about his refusal to have anything to do with Salma.

Thursday, 27 June

I am arranging for the best student of English in the third year of each of the four Syrian universities to have six weeks in Britain. The condition is that they have not been to Britain before. This will exclude those from privileged families. The six weeks will include some language learning, a British studies course and two weeks at the Edinburgh Festival. The four selected students – all girls, Zaina, Iman, Maha and Maha – come to the British Council and have breakfast with the staff. The girl from Homs is one of the nine children of a government official (whose salary cannot be more than 5,000 Syrian pounds [£72] a month). The father comes to breakfast as well. The Aleppo girl brings her mother who does not shake hands with me; instead we bow to each other. The mother is anxious; should her daughter take some of the family gold, in case she runs short of cash? Vanda and Motaz do a superb job putting them at their ease. Firas and Samer also come and I rave about the places they are bound for – the Royal College of Music and RADA, "the best places in Britain and therefore the world!"

Friday, 28 June

I go to two parties. The first is a farewell to the Bulgarian flautist, Momchil Georgiev, who has been at the Institute of Music and Drama. We have some live music – a 15-year-old violinist and the grim Belorussian choir trainer sings some *Carmen* in, I think, Russian. Then to a Canadian party on a roof with cheerful Russian dancers from the Meridien Hotel. People look on from neighbouring balconies and rooftops.

Sunday, 30 June
Dr Maha, one of our students, is causing trouble. She is the wife of Wahib Tannous of the Central Command of the Ba'th Party and is throwing her weight around and having tantrums. Abdul Majid of the University at Homs calls and asks for indulgence – "You know what Syria is like," he pleads. "The trouble is," I explain, "we treat her like everybody else."

Monday, 1 July
Dr Maha comes to see me, her hair done up in a fashionable mop. I talk to her "like a father" – she was born in 1959 and so is 20 years younger than me – and reassure her about her English. She does not complain.

Tuesday, 2 July
My Line Manager phones. There will be redundancies later this month. Names will be decided this month and "the executions will be, as in China, immediate." Where will I be on the night of 23 July?

Wednesday, 3 July
I bump into the painter Hala al-Faisal on my way to work and am invited in to coffee. She has a streak of grey in her black hair. She introduces me to her brother, Fawwaz, a neurologist based in Los Angeles, and her son, now aged 16, with the trace of a moustache on his upper lip. A friendship unrelated to work or writing. She wants to paint my portrait.

Thursday, 4 July

I do a financial end-of-month check. That is the most exciting thing to happen all day.

There is much to worry about but, as I shuffle towards the twilight of life, I think, "Cor blimey, I've been a lucky sod." I worry about the redundancies. I am moderately confident, and may be a survivor of purges, a kind of British Council Gromyko.

Friday, 5 July

I come to Iskenderun for a Turkish long weekend. It happens to be the anniversary of the annexation of the sanjak of Iskenderun by Turkey. I wander round the town and come across people gorgeously dressed. Turkomans and "Sons of Turks" from Marash. Bandoliers, Kumkale hats and splendid scarlet waistcoats. One man has whiskers he must have cultivated for years. A boy, in antique military gear, has a long knife, suitable for slitting throats, and is encouraged by his elders to strike aggressive poses.

Monday, 8 July

During the morning Bouthaina Shaaban calls. She is most distressed. Permission for her to go to the Cambridge Literature seminar has been cancelled. She had got everything ready – house, family, transport. She is heartbroken. Netanyahu has gone to the United States and it is likely that President Clinton will telephone President Assad. The latter President trusts Bouthaina on delicate political matters. We talk about translation. Apparently Ghassan Malih received US$500 for translating one of Sa'dallah Wannous's plays. Sa'dallah got nothing.

I go to the Ballet School's annual presentation. The star is undoubtedly Razan Isa. She has tremendous stage presence and her movements are majestic. Even when she is in the wings, immobile, she still has an allure. There is such a graceful confidence that if she makes a false move you feel the taped music is at fault. Others are quite good and Razan is the first to applaud them.

Tuesday, 9 July

The vast lobby of the Sheraton Hotel looks like some high-class brothel. Gulf Arabs cruise around as do a large number of women of different ages and nationalities – all looking like prostitutes.

Wednesday, 10 July

We have an office cleaner who is sloppy and inefficient and nobody wants her. She refuses to quit. Ayoub found her and (rightly) has a sense of responsibility. He talks to her. "They want to get rid of you. They are quite ruthless and will not be deterred by any threat from Social Security. And nobody will take up your case if it affects UK-Syrian relations. You should resign and get benefits. If you are sacked you get nothing."

I hear Alan Waddams, the European Ambassador, give a talk on Europe: Myth or Reality. Many of the questions display what Alan calls "regional narcissism. The trouble with Arabs is that they talk politics and not economics. Only about three per cent of Syrian trade is with other Arab countries." Sadiq al-Azm comments, "You're sounding like a Marxist."

Peter took a fortnight's leave – seeing his eldest son, Paul, graduate from the University of Brighton, and taking a family holiday in Mallorca.

Tuesday, 23 July

I phone my Line Manager and am reassured that I am not being made redundant. "There was never any danger."

That is what I expected but I am greatly relieved. It ends eight months of anxiety. I am out of sympathy with much of the new British Council. I believe in the practice of global cultural relations, rather than the servicing of an international bourgeoisie.

Back in Damascus.

Thursday, 1 August

The mother of Saliha Sanqar, Minister of Higher Education, has died and I attend the funeral with Motaz. A lot of us stand outside the mosque. It is an opportunity to network. I talk to Wahib Fadl, Minister for Presidential Affairs, Dr Wahib Tannous from the Central Command of the Party, Dr Iyad Shatti, Minister of Health, Abdul Majid Sheikh Husain from Homs University and the Deputy Minister of Higher Education, Muhiuddin Isa. I am the only foreigner.

Lattakia.

Friday, 2 August

I am reading *Nomad* by Robin Maugham, about British intelligence in this town during the Second World War. He talks of the Sharifi brothers who drank araq from a teapot during Ramadan at the Casino.

During the afternoon I go for a walk by the sea, past a huge Friday market where loads of junk is sold, mostly second-hand clothes. I buy a comb for 10 Syrian pounds (15p) and end up at Railway Roundabout. I walk back to the centre of the city past what must have been country villas in grand gardens – most have gone to seed.

I am collected by Ahmad al-Sufi and his wife, Majida Bouzo, and we go out to dinner. I have translated several of Majida's stories. Majida was at school in Damascus in the same class as Rana Kabbani, Rana Saadeh and a daughter of Cynthia and Solhi al-Wadi.

Saturday, 3 August

Sa'd Rabia calls and we walk into town. An autodidact, his father was an immigrant teacher from Iraq and he hopes himself to go to the Emirates to teach. He is full of information about people and places. He points out one large villa. "That is known as the House of God," he says. It is the family home of Sulaiman Murshid. We go to call on Abdul Qadir al-Rabi' at his flat. Abdul Qadir is a musician, philosopher and dissident. He has been in prison, and has been lucky enough to have some of his stories published. I actually do not think they are very good, but he has hopes of a selection being translated and published in the United States. He talks incessantly.

A Lattakia doctor friend drives me back to Damascus. He is full of information. Two sons of Jamil al-Assad, brother of the President, are bullies, rich on trading drugs. They bully people into selling land at rock-bottom prices. Bushra, the President's only daughter, defied her father in marrying someone who had been dismissed by her father. He had already been married and had four children. He tells me of human rights abuses. There have recently been campaigns against Turkomans. One was killed after being tortured; the police alleged that he had hanged himself. A medical colleague, a Turkoman surgeon, was dragged off from the hospital where he worked in front of colleagues and patients. My friend, who has been close to senior Ba'thists went to complain directly to the head of the intelligence department responsible. "Why do you have to humiliate him in front of other people?" There was no answer, but it was clear that the aim was just that – to humiliate him in front of others.

Sunday, 4 August
Back in the office we celebrate Motaz's birthday. It is also, he points out, the birthday of the Queen Mother – there is a 60-years' age difference.

Monday, 5 August
Last month the Jerusalem office of the British Council wrote saying they had heard we had an exciting Literature programme and seeking

advice. I suggested talks on translation. They are suggesting that I go there for a week.

In the evening Bouchra invites me to a family party. Her eldest son, Ala al-Din, is home from Volgograd where he is studying medicine. We call on some relations in Mezze – three brothers. One is a colonel in the Syrian army, and another a building contractor based in Saudi Arabia. Their aged mother and assorted young people make up the rest. I am the only person not related. It is the usual relaxed agreeable occasion.

Tuesday, 6 August

The Defence Attaché in the Embassy tells me he proposed that the Embassy send a message of congratulation to the Syrian athlete, Ghada Shu'a, who has won a gold medal for the women's heptathlon in the Olympic Games. She is a Christian and used to cross herself before every race. The Embassy refused. But I have done so, on behalf of the British Council.

I have dinner with my landlord and his son, Sam'an, who is a professor in Las Vegas. He is a United States citizen and is a right-wing conservative Republican, though he also has property in Damascus and Bloudan. He wonders whether the CIA are deliberately promoting Islamic fundamentalism. He is interesting on American schools, and on protests against discrimination from Hispanics and blacks. This leads to litigation that is bankrupting the public education system and enriching lawyers. It was all the fault, in his view, of Lyndon Baines Johnson and his liberalism.

Saturday, 10 August

Rosemary Halsted, Lady Jane Digby's great-niece, has sent me a photograph of a Damascus drinks seller, Abdul Rahim, to pass on to him. I walk into the city, find him and he gives me a glass of blackberry juice, in Arabic *tut shami*, literally "Damascus mulberry".

Georges, Laila, their son, Sam'an Ladhkani, and his two children, George and Diana, take me to Bloudan where they have a flat. Georges is a bit deaf but otherwise totally alert. He has never driven a car but has walked extensively, all over the mountains from Bloudan. It used to take three hours to walk from Bloudan to Heshbon in Lebanon.

"I once climbed Mount Hermon. I went with five other young men, six girls, two mules and a muleteer. We camped at the top. Sunrise on Mount Hermon is amazing. The sun is a huge orb that seems to be a metre and a half in diameter. It casts a shadow that stretches as far as the Mediterranean."

"When was that, Georges?" I ask.

"1922."

Young George, ten-years-old, is frightening. He is ferociously bright and confident, top of his class. "Nobody dares play chess with him!"

Sam'an and I go to the Grand Hotel to see some rooms. We go up in a lift with two Russian girls, well dressed and heavily made up. The great majority of the residents in the hotel are from the Gulf.

Tuesday, 13 August

The Ladhkanis come round for a drink, and I show them a film of the opera. Sam'an is enthusiastic. He would like a copy to show his American friends in Las Vegas. It gives Syrian exiles and emigrants a pride in being Syrian. They are all very pro-British. Georges and Laila tell me that they argued with pro-Axis neighbours during the Second World War. Young Sam'an had a potty with pictures of Hitler and Mussolini on the bottom.

Thursday, 15 August

I decide to go to Turkey for the weekend. I drive at speed and north of Hama a car overtakes near me. I brake and the car goes out of control. It slithers on the road and turns over. I find myself sitting sideways, the windscreen shattered and the passenger door bashed in. The safety belt has saved me and I am undamaged apart from two scratches on my right hand. I unfasten the safety belt, open the door and clamber out on to the top of the car, in fact, the driver's side stuck in the air. Immediately there are hands helping me. I jump down. People right the car. Both front tyres have exploded. People gather my belongings and I am taken in one car – by an Aleppan called Adolf Turkoman – and then by another car – by a Syrian from Glendale Los Angeles – to the local police station. I am in a state of shock but calmly work out what has to be done. A crane collects the car and brings it to the police compound. The captain, Naqib, and I make a report together, vying with each other to get classical Arabic phrases into it. Another policeman takes me to a bus bound for Aleppo. On the way he asks if I can get his 25-year-old son a job in England.

At Aleppo I have a beer on the terrace of the Baron Hotel and spend time chatting with Sally Mazloumian. She talks about Kim Philby who used to stay here. He had a warm smile that she later realised was treacherous. A tourist passes by, wearing a keffiyeh. He suffers, Sally says, from what her late husband, Koko, used to call "arabitus".

Friday, 16 August

I toss and turn all night. I am not at all comfortable. The nightmare of being behind the steering wheel of a car that is out of control. Thinking of what might have happened. I did two foolish things. I was driving too fast, and I should not have braked. Thinking of what might have happened is not very useful. At every instant there are an infinite number of possible courses of action. I might have chosen not to have gone to Turkey. And so on. But what happened happened. I was lucky and I was unlucky.

But now I start on the administration of clearing up. It is all very interesting in a bizarre sort of way. I walk up to Sulaimaniya in the Aleppo industrial suburb. It is beyond Villat and in the Armenian quarter. I find the Peugeot agency and meet the *muallim*, the boss, an Armenian called Dikran, whose Arabic is strange. I arrange for my car to be brought from the police station at 11 o'clock. Fortunately it is not a day off for Armenians. I wait and wait. I have a meal at Wanis's (Armenian) restaurant and phone Adolf who lives nearby. I spend the afternoon with his family. He is a Catholic married to an Armenian who teaches music. The car is towed into the garage at 4. The front axle has snapped and much bodywork needs to be repaired. It will all cost about 80,000 Syrian pounds – over £1,000, but things are under control.

I am exhausted, shaky and depressed. I take a bus back to Damascus.

Saturday, 17 August

I have a much better night. I make a personal audit. I am just a little stiff and have waves of depression, but I can see these coming and can put up the necessary psychological resistance. I am haunted by those three seconds of swerving frighteningly out of control, ending up, clump, in the ditch.

Sunday, 18 August

Cornelia Khaled, who is shortly off to Harvard for a year, takes me to the Zenobians, a group of Anglophone women. The (British) Ambassador's wife is in the chair and I give a talk on translating *Sabriya*. There are over 30 present including Maha Kabbani (mother of Rana), Warqa Barmada and Brigid Waddams. I explain why I translate, the wish to do something Syrian, the need to promote Arabic literature. Questions are about women's literature. Can I, as a man, empathise?

I have dinner with the Ambassador. The other guests include the archaeologist Peter Parr who is working on Tell Nebi Mend, and Hayan Atassi, who reckons that the Ambassador's Residence would go for US$3 million.

Monday, 19 August

We are sacking one of the staff. I have been getting advice from our landlord, Haidar Bouzo. It is costing US$300 but is worth it. He is a former Minister of Labour, is the best lawyer on labour matters and has contacts that will help us get rid of the member of staff.

In the afternoon Hassana Mardam-Bey takes me to tea at her house. I have visualised the house as the one in *Sabriya*, but Hassana points to a tree, observing, "This lemon tree is not strong enough to hang yourself from." Hassana's brother shows me notebooks belonging to their grandfather who studied in Britain in the 1920s. They are meticulous and encyclopaedic.

Wednesday, 21 August

One of the students whom we sent to Britain for six weeks calls with a thank-you present. She talks of her time with wondrous excitement. At Exeter she went to the cathedral for a communion service. People were surprised – she is a Muslim.

"Are all Syrians so open-minded?" she was asked.

"Mostly. Not all," she replied loyally and honestly. She tells me how beautiful she found the music. She says her spirit is still there although physically she has come back to Syria.

Saturday, 24 August

I review two books for *Asian Affairs*. One is the splendidly illustrated book on Kurds by Jonathan Rugman. I note that Ocalan, the leader of the PKK, has a flat in Jaramana. The other is on Lebanon by

Elizabeth Picard who observes that Lebanon has preserved features of Ottomanism.

Monday, 26 August

I have a visit from Mai Memerbachi. She is from the family Bandki in Aleppo. The name was originally Bunduki, meaning "from Venice" (Bunduk in Arabic). Her mother was British, hence her blonde hair. We talk archaeology and other ideas. She has lots of ideas for Syria but is thwarted by bureaucracy, inertia and the *mukhabarat*. She has a son at Harrow and a daughter about to start at the University of St Andrews.

I also have a visit from the private secretary and the personal detective of the Duke of Kent – due here in a few weeks. They are cool about my proposal for him to have a breakfast at the office and to be taken into an English class. So it will be talk, meet people and an orange juice. But it may not happen at all, for he could be called to see the President.

Tuesday, 27 August

I have a visit from Laila Malih who teaches English at the University of Kuwait. She did her doctorate on Arabs who wrote in English and we have an interesting chat about *Black Vanguard* by Edward Atiyah. In Omdurman I used to know Ishaq al-Khalifa Sharif, a grandson of the Mahdi, and the model for one of the characters. One of Laila's brothers has translated into English a play of Sa'dallah Wannous. Another is a film director.

I go to a farewell party given by Mai Memerbachi to say farewell to the Ambassador. She gives me a copy of a book on Aleppo by her cousin, Marie Seurat. Among the other guests are the economist Nabil Sukkar and Firas Tlas, businessman and son of the Minister of Defence.

Thursday, 29 August

Abdul Majid, the Rector of the University at Homs, tells me he is unable to go to Bristol. He had to get permission from the Minister of Higher Education. She put the request in a drawer and just forgot about it. He is very upset as he was hoping to attend the wedding of the granddaughter of the dinner lady he befriended when he was a PhD student at the University of Bristol. It is reckoned that the Minister fears Abdul Majid as a candidate for her job.

I go to the United States Ambassador's Residence for a party to welcome my new opposite number, Evelyn Early. I meet lots of people. Hala al-Faisal, the painter. Abdul Salam al-Ujaili who greets me warmly and whom I introduce to Alan Waddams. Sadiq al-Azm. Mamduh Udwan. Riad Ismat. Nuhad Abdullah. Cynthia and Solhi al-Wadi. Solhi is very amused when Cynthia and I find ourselves chatting to each other in Arabic.

Friday, 30 August

I go with Bouchra and Ahmed to a shop in Doumar owned by their son and his brother, selling sweets and coffee. We are invited to help ourselves to paper napkins, ice lollies and sweets. Ahmed and Bouchra used to have a house nearby. It cost them 50,000 Syrian pounds in 1980. Now flats cost up to two million Syrian pounds.

We go to the house in Raihan that belongs to the family of Nadia al-Ghazzi's father who was Prime Minister of Syria in the 1950s and from an old Damascus family. Bouchra's grandmother used to live nearby and Bouchra knew Nadia when she was a little girl. The fountain in the courtyard is playing and we sit around eating fruit with Nadia, her photographer daughter Rasha, and a businesswoman, Ghalia Kaylani, a cousin of Hassana Mardam-Bey. We are shown round the house. The kitchen is changing its functions. Instead of being a dirty hole with store and bakery, a place for women and servants, it has become a kind of salon where family and guests meet and chat.

Peter is away in Britain for a fortnight.

Wednesday, 4 September

I phone Mrs Dowling, former dinner lady at the University of Bristol. I pass on Abdul Majid's greetings and regrets that he cannot attend her granddaughter's wedding. She is very friendly and has no idea what Syria is like. "It's hot," I tell her. "There are lots of nice people like Abdul Majid, but things are sometimes a bit confusing."

Back in Damascus.

Sunday, 15 September

The Embassy is getting busy for the visit of the Duke of Kent. They think it is the first ever royal visit to Syria but I point out that Albert Edward, Prince of Wales came here in 1869.

Monday, 16 September

Chris Simpson of Magna Carta is here, with his wife, Linda. I first entertained them in Yemen in 1981. We get on very well in spite of his heartiness and reactionary views, referring to "teachers, social scientists and people of that ilk". We have a jokey relationship. We take him for dinner at the Marouch Restaurant and at one point I say, "Tell me, Chris, how do you cope with hero worship?" There is a split second when he seems to take the question seriously. Linda snorts and we both collapse into helpless laughter.

Tuesday, 17 September

I have a call from Narendra, the benign upper-class Indian who is a great friend of Robyn Davidson, who has introduced us. He is charming, with a farm on the outskirts of Delhi, an orchard in the Himalayas as well as his main home in Jodhpur. He is a Member of the Indian Parliament and his son, who was at Millfield School, is training for the 2000 Olympics at Sydney in the three-day horsemanship event. Narendra has a project developing pistachio nuts in the Euphrates valley, part financed by the Deputy Prime Minister of Kuwait, Sheikh Nasr al-Sabah.

Theresa and I call on Ulfat Idilbi whose son, Ziad, died during the summer. She is in great distress and seems to have been weeping a lot. "He had been so fit. He did not smoke or drink and had a happy personal and family life. His father lived to the age of 90, *his* father to a hundred." She is cross that everybody, but herself, knew how ill Ziad was.

Saturday, 21 September

The Minister of Culture has asked me to check through the translation of one of her speeches. Much is rubbishy verbiage but I faithfully edit it all.

Monday, 23 September

The new British Ambassador, Basil Eastwood, comes for a British Council breakfast. It is a jolly occasion and at a private meeting I press for the opening of a branch in Aleppo. He is ready to use the forthcoming visit of the Duke of Kent to further that.

I go to the Saudi National Day party at the Sheraton Hotel. I drop into the bookshop and am glad to see *Sabriya* on sale. At 1,000 Syrian pounds (about £15.) I tell them I am the translator and ask them to display it more prominently. I complain about the price, pointing out that I get only 50 Syrian pounds for every copy sold.

Tuesday, 24 September

I go to see George Jabbour, at his request. He is a strange conspiratorial man. He would not come to my office so I go to his mother's house. She is 89, diminutive, chirpy, physically alert but as deaf as a doorpost. Conversation is difficult.

George suddenly starts talking about Masons.

"Are you a Mason?" I ask.

"Masonry is forbidden in this country," he answers.

"That's not an answer to my question."

"My father was a Mason and I was interested as a young man."

He would like to have some time with the Duke of Kent who is Britain's top Mason.

"You can recognise a Mason," he goes on, "by introducing seven into the conversation."

George is interested in human rights organisations (perhaps more than in human rights) and was Syria's representative at one international human rights function.

Wednesday, 25 September

Rana Saadeh drops in. She has been translating material about the forthcoming visit of the Duke of Kent. If you translate "Mason", she says, the suggestion is that he is an atheist. If you translate "Freemason", the suggestion is that he is a Jew.

Friday, 27 September

We walk round Jabal Kasiyun, about three miles. The scenery changes constantly and Damascus is half hidden by haze. We hear boom boom coming from the west. Is there military activity in the Biqa'?

We go to lunch at the house of Awad Amoro, the Castrol agent. He is Palestinian, with a British passport, has a business in Docklands and a factory in Barking. His wife is what my father would have called a "fashion plate". The house in the Ghouta was built in 1980 and was based on something Awad had seen in a magazine about Chinese houses. The garden is a fruit and vegetable orchard. There is a swimming pool and a tennis court. The family is friendly and unpretentious.

Monday, 30 September

I have a staff meeting to discuss the Duke's visit – cleaning, flowers, refreshments. We time the visit to the minute, with each person knowing where he or she will be. One teacher comes up with a bright idea. The Queen's coronation dress was made of Damascus brocade. What about presenting the Duke with a tie made from the same brocade? I ask the teacher to get one straightaway.

I go to the Ambassador's Residence where I was one of a select group to dine with the Duke. But the personal detective insists at being at table so I have to drop out. But I do attend the briefing meeting and have been asked to speak for four minutes on the work of the British Council. The Duke arrives. He will be 60 next month. He stoops, his chin recedes and he seems to have some of Charles's mannerisms. He listens to the briefing and, unlike his cousin Gloucester in Tunis ten years ago, does not fall asleep. The Embassy Spook talks of the internal situation – there are 100,000 people in internal security, and that is a conservative estimate. The Defence Attaché talks of the army, a quarter of a million men strong. I do my piece and then, with others not dining, depart.

Tuesday, 1 October

I go to the office of the Prime Minister early and hang around, waiting for the arrival of the Ambassador and the Duke. I stroll into the conference room and am handed cards with names on. Would I distribute them around the table? So I fix the placement, putting the Duke in the big chair, the Ambassador on his right, the Private Secretary on his left. I put myself at the end, opposite the Duke. But I am aware that there are likely to be more bums than seats. The chairman of the meeting is Dr Salim Yasin, Deputy Prime Minister. The Syrian side includes the Minister of Electricity and prominent businessmen such as Ratib Shallah, Abdul Rahman al-Attar and Saeb Nahhas. The room fills up. Courtesies and then the Duke invites comments around the table. When it is my turn, the Duke asks me – remembering my name – what I want. I make a bid for a branch of the British Council in Aleppo. The Deputy Prime Minister raises the matter of a cultural agreement.

Wednesday, 2 October

There is a sense of excitement at the office. Mamduh Udwan turns up and I invite him to stay. I have organised things carefully, and we have a final rehearsal so everybody knows where they stand and what they have to do. The Duke arrives at 9.40. I brief him for four minutes in my office and then I introduce him to all the staff. I end by presenting him with the tie. He leaves us, his work over, and as he gets into the car, with the Royal Standard flying, he takes off his jacket. He is to be taken round the old city by Hussein Hinnawi.

Friday, 4 October

We go up to Bloudan and walk for a mile or so on the track that leads to Helbun. The track goes among orchards and we meet two brothers, gathering apples, packing then in crates to store in their house for the winter. There is a spring in the middle of the track – a trickle of water appears from nowhere.

Back in Damascus we go to the Latin church and get seats in the front (thanks to Ghasan, the Jordanian from the Institute of Music who is actually the *mukhabarat* agent there). Solhi al-Wadi and the orchestra play some Mozart, some Vivaldi and some Albinoni. It is done with great panache. The church is absolutely packed and there are dozens standing. Every pew is taken. I marvel at the following that Solhi has built up over 30 years.

"All ages," I say to Riad Ismat.

"And all classes," he replies.

Sunday, 6 October

I call on Solhi. He talks of his childhood, how he ran away from school. His parents were summoned and his mother gave him a humiliating wallop. He talks of the family 240-*dunum* estate near Baghdad and how his father suspected him of socialist leanings because he thought the peasants should be educated.

Tuesday, 8 October

I take a bus to Homs. Abdul Majid of the university calls at the hotel and takes me to the Artists' Syndicate where we see Hala al-Faisal. We have a beer with her and with Munzir al-Haik the Homs historian.

Wednesday, 9 October

Farhan Bulbul, the Homs playwright, calls at the hotel. He teaches once a week at the Institute of Drama and we go to the Arab Cultural Centre and then to the Tlas bookshop and meet Maha, the Christian wife of the manager, Munzir al-Haik.

At the bus station I fall into conversation with an ill-shaven part-time journalist working for the busses called Ali Samandar. For some reason we are soon talking about the concepts of *zahiriya* and *batiniya* in Sufism – about which he is writing a book.

I spend the evening in Lattakia with Munzer Muhammad, Dean of the Faculty of Arts. He is one of the few mind-expanding scholars in the country. He gives me two books of theology written by his father, Sheikh Muhammad Salih, an Alawaite man of religion.

Thursday, 10 October

Munzer tells me that at the meeting of the Duke of Kent with the Deputy Prime Minister last week the television news cameras panned on my face as I was making a bid for a British Council office in Aleppo. I seemed to be at the head of the table.

I have a problem with one of the senior teaching staff. She has written what seems to be a confrontational letter. I reply and wonder about my own management style. It is a combination of Marlon Brando as The Godfather and Clement Attlee: benign, tolerant but deep down utterly ruthless.

Saturday, 12 October

I wrote a note for the Ambassador on the Rector of Aleppo University. The Ambassador has been to Aleppo and found him supportive.

"I did not say in my note that he is a corrupt bully."

"Well, I did find him a fat slob."

We go to a recital at the flat of Marjorie Ransom of the American Embassy. The musicians introduce their work with enthusiasm. I have never heard of Amy Beach before. Muhammad Shahrur is there, expounding texts of the Koran.

Sunday, 13 October

I take the Ambassador to call on the Minister of Culture. All is cordial. She brings up the triumph of the opera – the first in this part of the world apart from Egypt. (She ignores Israel.)

In the late morning a television crew comes to the office to interview me. When I talk in Arabic I seem to be looking into the middle distance and not at the camera. It makes me look shifty.

We are invited to a party with our neighbours, Rima and Ghaith. The party is mostly made up of Christian merchants. Some we know, like Razek Memerbachi, but others include Nazir al-Assad, an oily relation of the President, and a man called Yusuf who exports tomato paste to Italy.

Monday, 14 October

I have a call from a poet, Marius Kociejowski, who arrives at the same time as Hala al-Faisal. She takes him off on a tour of the old city.

Tuesday, 15 October

I have a phone call from Muhammad Khudr, the Syrian Ambassador in London. He invites me to come to London and give a lecture on the British contribution to archaeology in Syria. I stipulate that I must have a return air fare. He agrees. It will be a great opportunity to promote the idea of commercial sponsorship of archaeology.

Wednesday, 16 October

I have a very curious dream. A girl is walking along a road, wearing a blue silk headscarf. A gust of wind suddenly rips it off her head, right up into the sky. It flutters and lands on the nest of an eagle/hawk/stork/falcon which is on the top of a St Simeon Stylites-type column. The bird has talons that tear flesh and are covered with dripping blood. It comes down to us and speaks English, saying it will surrender the headscarf on the condition that it can have a puppy that will keep it company – for it is lonely – on the column.

Thursday, 17 October

I have a visit from Muhammad Mustafa, the Damascus representative of Hamas. I apparently met him at the Saudi National Day with George Jabbour. He explains Hamas to me. The resistance is just one of their activities. They also have social, educational and charitable work. Charity extends to all, regardless of religion. All Israeli adults are legitimate military targets because they all do military service and are in reserve for years. They are not against Jews but against Israelis as occupiers, just as Europe was against Nazi occupation, though both sides were Christian. "We resisted the Turkish occupation though we were fellow-Muslims."

Sunday, 20 October

Theresa goes to a meeting of the Zenobians, the Anglophone women's organisation. She tells me someone said, "I have heard two people *raving* about *Sabriya*." And someone else said, "I believe it is also in Arabic."

Monday, 21 October

I have the idea of a British Council calendar exploiting our greatest asset – our staff. I propose the idea of pictures of us all with comments about us and the work we do.

In the office we all watch the news and see Chirac losing his cool in Jerusalem. We all have smiles on our faces. Chirac talks English with his Israeli bodyguards who do not let him talk directly to Palestinians. It emphasises the emptiness of Netanyahu. "What is needed, Sir," as King Hussein says, "is not the arrogance of power but the kind of vision Rabin had. Perhaps you'll have it one day."

Thursday, 24 October

We go to a party at the Italian Ambassador's Residence. We meet General Gharib, born in Antakya, and head of immigration – a useful contact. His Christian wife, an artist, is also from Antakya. Another guest is Wafa Sidawi and her daughter, Rania. Wafa runs an art gallery. The daughter used to be the girlfriend of Basil al-Assad. She is tall, beautiful, Christian, with a low-cut dress, and trousers that show up her figure. What a life she must have had. Can others touch her? What does she make of the cult of Basil?

Friday, 25 October

Today is the day of the Terry Fox annual charity run in aid of cancer research. We register by buying a Terry Fox T-shirt. Seven or eight hundred people turn up at the back of the Sheraton Hotel. It is largely a European expatriate event but there are plenty of Syrians of a certain class: the Armenian businessman Nubar, Razek Memerbachi, the Yazijis, Hanan and Alfredo, a lot of children from the Damascus Community School. Some participants look professionally athletic. It is not so much of a run as a walk of five or six kilometres. We have a police escort and I am reminded of Aldermaston marches in the early 1960s. Up one slope three girls on skateboards are, snake-like, clinging on to a police motorcycle.

Saturday, 26 October

Brigid and Alan Waddams come round for dinner. Alan, the European Ambassador, talks of the Business Centre the European Union are promoting. The government and the universities do not like it because it is outside their control, but everybody else does, and there is support from Bashar al-Assad and Wahib Tannous.

Monday, 28 October

I have a visit from Alexis, the new French Cultural Attaché. He speaks impeccable English, is a specialist in 18th-century English literature and is currently translating *Clarissa* into French.

Tuesday, 29 October

I am preparing for the visit of a senior colleague, Edmund Marsden. He was Director here in the early 1980s. I phone him, having sent him a draft of the programme for his one-day visit here. He would like to visit the Higher Institute for Music.

"Is it a white elephant?" he asks.

"No," I reply. "It is the only part of the higher education set-up that is vibrant with activity and creativity."

"In my day, Solhi only had a 14-piece chamber orchestra."

Thursday, 31 October

I write to Mary Lovell who sent me a copy of *A Scandalous Life*, her biography of Lady Jane Digby. I tell her that her friend, Hussein Hinnawi, who had located Lady Jane's Damascus house, was the guide to the first British royal visitor to Damascus since 1869 when his great-grandfather camped next to Lady Jane's house. I tell her that Lady Jane's watch was inherited by Ulfat Idilbi, whose *Sabriya* I send her.

Mamduh Udwan calls. I have translated one of his plays and am arranging for a British director, Penny Black, to come to Damascus with two actors to stage it here in English.

For my headquarters I write a note on my relations with the Ministry of Culture: complex, fruitful and successful but against the grain of current British Council thought. I describe the Minister's modus operandi as being that of a court. I adapt and comply accordingly, and thereby achieve my objective of promoting the values of an open and plural society.

Friday, 1 November
We go to Bosra. It is the first time I have been there since the triumph of the opera. I am strangely moved and almost in tears as I look around. How on earth did we get all that together?

Monday, 4 November
I meet Edmund Marsden at the airport at 3.30 am, bring him home and two hours later we start a busy programme. It was said of Gladstone that he would do in four hours what most men would take 16 hours to do. And Gladstone would work a 16-hour day. Edmund is like that. We call on three Ministers, have lunch with the Minister of Culture and, in the afternoon, go to a rehearsal of the orchestra. More meetings – Edmund does not take a rest – and a party for old friends in the evening.

Tuesday, 5 November
I take Edmund at 7 to the airport and see him off. The airport is

evacuated for a visit by the President of Guyana, Dr Cheddi Jagan.

In the evening we host a party for Susannah Self and her husband, Michael Christie. Susannah was a marvellous witch in the opera and is back to do a recital at the Institute for Music. She is a granddaughter of John Drinkwater and a cousin of Will. Another guest is Richard Gott who is here with Rana Kabbani. I ask Richard, who has been a specialist on South America, why Cheddi Jagan should come to Syria. He reckons that Jagan and Assad are both still in a time warp: the Bandung generation, with a belief in Third Worldism. We have as guests several people from the Institute, young people, and also Solhi, who ends up totally plastered.

Wednesday, 6 November

I have lunch with Richard Gott and Rana Kabbani. Rana is complimentary about *Sabriya*. She talks of the Prince of Wales whom she advises on Islamic matters. Someone from the Foreign Office – I probe and learn that it is John Shepherd – tried to persuade Charles to make a speech in Saudi Arabia, saying that that country was a place of freedom and openness. Charles refused.

I see an interview I have given for Syrian television. I seem to go into autopilot when I speak Arabic. I am fluent and speak intelligently of Sa'dallah and Syria. I am generally "pro". I smile, use my hands and have an untidy bookshelf in the background.

We go to another concert given by the national orchestra. The Armenian singer Talar sings an Azeri song and a 12-year-old Sudanese, Ibrahim Yaji, is the soloist in Beethoven's first piano concerto.

Thursday, 7 November

I go to Homs where Susannah and Michael are to give a recital. At first nothing has been prepared, but things improve. The Cultural Centre fills up, and there are plenty of Homs personalities – the historian Munzir al-Haik, the playwright Farhan Bulbul and others.

There are also younger people – Ramez and Nawar and other students from the Institute. The hall is full to capacity. Nobody slips away at the interval and there is a standing ovation at the end. Hala al-Faisal is there sketching.

We go on to Farhan's house and a video is played of the opera. All present are as excited as if the opera was last week. "Look at that, that's me," says one youngster. There are anecdotes and memories – the mad general, the strong wind at Palmyra. We are ready to go but Farhan shows us another video, of his eldest daughter singing a classical Arabic song on some public occasion. The house has a framed portrait of Umm Kulthoum, and framed posters of plays Farhan has produced. "Homs will talk about this for years," says one lady from the Atassi family.

Friday, 8 November
We take Susannah and Michael to Lattakia. At 5 we meet Sa'd Rabi who takes us through Sulaiba, the strongly Muslim area, along Quwwatli Street to a house with a closed projecting balcony, the home of Mahmud Ajjan. We are joined there by about 20 people. Mahmud is in his seventies, a violinist and composer. His nephew, Ziad, plays the oud; Ziad's daughter, Ghinwa (which means "song"), is a singer. I meet Monzer Masri, a poet and painter. He has a government job (or sinecure) which, he says, ensures a steady small income and gives him time to do a lot of reading. He also owns a shop and a factory for making shoes. He had a volume of poetry published in Beirut but the poems were condemned in Syria – especially one poem called "Dark" – and 2,000 copies were burnt. Some escaped the holocaust and Monzer has promised to get me one[8]. Someone refers sarcastically to the University in Lattakia, officially called Tishreen (after the October 1973 War) as Hittin

8 He never did!

University – after Saladin's victory over the Crusaders in 1191. Mahmud and Ziad play duets on their instruments, no harmony, but with a vigorous beat working to a climax. Then Michael and Susannah perform. She sings some Dowland songs; her strong voice fills the room and drowns the traffic noise outside.

Saturday, 9 November
We take Michael and Susannah to Saladin's castle. Susannah sketches and I drink honey-flavoured tea and chat to the custodians, the brothers Ali and Mahir, who were born in the castle.

Monday, 11 November
I am called in to see Wahib Tannous, the senior Ba'th Party official for higher education. He greets me warmly with a kiss and we chat. He asks about medical postgraduate placings for Dr Basil Sulaiman Qaddah, whose father, according to the Minister of Culture, opposed our opening up in Aleppo. It will be good to do a favour for his son. I ask Wahib if I can bring the Ambassador to see him. Of course. I hint at the idea of a visit to Britain as part of a series of high-level policy trips.

Wednesday, 13 November
We have dinner with Brigid and Alan Waddams. Alan accompanied a senior European delegation to call on the President. The Irish Foreign Minister, Dick Spring, talked about Arab unity.

"Would Syria like any help, from our European experience, in advancing Arab unity?"

"The important thing," President Assad explained, "is the will to unite. When that is there I will gladly seek assistance from Europe."

I ask Alan how the President looked.

"He seems tired and disappointed. He looks grey and seems to be a little deaf. The Foreign Minister, Sharra', and Buthaina have to prompt him. He looks round and asks "*Shu? Shu?*" ("What? What?") He can put on the avuncular bonhomie, but unhealthy skin and swollen ankles suggest an ill man. If he died tomorrow I would not be surprised. Nor would I if he lasted five years."

Alan thinks he wanted to wrap up a peace deal with Israel before he died, and the election of Netanyahu was a bitter disappointment.

Thursday, 14 November
George Jabbour shows me a letter he has received from Wafic Said, whose offer of a £20 million Business School has met resistance from the University of Oxford. The letter confronts criticism from the Arab world. He is obviously angry and refers to his pride in being the son of one of the founders of the University of Damascus. He has done a lot for the Arab world with support for scholarships and the promotion of understanding. He offered support to the University of Damascus but has not received a reply,

Saturday, 16 November
I am reading *The Political Economy of Syria under Assad* by Volker Perthes. He is full of little insights. People have fallen for the propaganda and personality cult here and think Assad is important. Perhaps he is. Perhaps he is not. Lots of things may manage to carry on perfectly well without regard to him. Syria, it seems, is a whole accumulation of little pockets of power and authority. Everything is negotiable (with bribes). Everything is arbitrary (if you can get away with it).

Sunday, 17 November
I call on Ulfat Idilbi. I plan to translate another of her novels, *Grandfather's Tale*. She has been reading the Norwegian novel, *Sophie's World*, which in Arabic translation sounds like "Sufi's World". A photograph of her late son, Ziad, dominates the mantelpiece.

Tuesday, 19 November

I receive the copy of a review the late Robert Tewdwr Moss did of *Sabriya* in the *Literary Review.* (He was apparently murdered by a queer-bashing British Muslim convert.) It is interesting but wrongheaded. He sees the novel as an aspect of government-controlled literature in Syria. The Arabic version was first published by the Ministry of Culture and then by the publishing house of the Ministry of Defence. But it is the Party that has jumped on the bandwagon of Ulfat.

Wednesday, 20 November

Solhi is going off to Kuwait and is dreading not having access to "the water of life" as he calls whisky. I phone Carl Reuter, my opposite number in Kuwait. Does Carl have access to whisky? Can he get a bottle to Solhi? Yes, of course, is the answer.

Thursday, 21 November

In Aleppo I go with the British Honorary Consul, Tony Akhras, and call on the Governor, to press the case for a British Council liaison office in Aleppo. The Governor, Mustafa Miru, has recently been awarded a PhD. I congratulate him and ask what the subject was, fearing that it may be on the economy of Hasake or something equally boring. But, no, it is about the Lebanese writer, Amin al-Rihani. We then talk about a Centre. It will encourage trade between Britain and Aleppo (not Syria, I say). He gives his blessing and I invite him to the opening.

Saturday, 23 November

Ann, my opposite number in Beirut, calls and we have lunch together. Her Director of Studies has been sacked, partly for incompetence, partly because he spent time chatting up Syrian soldiers, shoeshine boys and concierges, giving them his business card.

Wednesday, 27 November

I am invited to the unveiling of a bust of the President in the forecourt of the Ministry of Higher Education. I go along in good time. Students are chanting, dancing and playing drums. After the unveiling I am invited up to the Minister's room for a coffee with her and her Deputy Ministers and assorted university senior staff. I am the only non-Arab present. It is a questionable activity but I want to identify with Syria.

The Defence Attaché, Dick Clarke, tells me of a meeting of Defence Attachés when he crossed swords with the Turkish DA who objected to Dick's criticism of Turkey's behaviour at Suez (in 1916, not 1956). You didn't know how to use German landing equipment, Dick said. "The British know what they are talking about," the Spanish DA intervened. "They did for us in 1588. They knew how to sail at night." And the Polish DA joins is, "They helped us out in 1939."

Saturday, 30 November

Geoffrey King is back with two surveyors, bound for Homs. We go to the office of Hayan Atassi and his General. The General suggests we call on Mustafa Tlas, the Minister of Defence, on Thursday. Tlas has written to the Governor of Homs stressing the importance of Geoffrey's survey of the citadel site at Homs, saying it is part of Syria's heritage that goes back thousands of years. It becomes clear that the historian of Homs, Munzir al-Haik, is a key player. He seems to be Tlas's "civil arm" in Homs.

Monday, 2 December

The Ambassador asks me to read a paper on the Alawites, produced in the Embassy a few years ago. It is an extraordinary piece, much of it cribbed from something written by Evans-Pritchard when he was in intelligence in Syria during the Second World War. It fails to mention the significance of Sulaiman Murshid or the complexities (class, rich and poor, rural and urban, migrants from the Sanjak of Iskenderun) of it all. The author of the paper does not seem to have spoken to any Alawite about their beliefs. And there is a touch of the Learned Elders of Zion about it. The Grand Council, and all that. I make extensive notes, rubbishing it.

I have lunch with Kamal Abu Deeb, Professor of Arabic at the School of Oriental and African Studies. He hates Salma Khadra Jayyusi whom he sees as arrogant, dishonest and corrupt. He has written a scathing review of her Palestine anthology, to which I contributed.

In the evening I go to see Sa'dallah Wannous. I have a cordial welcome and propose translating some of his plays. He agrees, provided that Salma Jayyusi is not involved. He is wearing a dressing-gown and a woolly cap. His face seems bloated and he tires quickly. "I am chemical man," he tells me. He has chemotherapy treatment at the Shami Hospital and has had over 30 sessions. But his mind is alert. He tells a story of Bertold Brecht, how he used an English word in a translation. It was pointed out to him that it was not a German word. "It is from today," Brecht said.

Wednesday, 4 December

I drive to Homs and go straight to the citadel, joining Geoffrey King, General Ahmad Yusuf, Munzir al-Haik and a group of journalists and officials. We see the site of the mosque. Recent rain has shown up the markings of a 40-metre-square construction that, with a *qibla*, faces south. Part of the square has been eroded by the wearing away of the southern edge of the tell. A mosque known as the Sultan Mosque was here in the 18th century. The Egyptian Ibrahim Pasha occupied the tell in the 1830s and then it became a rubbish dump. The French cleared the place in the 1920s and constructed barracks.

The General takes us to call on the Governor who is fascinated by the exposed mosque site. A year ago when the tell ceased being a military site, there was an agreement that the archaeologists would have the northern part of the tell and the southern part would be a coffee garden. But the potentially more interesting archaeology is located in the southern part.

Thursday, 5 December
General Ahmad Yusuf takes Geoffrey, Munzir and myself to call on the Minister of Defence, Mustafa Tlas. There is heavy security but the General is greeted with a friendly grin from one of the guards. We are ushered to the office of the Minister's secretary, General Nasif Khair Bey. Then into the Minister's room. He has a dashboard of decorations on his chest and a big smile. Behind his desk are books, including English and French dictionaries, and an out-of-date reference book on weaponry. He has plenty of pictures of the President, including one of him as a young man, perhaps when Tlas first knew him. Geoffrey briefs him on Homs. Tlas offers any assistance – manpower, engineers, cement, and a helicopter to do a photogrammetric survey. We stay for half an hour and the meeting ends with him presenting copies of the books he has "written". It is all very cordial and I think of offering to do an archaeological survey of his home town, Rastan.

Tuesday, 10 December
Solhi tells me he is grateful to me for two things – the opera, and the whisky in Kuwait. Does he put them on the same level? I discuss the idea of the Institute putting on my translations of two Syrian plays – *The Mask* by Mamduh Udwan and *The Elephant Oh Lord of Ages* by Sa'dallah Wannous.

Wednesday, 11 December
Blake Morrison's book, *And When Did You Last See Your Father?* has

been translated into Arabic. I fax Blake inviting him to a launch here in April.

Saturday, 14 December
I am translating Sa'dallah's play and am having difficulties. There is no problem getting the meaning but I am not getting the brio of the Arab text into English. I feel my present version is mechanical. The challenge is the dialogue that has to be spoken. It is different from translating a novel or story that has only to be read. I am now translating something with a production in mind.

I call at the Ministry and talk to the novelist Hasan M Yusuf, Ghinwa Ma'mari and Hisham Dajani. They are all part of a Sa'dallah circle. Hasan Mim – as he is called – calls regularly, Ghinwa acts as a secretary and Hisham studied with him in Cairo in the 1960s.

Wednesday, 18 December
I go to Aleppo to see a potential site of an office for the British Council. The Honorary Consul, Tony Akhras, and his sons take us to a flat in the Sabil quarter that seems ideal. It only needs rewiring and a coat of paint. They tell me that the largest foreign community, after the Armenians, is the Canadian-Syrian. There are also large numbers of both Greeks and Turks.

Thursday, 19 December
The Ambassador and I are to call on Wahib Tannous at the Ba'th Party headquarters on Sunday. This is a breakthrough. The Embassy acknowledges the Party and the Party is receiving a western Ambassador.

Sunday, 22 December
I accompany the Ambassador on a call on Wahib Tannous. It is all in Arabic and the Ambassador asks about the philosophy of the

Party. Syria, we are told, is very democratic and there are elections at all levels – peasants, academics, capitalists and so on. But in the course of the discussion some interesting points emerge. Thirty per cent of all Syrians are in receipt of education, free, from the state. And between 15,000 and 20,000 Syrians are studying abroad, again courtesy of the state.

Tuesday, 24 December
I take Gabriel – here for the Christmas holidays – for a walk into town. We go to the Hijaz railway station and have a coffee and a Pepsi in a converted railway carriage with its décor dating from about 1914. Most of the clientele are European tourists. Alcoholic drinks are served, a "cool" place for Gabriel and his Damascus mates.

Monday, 30 December
I go to call on the Mardam Beys, a condolence call for Salma Mardam Bey who died in London last week after years of cancer. I see Jacques Hakim, Ratib Shallah, Nabil Sukkar and various members of the Mardam Bey family.

Tuesday, 31 December
We take Gabriel and Nathaniel to Faraya in Lebanon for skiing. But there is not a lot of snow. We spend the evening – and see the New Year in – at a restaurant, where there is as much food and booze as you want: US$30 a head. The patron and his wife preside and a dozen waiters (including one from Homs) fill up glasses and keep the Coca Cola and araq flowing. Balloons and comic hats are handed out at midnight.

Laila and Georges Ladhkani.

Rosemary Halsted tidies up the grave of her aunt, Lady Jane Digby.

Vanda with Chris and Linda Simpson of Magna Carta.

Musicians at Lattakia.

The Duke of Kent with Mamduh Udwan.

Susannah Self with musicians at Lattakia.

1997

Thursday, 2 January 1997

Vanda brings in news that dominates our thoughts all day. On Tuesday afternoon a bus bound for Aleppo was targeted by a bomb planted in the luggage. All passengers were killed and there was extensive damage in Baramke. One lady sitting in the front thought she had been spared, left the bus rejoicing and dropped down dead.

There is a news blackout on the story. Hospitals have been forbidden to say anything. All is referred to Security. Journalists have been told not to file anything. AFP eventually breaks the embargo and Simon Ingram is on the BBC commenting how the rumour mill in Damascus is working overtime. Nobody has claimed responsibility. The Muslim Brothers? Lebanese dissidents? There have been bombs directed at Syrian targets in Lebanon lately. Later on, the Syrian government, forced to acknowledge what the world knows, unconvincingly blames the Israelis.

Sunday, 5 January

Wa'il Barazi phones. I have written (in Arabic) an introduction to his translation of *And When Did You Last See Your Father?* by Blake Morrison.

Theresa and I go to a production at the Kabbani theatre of Sa'dallah Wannous's play, *Yawm min Yamanna* (*A Day in our Times*), about a girls' school whose pupils moonlight at the local brothel. The head and the local religious authorities take no action as the madam of the brothel has donated money to the mosque. I talk to the director, Ajaj Hafır, who did a PhD in Leningrad on Sufism and drama. He tells me very little was cut by the censors. The theatre is packed and there is plenty of applause during the play.

Monday, 6 January

The Embassy view of the bombings is that the Syrian authorities do not have a clue about what has happened. There is a gap in the security and in the intelligence.

I receive a letter from the Minister of Defence, "top secret and immediate", about Geoffrey King doing an archaeological survey of Rastan.

Tuesday, 7 January

I receive a cheque for 100,000 Syrian pounds from the insurance company – £1,500. That concluded the formalities about my accident last August. I drive too fast. This was a warning. It was "an accident waiting to happen". I was lucky. Nobody else was involved and I did not kill or maim myself.

Wednesday, 8 January

There were survivors of the New Year's Eve bus explosion. Michel Khoury was sitting next to the driver and felt a huge ramming as if another bus had driven into it. He looked behind him and saw utter devastation. His ears were damaged and, after medical treatment, he was held by the security forces for 48 hours. They asked him if he had any enemies. It is interesting: their first reaction is to think of personal vendettas. Another student at the Institute of Music and Drama, Ali Sulaiman, was less fortunate. He was not on the bus but close to it. He has lost his eyes and his nose. He is in hospital and

Solhi visited him yesterday. His eyes are bandaged and he does not yet know that he is blinded for life.

Solhi tells me that the President once invited him to take Syrian nationality. Solhi, the Iraqi pan-Arab, replied, "I'm waiting for there to be an *Arab* passport." Assad smiled enigmatically.

Thursday, 9 January

We have tea with teachers, Jed and Pasha, at their flat. The other guests include RobinYassin-Kassab, who has a Syrian father and a British mother and was brought up in Britain. At sunset he goes off with another Muslim teacher to pray, while Jed opens a bottle of wine.

Thursday, 23 January

Having returned from a fortnight away, meeting colleagues in Brussels and London, I come down with bronchitis. I go to the Shami Hospital for tests. I am laid on a couch, my temperature is taken, my pulse measured and I am asked to say 99. (In Arabic you are asked to say 44.)

Tuesday, 28 January

The Number 2 in the British Embassy calls. He says the Embassy do not know enough Syrians outside business circles and what I call the haute bourgeoisie. Can I help? I say I pick up a lot of political gossip but I do not seek it out. It is not my job. People say things to me and I know I have a wide range of contacts, from Hamas to the Ba'th Party. My relationships would be poorer if it was known that I was a channel of the Embassy.

Wednesday, 29 January

We have arranged for Nadir, a computer whizz-kid from the British Council in Jordan, to advise us on a new project, called OVID, or the Overseas Information Database. But he is held at the border because of his laptop computer which the customs people cannot make head or tail of, but instinctively suspect. We have to get a letter from the Director of Syrian Customs to say that we will guarantee that he will take it out again. Ayoub takes the letter to Dera'a. Nadir has spent over six hours at the border.

Friday, 31 January

We go for a walk around Jabal Kasiyun with two teachers, Robert and Pat. Robert is a dour man in his forties, and started a PhD in Sociology on a subject I do not understand. In the early 1980s he was a dispatch rider in the City of London, earning as much as £500 a week, all tax-free. He made lots of money, bought a van and filled it with the latest music and drove to Greece where on a beach he met his present wife, her sister and brother-in-law, all naked. They were old-fashioned liberal socialists. Robert is well read and we talk about Gibbon. He was teaching aeronautical technical terms to Lufthansa staff and read Gibbon as an antidote. He goes on to observe how a lot of aircraft language is derived from ships – captain, cabin, steward, embarkation. Pat was for a while a contemplative nun.

Monday, 3 February

The lawyer Jacques Hakim charges US$ 2,000 a day if he has to be in court.

I have a call from Samir Abdu who has translated a lot of Bertrand Russell's work into Arabic, and, as a young man in 1965, called on him.

We break the Ramadan fast with a party in the office, with Pamela and John Bunney as guests. They were in the Embassy here 20 years ago and are currently posted in Saudi Arabia. I arrange for there to be no alcohol because we wanted Ayoub to attend. But he has to be Acting Imam at his local mosque for the sunset prayers.

In the evening John and I call on our landlord, Georges, on his 99th birthday. He is neatly dressed in a brown suit and we chat for a while. He ought to achieve his ambition of living in three centuries.

Thursday, 6 February

We drive to Aleppo and have a drink with Sally Mazloumian at the Baron Hotel. She has now been 50 years in Aleppo and, a great-grandmother, looks well. She is mourning the death of Pamela Digby Churchill Harriman whom she once nursed years ago.

Wednesday, 12 February

I join Embassy colleagues in Homs. There is no news about appointments made to see the Party Secretary, the Chief of Police and the Governor. We do get a message from the Governor's office: "Please do not call on me. I shall be embarrassed as I do not have permission to receive you." So we hang around in the hotel. The Ambassador plays trick-track with his Deputy and teaches it to the Commercial Attaché.

Later in the day we go to the citadel and I give Embassy colleagues a talk on the spot about the excavations, emphasising the political, economic and social aspects, then about the exciting traces of the mosque.

Thursday, 13 February

I have dinner at the German Archaeological Institute and chat with the Danish scholar Peder Mortensen. He is the son of an art historian and inherited all his books, and then added plenty more of his own. He measures books in metres. He met Kim Philby in 1958 and has kept his visiting card.

Friday, 14 February

I go to the Meridien for the wedding of Wada' Atassi, the son of

Warqa Barmada, a grand society wedding. I sit with Marya Atassi, who lives in Cairo with her Egyptian husband whom she met in Sharjah. She tells me that the wedding dress is likely to have cost US$2,000.

Saturday, 15 February
I go to the Ebla Cham for a concert. There is a mixture of music – "Fingal's Cave", an Azeri piece by Ali Akbar, a song from *Carmen* and one of Solhi al-Wadi's compositions – a cross between Brahms and Shostakovitch.

Tuesday, 18 February
I am reading the devastating critique of the Assad regime by Michel Seurat[1]. He argues that politics has been banned from the country but the Sunni Muslims are lying in wait. Their time will come.

Wednesday, 19 February
Our office is in e-mail contact with London. We are not the last in the Middle East to link up – we are ahead of Bahrain and Morocco. But Syria is probably the country that is most hostile to information technology.

On my way back from seeing a visitor off at the airport I see what looks like some coloured paper in the road, turning in the wind. At the last moment I see that it is a cat writhing in agony. My wheels strike it and I hope kill it. I have very little remorse or anxiety, though that night I dream of a cat sleeping on my bed.

Thursday, 20 February
I drive to Beirut. There are lots of heavy lorries going over the mountain. The driving is appalling. Slow lorries overtaking even

1 Michel Seurat, *L'Etat de Barbarie*, Seuil, Paris, 1977.

slower lorries without any anticipation of what may be coming in the opposite direction. Cars are forced into the gutter. There is mist and heavy rain all the way to Beirut.

Friday, 21 February

I go to the Madina theatre and meet the director, Nidal Ashqar. She is fiftysomething and trained at the Royal Academy of Dramatic Art. I then see a production of Sa'dallah's play, *Isharat wa Tahawwulat*, which is very hard to translate. It is located in a late-Ottoman city and put on as a pantomime with plenty of music and dance. All the cast are on stage most of the time. The curtain is a huge trellis *mashrabiya*, and the general décor and costume is like an orientalist painting. The theatre is not full. Nidal has brought out a feminist, rather than a class, interpretation of the play. In deference to the censors they had to make some cuts toning down the political aspects and were unable to refer to the Mufti.

Saturday, 22 February

I drive north and search for and finally find Akkar castle, a Crusader castle up a valley in northern Lebanon. There are no signs to it and I have to ask constantly. I walk the last stretch through a full and cold mountain stream. The entrance is blocked by thorn bushes, presumably to prevent animals entering. There is no sign of care for the castle, and wheat is growing in the ruins.

I drive on to Aleppo and have dinner with the Consul, Tony Akhras, and his son, Alexander, Iskandar, who will be succeeding him as Consul after the Queen's Birthday in the summer. There has been heavy snow in the country. The Damascus to Homs road is closed, as is the road from Damascus to Beirut.

Peter was able to get back to Damascus.

Monday, 24 February

I have a call from Samir Chamsi Pasha, the Homsi British-based textile merchant. He is making a contribution (£1,000) towards the Homs citadel dig, and we discuss what British city Homs should be twinned with. Leeds is comparable in size and location. There are Leeds graduates in Homs. Homs, like Leeds, has been a textile city. His family moved their activities to Beirut in 1960 during the union with Egypt to escape from the socialism of Abdul Nasser. They then relocated to Britain in the 1970s because of the Lebanese Civil War.

Tuesday, 25 February

I go to a lecture at the Goethe Institute given by Frau Professor Dr Anne-Marie Schimmel. The auditorium is packed out and the lecturer comes in, a frail elderly lady. She speaks in German and there is a translator. She talks of the interest Goethe and Herder had in Persian poetry. There are several people in the audience I know, but plenty I do not – Syrians who have studied in Germany, East or West. There is a Germanophone community here.

Thursday, 27 February

Sadiq al-Azm calls. He seeks my advice on allusions in Salman Rushdie's *Satanic Verses*, some of which he is translating into Arabic. I tell him I am about to go on a week's lecture tour of Palestine and he gives me a letter for the poet, Fadwa Tuqan, whose niece is his wife.

I go to the French Cultural Centre for a discussion about translating Sa'dallah Wannous's plays into French. Three of the translators are present. Some students put on scenes from Sa'dallah's plays. One of our teachers is there and is not aware that I translate as well. "Being Director of the British Council," I tell her, "is my part-time job. All Directors are like that really."

Peter was invited by the British Council in East Jerusalem to give lectures on translation in Gaza, Hebron, Nablus and Ramallah. He went with Theresa and stayed first in Amman.

Friday, 28 February

A taxi takes us to the Jordanian emigration point, from where we take a bus a mile or so to the Allenby Bridge, The river Jordan is swollen with water, some of which, I reflect, is coming from Mount Hermon. A heavily armed Israeli soldier gives confusing signals and our Jordanian driver, enraged, shouts (in English), "Look at your back, you son of a bitch!"

I am asked by an Israeli the purpose of my visit. "I am the guest of the British Council," I say, looking her in the eye. She does not look me in the eye. The Jerusalem British Council driver, Ramadan, meets us and takes us on a dusty road through Jericho and up to Jerusalem.

We wander off on foot into the Old City, having a falafel by the Damascus Gate. Groups of visitors are pausing at the Stations of the Cross in the Via Dolorosa, singing hymns. We go to the Church of the Holy Sepulchre and join a queue to enter the shrine of the Holy Sepulchre. An American asks Theresa what the queue is for.

"The Holy Sepulchre," she says. He moves away and then returns to ask, "What's a sepulchre?"

We drift through the souks and spend time at the Western Wall. Many of the Jews pray and make a rhythmic movement, like clockwork toys. The Haram al-Sharif is closed.

Jessica Barry, a journalist, calls for a drink. She smokes six cigarettes in the hour and tells us of "Jerusalem Syndrome", where people are affected by a religious obsession. Two people were recently arrested claiming to be the Virgin Mary, each denouncing the other as an imposter.

Saturday, 1 March

We walk to the Haram al-Sharif and enter the Dome of the Rock and the al-Aqsa Mosque. I see the spot where King Abdullah of Jordan was assassinated in 1951. There is a mixture of people in the old city. Most sinister are the Israeli soldiers, heavily armed, and in groups of two or three. Single Jews walk around, heads bowed.

We walk through the city to Jaffa Gate and spend an hour at the splendidly reconstructed citadel. The history of Jerusalem is on display panels. The display is good but Palestinians are marginalised – not even mentioned. Muslims and Christians are presented as incidental to the history of Jewish Jerusalem. They are defined separately so that the Palestinian population is seen as disparate. One panel refers in English to "opposition" to the Jewish state; in Arabic it is *muqawama*, meaning resistance. We walk back through the city to St George's Cathedral, a tranquil spot of Englishness.

At three, Ramadan collects us from the hotel and we set off for Gaza, along the Tel Aviv road and then south on the coastal road by heavily industrialised Ashkelon. We enter the Gaza Strip at the Erez Crossing and are immediately in a different country. Ill-maintained roads, donkey-drawn carts, even groups of camels (well, one). The city of Gaza is even more depressed and depressing. Poverty everywhere. Gaza has a million people, three quarters of whom are refugees from central and southern Palestine. Most women in the streets are veiled. We end up at the Adam Hotel, thrown up recently on a beach that does not look at all inviting. We are joined by the lutenist, Bill Badley, who is doing a Channel Four programme on Palestinian music.

Sunday, 2 March

I do not sleep well: pre-performance nerves. This is the first time I have given a formal lecture on translation.

Ghada of the Gaza British Council takes me to call on Ahmad Dahbour at the Ministry of Culture. We are soon on very good terms. He has lived as an exile in various Arab countries and we talk about writers whom we both know: Abbas Shiblak, Mamduh Udwan, Sa'dallah Wannous. He tells me that Abbas grew up with the Palestinian novelist, Yahya Yakhlif, and is portrayed in the latter's novel, *Tuffah al-Mahjanin*. I fail to ask about the work of the Ministry of Culture.

We then go to the Islamic University of Gaza, which was founded in 1983 and has 6,000 students. The head of the English Department, Dr Nazmi Misri, is my chairman. I have an audience of about 25, academics and graduate students involved in translation. I talk in a mixture of Arabic and English and there is a great discussion. For ten minutes we discuss the difference between "Shut up" and "Be quiet". I introduce the idea of Arabic fiction being related to an oral tradition and English fiction to a book-reading tradition.

On to the Writers' Union where I meet writers Abdullah Tayir, Ghalib Ashkelani, Habib Hanna and Muhammad Nassar. All present me with copies of their work and we talk about how to promote Palestinian literature.

The Gaza British Council driver, Jamil, takes us on a tour of the camps – Jabaliya, Buraij and Beach – extensive and poverty-stricken areas: perhaps the most desperate part of the Middle East. We go to his house in Jabaliya camp and meet his wife, Sara. Gazans are not permitted to have either a port or an airport. They cannot automatically leave the Strip. Migrant workers go to Israel but cannot stay overnight. Five-hour permits enable some to go to Ashkelon for shopping. To the west of Gaza City are some Jewish settlements, constructed but not occupied.

Monday, 3 March
Trupti Desai, the British Council Director in Gaza, collects us with Isa al-Qarr, Public Relations Officer of UNRWA, and we visit the

camps to the south-west. We go to Middle Camp and Deir al-Balah. It has been raining heavily and conditions are appalling. Children play around barefoot and the gutters run with raw sewage. The main souk road is very narrow, the gaps between houses even narrower. Not far away are heavily fortified Israeli settlements that are like prisons, with barbed-wire fences and absolutely no contact with their human environment.

Gaza City has a sprinkling of villas, a fine one for Mahmoud Abbas and another fine Presidential Guest House, with notices that it was a gift from Britain. Chirac stayed in the Guest House and the road going past it is called Rue Charles de Gaulle. There is a fragile sense of hope in the appurtenances of state with postage stamps and Ministries in makeshift villas. Access to cars and drivers becomes an important symbol of authority. I am reminded of Juba in 1973. Big Brother Israel controls most things and dominates the economy.

Jamil takes us back to Jerusalem. Israelis and Palestinians have learnt to live with each other. There is a certain pragmatic modus operandi. Smiles and the occasional handshake veil a deep mutual hatred.

We call on the novelist Liana Badr at her comfortable villa in Bira by Ramallah. We start in Arabic but switch to English. She is very depressed by the situation. Netanyahu does not know what to do. The Palestinians have made so many concessions. She works partly in Jericho and sees a lot of Fadwa Tuqan. She says the conservatism of the Palestinians is a reaction to exposure of Israeli permissiveness – drugs and prostitution. I suggest that people who are deprived of authority exert what little they have in small ways like bullying women to wear the veil.

Tuesday, 4 March
The British Council driver, Ramadan, takes us to Nablus, through the mountains north of Ramallah. The Israelis control the road signs

and as we enter the city the sign naming it is in three languages – Shechem in Hebrew and in English transliteration, Nablus in Arabic. It is as if by not having "Nablus" transliterated thus in English there is a denial of what the Nabuls is (and the rest of the world) call their own city. The hills have illegal settlements, fortress-like, brooding, threatening.

The driver takes us to the classical site of Sebastia to the north. I collect a bit of the Palestinian soil and a stone to take back to Damascus to Ayoub. We return to Nablus and look at the old city, with one main street, flanked by large family houses belonging to the Tuqans and the Abu Ghazalis. We meet a visiting specialist, Trevor Holmes, who is restoring the 19th-century palace belonging to the Qasims, another feudal family of northern Palestine.

We are taken into the mountains to where the Samaritans live. They broke away from mainstream Judaism and live around where they think the Temple should be.

After lunch we go to the Municipal Library. The librarian (and my chairman) is Ali Tuqan, and my formal host is Abd al-Hadi, a kinsman of the nationalist, Awni Abd al-Hadi. There are about 60 in the audience: writers, translators and students from Najah University. I have carefully prepared my lecture which I give in Arabic. I start by saying how pleased I am to be in the city of Fadwa Tuqan and Muhammad Izzat Darwaza, and then talk for 35 to 40 minutes. There are questions and I reply in Arabic to questions put in English. I feel more relaxed but am drained at the end.

Wednesday, 5 March
Ramadan takes us from our Jerusalem hotel to Hebron. There is heavy traffic in Jerusalem. We go by Jabal Abu Ghunaim, which is threatened with a settlement. I am told that the Jewish population now exceeds the Arab in East Jerusalem. We pass through rocky countryside, with menacing settlements on the hills around.

We call at Hebron University which has been plagued with closures. There is no electricity and it is bitterly cold. Over the road are arches with improving slogans, one of which reads, ironically, "A soft answer turneth away worth." In the University President's office is a portrait of Muhammad Ali Jabari who was Mayor of Hebron for 40 years.

I talk in English to about 60 people including staff from the University of Bethlehem. I analyse a few pages of *Sabriya* in English and Arabic. That never fails to arouse and sustain interest. One student asks an articulate and challenging question about gender and translation. We have lunch at the university – cold soup and cold chicken in an unheated room. Those who can wear overcoats.

The British Council Director in Hebron, Na'im, takes us on a tour of Hebron. The Israelis evacuated a large part of the city only two months ago. They still control everything. We drive towards Kiryat Arab. Palestinian housing nearby has been forbidden. Unlike other places the settlement in Hebron is in the centre of the city. We go along to the mosque/synagogue. The main entrance is for Jews. Muslims have to go through two checkpoints at the side. Na'im points out the spot where the Jewish settler, Dr Baruch Goldstein, opened fire and killed 30 Palestinians at dawn prayer in February 1994. (He now has a hero's grave at Kiryat Arba.) We pause at the tombs of Abraham, Jacob and Joseph and their wives, and then stroll through the deserted souk. Wire netting is overhead, a defence against stones thrown by Israelis above. A group of Israeli soldiers, armed to the teeth, walk through the souk, reminding me of a scene in the film, *Schindler's List*. A month or so ago an Israeli soldier fired at Palestinians in the vegetable market. The Jewish settlement proclaims that it is reclaimed Jewish property stolen by Arabs after the massacre in 1929. Israeli control of the area has been intensified after the Goldstein massacre.

Back in Jerusalem we have dinner with Bill Badley, the Israeli dissident Uri Davis and his Finnish partner, Sirko. She first came to

Israel in 1973 to work on a kibbutz. The experience led her to be a founding member of the Palestine Solidarity Campaign in Finland.

Thursday, 6 March
In the afternoon Peter Skelton, Director of the British Council in the Occupied Territories, takes us to the Khalil Sakakini Centre in Ramallah. There are about 20 in the audience, including Liana Badr. Peter introduces me in English and I ask whether they would like me to talk in English or in Arabic. "In Arabic," they say. I talk about translating poetry. I am hesitant at first but it all leads to a good discussion. Among the audience is a bright, slightly dominant lady, Ilham Abu Ghazali, from Nablus, who teaches at Bir Zeit University. She tells me that she organised theatre in Nablus. They put on Sa'dallah Wannous's play, *The Elephant Oh Lord of Ages*, but it was closed down after one performance by the occupying Israeli military authorities.

We adjourn to a bar and then to a restaurant. Peter tells me he can no longer entertain in Jerusalem because of Israeli restrictions on Palestinians entering "Israel" – East Jerusalem. The Israelis are also pressurising the British Council and the Consulate General to move away from East Jerusalem to Ramallah where the Palestinian Authority has its government. Their presence is a constant reminder of the illegitimacy of their rule there. Some organisations have moved out.

Friday, 7 March
We walk through the old city of Jerusalem with Peter. Israeli soldiers are at key points, heavily armed in intimidating groups. Apparently the Israelis are always nervous on Fridays, fearing inflammatory sermons.

"Who chooses to live in Hebron?" I ask Peter.

"Brooklyn nutters," he replies.

We leave Jerusalem at 10, wind our way through the dusty hills to Jericho, passing the Monastery of St George and the house of Musa Alami. There is no problem with the checkpoint. We take a taxi to Amman. The driver is a graduate of the University of Jordan and for 20 years taught in Libya, Algeria and Saudi Arabia. He invested his savings in a taxi. We return by another shared taxi to Damascus.

What an interesting few days. In addition to reminders of *Schindler's List* (when Jews were victims) I am also reminded of Syria: armed soldiers everywhere, the fear of the people. In Israel and the Occupied Territories, the Palestinians are fearful of the Israelis; in Syria it is the people fearing the authorities.

Monday, 17 March

We host a dinner party, mostly for medical folk. The Communist MP, Dr al-Taqi, tells me that Sa'dallah Wannous was invited to call on the President, and made a whole lot of complaints about restrictions on freedom. Assad took it all on the chin. Muhammad Shahrur, the liberal Islamic scholar (and Professor of Engineering) has been told he cannot talk publicly about Islam. This is in response to pressure from the Muslim Brothers. He has not lost his job and the restrictions will be lifted in due course. Dr al-Taqi's mother was sent by her father, a tribal sheikh, to study in Paris in 1939. When somebody said, "She might lose her virginity there," the sheikh said, "Better there than here."

Tuesday, 18 March

One of the British Council teachers, Andy Williams, is a graduate in Drama Studies. He is spending a term teaching English through drama. He is using as a text my translation of Sa'dallah Wannous's play, *The Elephant Oh Lord of Ages*. We are working with the Higher Institute of Music and Drama to stage it next month under Andy's direction. I join Andy and his class at the Institute. The class starts with a warm-up, walking around the room with Andy calling out, "You're walking in the country. You're getting thirsty. There is an apple tree with juicy apples high up. You have to jump up to grab them. A dog comes along and attacks your leg. You have to shake him off…" and so on. I join in.

I talk to the students about translating the play. They have questions about particular points. Allah or God? I take a vote and get those who prefer one to explain why. I have translated *mub lagha* as "sensationalism". Why? It could have been "rhetoric" or "exaggeration". But we agree that the word is used pejoratively. But another reason for objecting to the word emerges. It is hard to declaim with outrage. Another student suggests it might be better if the characters were given names. Does it not otherwise depersonalise them? One character has only one line: "The elephant knocked down my one and only palm tree." She feels there is plenty of personality there.

I see Ghinwa, who acts as Sa'dallah's secretary. She tells me that Salma Jayyusi phoned Sa'dallah recently and he was furious and upset. He has been having more treatment lately and is not receiving visitors. I would like to take Andy to meet him.

Peter also translated the play, The Mask, *by Mamduh Udwan, and was collaborating with the Higher Institute of Music and Drama for the play to be performed in Arabic and in English on the same evening. The play takes about 45 minutes. The plan was to conclude the Anglo-Syrian evening of drama with the production of Sa'dallah's play,* The Elephant, Oh Lord of Ages. *Riad Ismat would direct the Arabic version of Mamduh's play.*

Wednesday, 19 March
At a reception I meet Mamduh who greets me with a bear hug. Our

show will be the first performance of his play. And the Elephant play will be the first performance of any of Sa'dallah's work in English. I meet the film director, Haitham Haqqi, and his wife, Layali, sister of Liana Badr whose *A Balcony over the Fakihani* I have translated. The sisters look alike. I met their father in Tunis. I feel I know the family and meeting Layali is like meeting a long-lost friend.

Thursday, 20 March

I call on the Minister and tell her I shall be leaving in the summer. I also tell her that the Chairman of the British Council, Sir Martin Jacomb, will be visiting Syria, coming overland from Beirut. She offers to give him a dinner and to arrange VIP treatment at the frontier.

Friday, 21 March

We go to the Syrian Orthodox Club in Bab Touma. The Director is Samir Abdu, Bertrand Russell's translator. I talk to a tiresome teacher of History at the University who is a doctrinaire anti-imperialist and talks about "anti-Arabism" in Britain. I tell him, "We are an island. We hate all foreigners. We make no exceptions for Arabs." I thought I was going to give a lecture in Arabic on translation, but instead it is a colloquium with six searching questions from Samir. There is much discussion of *Sabriya*, with complimentary remarks. At the end I am presented with a mosaic with the Lord's Prayer in Arabic and Syriac, and my name in the two languages.

Saturday, 22 March

We go to a recital by a German String Quartet playing Schubert, Debussy and Brahms. The place is packed with people standing in the aisles. This is thanks to Solhi's influence. He has built up a taste for western classical music among all classes of people.

Monday, 24 March

At an Embassy staff meeting most of the discussion is about two people sharing an office. One is a fervent smoker, the other a rabid non-smoker. The British public-sector policy is that there should be no smoking in a shared office. I suggest that resolving the status of Jerusalem might be easier. Someone also says the Embassy only had a waiting room because the previous Ambassador kept people waiting.

Wednesday, 26 March

Sa'dallah's secretary, Ghinwa, calls. Sa'dallah is in a bad way. The trend is constantly downward. He fluctuates from day to day, and even during one day. But he is at his most creative on Fridays. She works with him "and it is like working with a man who is not ill". She knew him at the Institute before he was ill. He was a "melancholy man" and when the cancer struck four or five years ago, she thought he would not last. But the illness has brought out all sorts of qualities. He is more tolerant and more positive. He is sustained by the support, interest and good wishes of friends, and by the growing appreciation of his work. I compliment Ghinwa on her improved English which she insists on using. I learn later that she has come in for an interview for a scholarship and by chatting with me for 20 minutes she has done the best thing possible by practising her English. And my complimenting her on her English has given her a boost of confidence.

Tuesday, 1 April

We have lunch with the Ambassador. The other guests are the archaeologists David and Joan Oates. David is 70 and frail but better than he was last April. There is much concern about the threats to the archaeological institutes, including a feud between Amman and Baghdad that goes back to a feud between Kathleen Kenyon and

Max Mallowan. They both moan about Mrs Thatcher who was mean towards archaeology.

Wednesday, 2 April
I accompany the Ambassador to Lattakia where we call on the Chamber of Commerce to be received by Kamal al-Assad and Faruq Joud.

The Ambassador is having difficulty getting permission to meet people, thanks to someone in the Ministry of Foreign Affairs. He is not allowed to see the President of the University who is not allowed to distribute invitations to university staff to attend our reception. But Ahmad al-Sufi and his wife Majida come. I get a kiss from both; Majida (a Kurdish Muslim) is actually wearing a crucifix round her neck.

We go on to dinner with Nuhad Abdullah who designs houses for wealthy and important clients. He designed one for Wahib Tannous at Mashtal Hilu. He talks about Alawite politics and how there are three main groups – the Haidaris to the north of Lattakia, the Khassis to the south and the Murshidis in the mountains and the Ghab. He tells us that the Minister of Higher Education, Saliha Sanqar, had the idea of a massive, iron-relief portrait of President Assad on the wall of the Ministry, but technical advisers told her that there was a danger that it could bring the whole building down. She should, he thought, worry more about the deleterious effect of East European PhDs in positions of influence in Syrian universities. He repeats his fears of a potential backlash against Alawites in Hama and Aleppo and what he calls the "civil war".

Thursday, 3 April
I accompany the Ambassador and the Commercial Attaché on a visit to factories in Lattakia. We go first to the government-owned Lattakia Spinning Factory. They have machines rented from the

Islamic Bank and these are operated in shifts. The Production Manager earns one sixth of what he could earn in the private sector. I ask, Why not move to Damascus? He comes from Lattakia and life is cheaper than in Damascus where he would have to move to. 2,100 employees work in shifts, earning 3 to 4,000 Syrian pounds a month, but they can double this with overtime and bonuses.

We go on to the perfume factory of Kamal al-Assad, located in stately villas in the countryside. There are attractive and well-qualified staff, including a PhD in analytical chemistry. I ponder and wonder whether it is all a cover for producing materials for chemical warfare. The third place is the Joud factory for processed food and producing white goods. They have 300 workers and have an annual turnover of US$110 million. Employees on the shop floor earn from 10 to 15,000 Syrian pounds a month. The whole plant seems efficient, relevant and dynamic.

We go on to call on the Governor who receives us with the Mayor and Chief of Police. It is not easy. We raise the idea of an English teaching package with the Chamber of Commerce. The Governor points out that it would need his permission and that there are facilities for teaching English in the schools and so on. He also points out that policy is centralised and its execution devolved, so "don't talk to me about policy matters". The Commercial Attaché says to me, privately, as we leave, "How do you say 'Bollocks' in a diplomatic way?"

Sunday, 6 April

When I come into my office I see an enormous spider, bigger than anything I have ever seen before, crawling across the floor. I pop a wastepaper basket over him, wondering whether he is poisonous and where his mum and dad, brothers and sisters may be.

Martha Munday, whom I knew slightly in Yemen, calls. She is very interesting on the status of women in Syria. The Ba'thist ideology is very liberal and the laws for women's rights – maternity leave, equal pay and so on – are as good as anywhere in the world. But there is a conflict between Ba'thist-driven law, and custom. There are also administrative decisions that affect women's rights. The Ministry of the Interior has issued a decree saying women should have the permission of their husband, father or brother to travel outside Syria.

I also have visits from three other UK-based academics, the charming Turkish scholar Vehbi, the Durham Arabist Paul Starkey, and the archaeologist Peter Parr. (It is the Easter vacation.)

In the evening we host a dinner party. Sadiq al-Azm talks of his son "who studied archaeology with someone called Peter something." "Parr?" I suggest. "He's standing over there."

Tuesday, 8 April

I am driven to Lattakia for a conference on translation at the University. Munzer Muhammad, Dean of the Faculty of Arts, gives a loyal speech celebrating the golden jubilee of the foundation of the Ba'th Party and pauses for applause at the mention of the President's name. Indeed there seems to be a spirit of intense loyalty. We also have a minute's silence for the death of Basil al-Assad – it is *three years* since he died.

The conference is packed with staff and students. No longer is there criticism of Moroccans and Algerians who betray their Arabism by writing in French. By contrast, Henri Zughaib, a Lebanese based in the United States, gives a stirring speech emphasising the importance of learning foreign languages so that Arabs can explain themselves to the world and translate their own literature instead of leaving it to orientalists. Another speaker talks of the words used in Arabic for "hospital". Usually the word is *mustashfa*, which is where you seek a cure. *Mashfa* is the word used in Syria and is more positive: it is the place where you obtain a cure.

Tuesday, 15 April

The Chairman of the British Council, Sir Martin Jacomb, and Lady Jacomb have invited themselves to Syria for a few days. Theresa and I meet them at the Lebanese frontier and bring them to Damascus. In the evening the Minister of Culture hosts a dinner for them. I sit next to her and she is warm in her support. She tells me that Sa'dallah is very ill and not seeing people. He has swollen up and the cancer seems to have reached his liver. It looks as if he has only days to live.

I accompany the Chairman and the Ambassador on a call on the Prime Minister. We spend an hour with him. He is cool at first but warms up, puffing at a fag or two. I feel a glow of pride, for the Ambassador has not been able to call on him yet. It is as if the British Council can provide access for the Ambassador. (The Duke of Kent also failed to see the Prime Minister.)

Thursday, 17 April

I take the Jacombs to Homs and we climb up on to the citadel and I give them a guided tour. Some local youths stand around threateningly. In my talk I drop the names of Mustafa Tlas and Hafez al-Assad, and they melt away.

Sir Martin used to the Vice-Chairman of Barclays Bank whose board invited the Queen Mother for lunch. He got in touch with the Queen Mother's secretary.

"What would she like to drink beforehand – sherry or gin?"

"A gin and tonic."

"What during the meal, red or white wine?"

"Well, first red, and then white."

"And something afterwards? Brandy? Port?"

"Well, both."

Friday, 18 April

I take the Jacombs to Krak des Chevaliers and we are received by the castle's manager, a Christian called Riad al-Saghir. Riad tells us that there are 140,000 visitors to the castle each year and the number is rising. The village by the castle, Qalat al-Husn, is in three parts: a Christian quarter, a Muslim quarter and a Turkoman quarter. The last are descendants of the soldiers who were stationed at the castle in Mamluk times. It was the Muslims who lived inside the castle until they were moved out by the French in the 1920s. I ask if there are any accidents in the castle.

"None," is the reply. "Perhaps one every 20 years." As we leave we see a young man with blood pouring down his face being awkwardly carried by three comrades.

Monday, 21 April

At a reception hosted by my American opposite number, Evelyn Early, I talk to the artist, Fatih Mudarris, and his wife. She tells me that Fatih's father was the only boy of a family of five. He married a Kurdish girl for love and the family had him murdered, when Fatih was only two. When Fatih was 11 he insisted that his mother, who had been banished, come to live with them.

"Does he feel he is a Mudarris or a Kurd?" I ask.

"He feels he is Fatih."

Tuesday, 22 April

Kathy and Blake Morrison, and Penny Black and her acting colleagues arrive at 4 in the morning, and after a rest come to the office for breakfast.

The Syria Times reports that my translation of *Sabriya* is on the syllabus of 17 American universities. Very nice, if true.

In the evening we host a launch for Wa'il Baraza's translation of Blake's *And When Did You Last See Your Father?* Wa'il is there with his headscarfed engineer wife. The publisher, Khair al-Din al-Nashawati, perpetually smiles. I say a few words in Arabic, and Blake ditto in English. We sip our fizzy drinks and eat our sticky cakes. A book launch is a novel event in Syria.

Wednesday, 23 April

I take Kathy and Blake to the Arab Writers' Union. It is funded partly by the government and partly by the Ba'th Party and has 700 members, of whom 55 are women. Blake talks about his latest book about the James Bulger case, when an infant was murdered by older boys.

Rana Kabbani joins us for lunch. She has been to see Ulfat who is frail.

My Line Manager has arrived and he joins Penny and her team, the Morrisons and ourselves for dinner at the Ambassador's. I get Sadiq al-Azm to meet Blake.

"You're going to miss all this," says the Line Manager. I realise there is a buzz of creative and intellectual excitement – all promoted by the British Council.

Thursday, 24 April

In the evening we go to the theatre at the Institute of Music and Drama. It is a cosy terraced square. I meet Andy Williams's players who are nervous and excited. They then put on *The Elephant Oh Lord of Ages*. I am deeply moved as I watch: these are my words that others have learned by heart to declare to other people. The play has music composed and performed by Abdullah Shehada on the kanun. After that we have Penny's production of my translation of Mamduh Udwan's play, *The Mask*. Finally, Riad Ismat's production of the play in Arabic. Again, as I watch the English production I have a sense of ownership of the words. I look around the audience and see Mamduh sitting, watching thoughtfully, also with a sense of ownership. And a few rows down is Penny. Does she also feel she owns the show? The productions interpret the play in different ways.

The English is a psychological drama; the Arabic a farce. The Syrian actress, Hala Umran, is wonderful. She can give the utmost meaning to the slightest gesture.

Sunday, 27 April

Duncan Campbell and Julie Christie are due out next week. I phone Duncan and advise him that he says his profession is "Writer". Julie has an Israeli visa in her passport and must get a new one, even though, as Duncan says, "she was on the right side".

Monday, 28 April

At the weekly Embassy meeting the Ambassador observes that talking about the Bulger case was perhaps not the best way of promoting a positive image of Britain.

I have lunch with Ma'mun Abu Zaid, whom I knew in Sudan. He was one of the Revolutionary Command Council that, under Numairy's leadership, took over Sudan in 1969. He became Minister of the Interior. He is here as the guest of the Syrian government – he has known Assad personally since 1969 – and is staying at a hotel near the headquarters of the *mukhabarat*. Does Syrian intelligence keep tabs on what is happening in other Arab countries, using people like Ma'mun? He wants to come and live in Damascus.

I go to another performance of the plays. Our British Council student actors have got used to having an audience and get their sense of timing right. The auditorium is packed, with people sitting in the aisles and standing at the back.

Tuesday, 29 April

Duncan phones. He and Julie have their visas.

Warqa Barmada calls. Bushra, the daughter of the President, wishes to do a British PhD in molecular biology, Her husband, an army general whom she married against her father's wishes, also wishes to do further studies in modern Arab history. She has not been able to explain all this over the phone, and there seems to have been a chain of intermediaries. I suggest they should come and see us and we can give them the best of advice.

It is the last night of the plays. The Syrian actresses are brilliant. When Hala acts flirtatiously with the burglar, she unconsciously opens her legs, suddenly becomes aware of this and closes them and crosses them. She talks about her misfortunes to the burglar, they are both reduced to tears, and the burglar offers a hanky to Hala. People in the audience are in fits of laughter.

Wednesday, 30 April

We think about Duncan and Julie's visit. She hates publicity and fuss. She is here on holiday for a rest, to see the country. I am keen that she meets some interesting Syrians.

Thursday, 1 May

It is General Election Day in Britain. I phone a London colleague early and ask if he has carried out his civic duty. "I was queuing up at 7 am to get these bastards out."

Friday, 2 May

We open a bottle of champagne to celebrate the Labour victory. Actually it is pretty lousy Syrian plonk. Penny phones from the hotel and screeches with delight at the news. The main change will be in patronage. No longer will businessmen have a prescriptive right to rule. Scholarship, public service, care for others are restored as values.

Monday, 5 May

We take Duncan and Julie, who arrived last night, to Krak des Chevaliers. One of her requests was to see the spring flowers so we stop on the road up to Krak, pick some flowers and talk to a shepherd.

Wednesday, 7 May

In Aleppo Julie, Theresa, Duncan and I have breakfast at the Baron Hotel dining room under the gaze of a photo of a much younger Hafez al-Assad, taken by Koko Mazloumian, and looking like Basil Fawlty.

Tony Akhras, the British Honorary Consul takes me to call on the Muhafiz, the Governor, Mustafa Miru. We have acquired premises for an office in the Sabil quarter and he agrees to come and open it next month.

We also interview candidates for the new office, which will be a liaison office part-funded by the Commercial Section of the British Embassy. The main purpose of our work will be educational promotion. I hope it will lead to English classes. We have lunch with the candidates. All are impressive. I like one whose family have a factory producing *zuhurat* tea bags.

We have dinner with Sally Mazloumian. Her comment on the result of the election is odd: "I don't believe in Buggins's turn next." She left the boredom of post-war England in 1947, escaping to Beirut to become a nurse at a psychiatric hospital. Julie talks about her mother, Rosemary, who was trekking in the Himalayas when she was pregnant, ran off with somebody when she was 50 and wrote a book on lighthouses.

Thursday, 8 May

We drive from Aleppo to Palmyra. Julie wants to take a picture of one of the Bedu black goatskin tents, so we stop. We are invited into the tents. Theresa and Julie go in one, Duncan and I go in another. Our hosts are warm, calm and hospitable. A tank of a mother is sitting on the floor, children running around. Two sons are outside dipping the sheep.

At the Zenobia Hotel we sit on the terrace looking at the new moon, described in Arabic poetry as being like a pared fingernail. Talk – as it often does with Julie – turns to films. *Dr Zhivago* is now permitted in Russia. David Lean was apparently careless about detail and much of the Russian is wrong. Julie should be in Cannes where Kenneth Branagh's *Hamlet* is being shown. (Julie plays Gertrude in it.) But she prefers being in Syria.

Friday, 9 May

We drive back to Damascus, meeting heavy traffic at Umayyad Square. "The first traffic jam for 700 miles," observes Duncan. They are both enjoying life and are great guests. Julie radiates and brings out something positive in everyone she meets – small children, guides, passing strangers. Although she is a very private person 30 years of megastardom have had their effect. She is not vain at all, but there is a consciousness of importance.

Saturday, 10 May

We arrange a small dinner party. The weather is right and we arrange tables in the garden. Our first guests are Brigid and Alan Waddams. Duncan and Brigid share their journalistic experience. Then the film director, Haitham Haqqi, and his wife, Layali Badr. Haitham is not confident in English. Layali makes films for children. She tells us that her father, though a progressive, indeed a Communist, tried to marry her off when she was 13. She was able to postpone being married until she was 16, married a man ten years older, had two children and then was divorced after seven years. She has a reasonable relationship with her son, but the father turned the daughter against her. The other guests are Bouthaina Shaaban and her Iraqi husband, Khalil. They met at the University of Warwick where Bouthaina acquired the habit of being a *Guardian* reader, so there is a good bonding with Duncan. Bouthaina has been to see Sa'dallah today.

He is sinking into a coma. I did not let Haitham and Layali know who our star guest is and she says at one stage to Duncan, "Your wife is very beautiful. She should go on the stage." There is then a sudden realisation of who Julie is.

Monday, 12 May

Julie and Duncan come into the office for a staff breakfast. Although we have been protective about Julie's privacy, she blossoms with my Syrian colleagues, charming and interested, deeply responsive to individuals. They love her. Julie suggests a group photograph.

We take them to the airport. It has been a marvellous visit.

In the evening we go to an archaeological dinner. The United States Ambassador, Christopher Ross, comes up and congratulates me on the plays: a courageous enterprise and a thumping success. He also congratulates me on an interview I gave on local television – fluent and correct. I have forgotten all about it and tell him that I am on autopilot when I talk Arabic. I do not know what I am going to say, I do not know what I am saying or what I have said. Somebody at the party rambles on about D H Lawrence blowing up trains in Syria.

Wednesday, 14 May

At a reception I am told that Sa'dallah is in the Shami Hospital and in a coma. It is a matter of days then, I suggest. "Hours," is the reply.

Thursday, 15 May

Sa'dallah died during the night. I go to see his friend, Mona Atassi. She is in tears. Sa'dallah had completed another play only two months ago. There was talk of nominating him for the Nobel Prize for Literature.

At sunset I drive to Sa'dallah's house. The body will be taken to his village near Tartus for burial. Mourners will formally condole at the Arab Cultural Centre. Friends of the family come to the house. The sitting room is full of men and women together, many of them wailing, watching the news showing a recording of a lecture Sa'dallah gave last year. There is not a dry eye. Fa'iza, Sa'dallah's widow, comes over to thank me for the flowers I sent when we put on Sa'dallah's play. I tell her I plan to do an obituary for *The Guardian*. I ask about Ghinwa, who has acted as Sa'dallah's secretary. She has been brewing coffee, appears, all in black, utterly distraught. I give her a big hug. Words are incapable of expressing feeling, and a reassuring hug means much more.

Friday, 16 May

Sa'dallah's body is due to go from the Shami Hospital to Tartus at 10 this morning. We get to the hospital at 9.45. Crowds are gathering – Mona Atassi, Sadiq al-Azm, George Jabbour, Ali Qayyim (representing the Minister of Culture who is in Paris and not due back until Wednesday). Fa'iza and daughter Dima are in black, surrounded by women. The whole gathering is mixed, subdued, sombre. Posters displaying a photograph of Sa'dallah when he was fit and healthy, though brooding, are on railings around the hospital. People are attaching wreaths – dozens of them – to an ambulance that seems to be ready to take the body. I do not think they will last the journey. Eventually at half past ten the coffin is brought out on the shoulders of a dozen men chanting *La Alla ila Allah*. Traffic is dense, and the police cannot control it. But the cortège finally sets off.

I go to the office and write up an obituary and send it to *The Guardian*.

Saturday, 17 May

We go to a reception at the Norwegian Ambassador's Residence for their National Day. One friend, a university professor asks me how

I voted. I give my usual enigmatic reply. I am a public servant and have no politics, but I am delighted with the result. The Conservatives have been in for a long time – exhausted, corrupt. "We are more patient in Syria," he observes.

Tuesday, 20 May

Georges and Laila Ladhkani invite us to dinner. One of the other guests is an *abuna*, an Orthodox priest from the Russian minority in Kazakhstan, francophone, bitterly anti-Communist and pro-Yeltsin. The staff of the Russian Embassy here, he tells us, are all old regime folk who, apart from the Muslim staff, will not pass the time of day with him. Theresa asks a few questions about Yeltsin's health and *abuna* explodes.

"There is nothing wrong with Yeltsin's health. It is all a western misunderstanding."

Theresa says she is neutral and the priest turns on her:

"What I detest," he snaps, "is neutrality. It is a nullity."

Theresa is crushed and deeply upset. She wants to go home but is persuaded to stay. The priest leaves and the rest of us rubbish him. A hedge-priest. An ill-mannered fool. *Adabsiz*, a lovely old Ottoman word, best translated as "uncouth". Word of his rudeness will spread through the Damascus Orthodox community.

Wednesday, 21 May

I receive a fax of my obituary of Sa'dallah that appeared in Monday's *Guardian*. It has been improved with editing, reads well and has the heading "Living with a Deadly Elephant".

Thursday, 22 May

One of the British students studying Arabic in Damascus drops in. Qamran (but Englished as Cameron) Munir is from Sheffield. He is about to go back to help his Pakistani family in their takeaway business. ("People, white people, come from as far as Rotherham.") He plans to set up a business in dress fashion and design for Muslim women. "Correct" Islamic dress but stylish so they do not feel left out.

Monday, 26 May

I have a visit from Kurt Mendenhall, the American academic expert on the Alawites. He has been in Lattakia for a fortnight. Nuhad Abdullah's father-in-law was an early Ba'thist, wrote the National Anthem and was Minister of Education in the 1960s. He thinks Rifaat al-Assad is totally marginalised these days and talks of one Alawite religious leader, Abdul Latif Yunus, now in his eighties, who is important in the community.

I take the Ambassador to a *ta'ziya*, a wake, for Sa'dallah at the Arab Cultural Club. As we arrive a delegation from Suwaida who have come in two busses also turn up, and there are speeches. We greet brothers of Sa'dallah. The women's *ta'ziya* is at the house.

Bouchra calls. Her son, Ala al-Din, has been studying at Volgograd, and wants an attachment at a Syrian university. He needs a chit from the Ministry of Higher Education, so we go together to call on Omar Karmo, the Deputy Minister.

I have lunch with Olga of the Karim Rida Said Foundation. She has worked in Palestine. She tells me she is rude to Israelis on principle, and as proxy for Palestinians who are unable to be rude with impunity.

Tuesday, 27 May

In Aleppo I have dinner with Olga and meet her Syrian colleague, Hanifa al-Jabari, who has been building up a centre for the rehabilitation of children who are disabled either physically or mentally. She has raised money from upper-class Aleppines, and Olga is hoping that there will be support from the Karim Rida Said Foundation.

Wednesday, 28 May

I go the Ambassador's Residence for a meeting to brief the new Minister of State for Foreign Affairs, Derek Fatchett. He is on a whirlwind tour of the region. He was in Israel and called on the President there. Then on to Arafat. This morning he was with King Hussein in Amman and hopes to see President Assad tomorrow. He tells us that the Israeli President asked him to pass on his good wishes to Assad. Should he do so? The Ambassador briefs him on local politics, pointing out that both the President's parents lived into their nineties. I am called on to talk about the role of the English language. Of the schoolchildren who are asked whether they wish to study French or English, 90 per cent opt for English. Private language schools are proliferating. I say we are expensive but serve as a centre of excellence and, indeed, stimulate the learning of the language. I mention the factor of migration. Thousands of Syrians work in the Gulf where the working language is English. And satellite television has created an English-language environment. Derek Fatchett affirms the values of public service, saying that it was not pleasant when it was insinuated that people who worked in the public sector were somehow a drain on the taxpayer or were unable to get a job in the private sector. We are professional patriots, he says.

In the Ambassador's room there are photographs of the 15 previous Ambassadors, all except one: David Roberts, whose brother was a Conservative MP. But the politics is accidental. The Beirut Embassy (where he also served) is arranging for a copy to be sent.

I enjoy being a fly on the wall on these occasions, watching British policy on the Middle East in the making, observing a new Minister feeling his way into the job.

Thursday, 29 May

I accompany the Ambassador and Minister of State to the office. He meets all the staff and we brief him. My Syrian colleagues are excellent, with bright smiling faces. The Minister says our reputation is high and other British Council offices should learn from us! It is a great fillip to the morale of us all.

He leaves us in a motorcade with blaring sirens for a call on the Foreign Minister. We all feel good.

Friday, 30 May
Theresa and I go to call on Fa'iza Shawish, Sa'dallah's widow. I give her a copy of my obituary. The flat is quite modest but I notice for the first time the works of Marx and Engels on the bookshelves. I have never thought out the matter of his having been a Communist.

Saturday, 31 May
We collect Nadia al-Ghazzi and Bouchra and her two daughters – Mayas aged 11 and Lilas aged eight – and go to a restaurant in the Barada valley. Bouchra knows the owners. The restaurant has its own zoo – a peacock, a hyena, a wolf and a couple of monkeys. Bouchra is a lovely person – independent, smoking between courses, but modest and conventional in so many ways.

Sunday, 1 June
I go for a walk in Jahiz Park and bump into the archaeologist, Adnan Bunni. He tells me that my obituary of Sa'dallah has been translated and has appeared in yesterday's *Tishreen*. I get a copy and check the translation. I wrote that he came from an "Alawite" family. This has been changed to a "popular" family.

Tuesday, 3 June
I phone Ann, British Council Director in Beirut.

"I feel part of the new government," she says. "Gordon Brown's father was my school chaplain at Kirkcaldy. Tony Blair went to the school my son is at, and Robin Cook was in the same class as me at university. It's people like me running the country. God help us!"

Thursday, 5 June
In Aleppo Theresa and I brief the two girls who will run the British Council side of the office. Rawa's father emigrated to Venezuela in the difficult times of the union with Egypt, then returned, married and had five children of whom Rawa is the youngest. She has the personality of one who is – not spoilt – but cherished as the youngest, one who charms and plays up to older people.

After lunch we head east to Rusafa, one of my favourite sites. As usual we have the place completely to ourselves. We go on to al-Raqqa, which Theresa is very fond of. We check into the Karnak Hotel and are told we are the guests of the Muhafiz, the Governor, and our room is upgraded to a room that is equally tatty but has more space and a large bowl of fresh flowers.

Friday, 6 June
Muhammad Abdul Hamid Hamad from the office of the Muhafiz calls. He is in his late forties and has degrees in Philosophy and Psychology – he did a dissertation on Pavlov. He has traded in cloth in New York and has also been on a course at the Osmania University, Hyderabad. He is writing a history of the small state that was set up in al-Raqqa after the First World War. We drive around the town, which has plenty of parks, and visit the museum that used to be the government office in the 1920s.

We go to Gut Bridge, single lane, built by the British army – as an inscription explains – in 1942 – at a time when the Euphrates was in flood. It was constructed from oil wells and pipes that had been damaged "by enemy action". It is still functioning.

We cross the bridge and Muhammad takes us on to call on Sheikh

Jumʻa, *mukhtar* of the village of Kasra,. (Kasra means here a bend in the river.) Tea and a late breakfast is brought out and we meet his wife, Umm Jasim, and seven of their eight children – the eighth is away doing his military service. Umm Jasim smokes continuously, lighting a new cigarette from the older, thereby saving matches. The girls, the *mukhtar* assures us, are liberated.

We drive on to Halabiya and dip our hands in the Euphrates and on to Deir ez-Zor for the night. We walk around the town at sunset and over the suspension pedestrian bridge. The paths are crowded with people strolling around, stopping at cafés for soft drinks.

Wednesday, 11 June
I have a regular morning walk by Tishreen Park, ending up at the office. Today there are preparations in the park for a flower exhibition. Florists are asleep at 7.30 am on mattresses on the ground in the open air.

Thursday, 12 June
Linda Schatkowski-Schilcher calls and we have lunch together. I used to know her 26 years ago in Lebanon when she was starting her research on the Damascus families. She is full of ideas and observations. The girls of Damascus wear the headscarf to avoid hassle. Many Jews in the United States are fed up with Netanyahu. It is hard for academics to be openly pro-Palestinian. She makes conscientious efforts to cultivate liberal Jews.

We have a farewell dinner at the house of Vanda and Nabil Batal. Bouthaina Shaaban is one of the guests. She tells me that Assad and Fatchett talked about cultural relations – she was interpreting – and how Assad approved. On one of his many visits, Warren Christopher turned back as he was leaving to say something. "Oh God," the President thought, "an afterthought about human rights". But it was to congratulate Bouthaina who had just had a baby. She tells me she has to get security clearance to come out and meet foreigners, but seeing me is all right.

Friday, 13 June
At 5 we collect Bouchra, her son Husam and his new fiancée, Ghalia Zenberakci, and the little girls and go to Raihan and spend three hours at the house of Nadia al-Ghazzi.

The house was built in the 1940s. Bouchra brought me here in 1971. Nadia's husband died in 1993, and as her brothers were not interested in the house, Nadia has worked on it. She has opened up rooms, installed a kitchen unit and had a marble staircase built.

Nadia herself is a quiet, unassuming woman, a lawyer and short-story writer. She has established an independent life for herself since her husband died. She says the extravagant Sheraton weddings only started in the 1970s, initiated by Syrians who had become rich in the Gulf. The pinnacle of vulgarity was when a bride arrived at the Sheraton on a camel.

Ghalia is 15 and comes from Midan and met Husam when she came to his chocolate shop. We sit chatting around the *bahra*, the fountain in the garden – the quintessence of Damascene sybaritism.

Monday, 16 June
We go to what is likely to be our last Queen's Birthday Party. I talk to Dr Ahmad al-Taqi who is active – with Muhammad Shahrur – in an organisation dealing with violence against women. He has been a champion of Sa'dallah who was – I learn – a member of the Communist Party. "It was the only way in which independent thoughts could be expressed," he says. "It represented an escape."

Tuesday, 17 June
I am in Aleppo to sack one of the newly appointed staff at our centre. I stay at the Qasr Hotel near Bab al-Faraj. I stayed here on my first

visit to Aleppo in 1962. It was then called al-Nasr Hotel. In Arabic a dot is added. In English the name changes from Victory to Palace. Today it seems to cater for Russians.

Wednesday, 18 June

I have a most uncomfortable night. The bed is not comfortable and there is a constant din outside. But my sense of nostalgia is satisfied. I take a bus back to Damascus, sleep and read the rest of Ivor Lucas's memoirs[2] – he was Ambassador here in the 1970s. He has kept a diary all his life. This explains why there is a vividness and contemporaneity in his account.

Cicely, the daughter of the Ambassador and Alison Eastwood, has been killed in a road accident in Zambia where she was doing a gap year. The family have arranged a moving *ta'ziya* for her at the Residence. They display a letter the Ambassador wrote to her godmother at 6 in the morning after a sleepless night, describing her impracticality, her scattiness, her untidiness, her enthusiasm for life, her idealism, her energy, her creativeness, her intelligence.

Thursday, 19 June

I receive my Line Manager's assessment of my performance. There are six categories: Outstanding, Excellent, Good, Satisfactory, Unsatisfactory, Unacceptable. I am given Good, just above average. I am intrigued and a little demotivated. But basically I cannot be bothered about what other people think of me or my work. I am coming to the end of five wonderful years in Syria.

Friday, 20 June

We call on our landlord neighbour, Georges, who has been unwell. He has had a haemorrhage and is beginning to look his age. He says

---

2 Ivor Lucas, *A Road to Damascus*, The Radcliffe Press, London and New York, 1997.

his body seems to be full of water, his legs are swollen and his heart is weak. But he is determined to reach his hundredth birthday next February[3]. There is nothing at all wrong with his mind. Laila serves up cakes on paper napkins with *Ahlan wa sahlan*, welcome, printed on them. She is not very happy about this – "It is very Muslim".

Sunday, 22 June
We go to the wedding of my colleague Souha in the Church of the Holy Cross, which fills up. We leave the church, greeting bride and groom. I kiss both, being European for the former, Arab for the latter.

Later – at ten pm – we go to al-Waha Restaurant for the wedding dinner round the pool. There is a bottle of whisky and a bottle of araq on each table. As bride and groom come in at half past ten a flock of doves is released. Souha is still wearing her trousseau. We leave at about 1.30.

Monday, 23 June
We have tea with Hassana Mardam Bey at the family house. Her mother is a cousin of Nadia al-Ghazzi and they are also related to the Salams of Beirut and the Kabbanis. The house is a remarkable oasis of spacious tranquillity in the heart of the souk area.

Wednesday, 25 June
In Aleppo for the final arrangements of the opening of the British Liaison Office (including the British Council), we go to see the bimaristan, the old hospital. It is locked up and the bell does not work. A passer-by knows where the *haris*, the guardian, lives – round the back. We are accompanied by Omar al-Hallaj, a graduate of the

3 He died in February 2001 just after his 103rd birthday when his family and friends gave him a birthday cake with one large and three small candles.

University of Texas at Austin in Islamic architectural history. I observe that the architecture and physical planning of southern Aleppo is quite different from the north. "That," explains Dr Omar, "is because it is mainly Mamluk whereas the north has been overlaid with Ottoman work."

Back in Damascus we have dinner with Father Luis, the Argentinian priest. It is a simple meal on a monastic refectory table, served by a southern Sudanese. Among the other guests are the Argentinian and Venezuelan Ambassadors. Talk is of the Syrian communities in South America. We are joined by a Colombian girl and her Spanish Arabist boyfriend. She talks of her small home town where a Syrian became mayor and wore a tarbush. There should be nothing strange in an Arab becoming mayor, *alcalde*, a Spanish word from the Arabic. There is talk of the tensions between north South Americans and south South Americans, the former feeling they are closer to the United States, the latter to Europe.

Thursday, 26 June

We have lunch with the Australian Ambassador and his wife, Amanda, and Zaki, a son-in-law of Solhi al-Wadi. Amanda is British and used to be active in Bristol Labour politics. Zaki is a great admirer of Margaret Thatcher.

In the evening we go to the farewell party for us hosted by the Ambassador. About 80 turn up. Solhi arrives with a small orchestra. He introduces the music and talks about the birth of the opera. "I thought I was half-mad," he says, "but Peter was totally mad." We then have some excerpts from *Dido and Aeneas*. Tears well up in my eyes – and I have forgotten to bring tissues. Lubana sings an aria from *Madame Butterfly*, singing with control, confidence and power. Finally the Arab instruments start "For he's a jolly good fellow", arranged by Solhi for small orchestra and small chorus.

Friday, 27 June

I go to the airport to meet my Director General, John Hanson. The place is crowded with Iranians, largely pilgrims, who have been to the Shi'ite shrines in and around Damascus. I find a quiet spot to wait and read Nigel Lawson's memoirs. My neighbour is a girl in a chador and jeans. She is Hedia, speaks excellent English and is married to a dentist in Tehran. She has been in Damascus for a week – not as a pilgrim but trying to get a visa to Canada. She failed and is very disappointed. She tells me she cannot discard the chador in Damascus because of other Iranians. She is fascinating and we exchange addresses. There is an announcement of John Hanson's flight and I have to move on. "Is it permitted to shake hands?" I ask Hedia. She glances round at her fellow-citizens and says, "Not here".

Saturday, 28 June

We go in convoy to Aleppo, a British Council car and a Ministry of Culture car.

At Aleppo we attend the Aleppo Queen's Birthday Party and I am busy bringing people – university, the Governor and others – to meet John Hanson. Sally Mazloumian says the last British Council people when the office closed in 1956 were a Mr Warrington and a Mr Peter Marsh.

Sunday, 29 June

I have carefully planned the opening of the office and all goes without a hitch. The Muhafiz arrives bang on time. He cuts the tape and makes a speech. John Hanson makes a speech in English (a speech I wrote) and I put it into Arabic. He talks about Amin al-Rihani (the subject of a thesis the Muhafiz wrote), about him being both an Arab nationalist and a citizen of the world, a role model for us all. John tells me the Muhafiz was clearly pleased with his speech as I interpreted.

We later take John on a tour through the old city. On the way we come upon a man lying on the ground, having an epileptic fit, being comforted by traders. The dim lights, the dress, the human situation of frailty – it is a scene that could have happened any time in the last five hundred years. It is as if we have arranged some street theatre.

Monday, 30 June

I have arranged to hand John Hanson on to my counterpart in Turkey at the Temple of Daphne south of Antakya, Antioch. We leave Aleppo at 10. The Minister of Culture has arranged for VIP treatment as we leave Syria at Bab al-Hawa, but we have to queue up like anyone else on the Turkish side.

We take him up to the citadel above Antioch, to the stunning view of the city immediately below and the coastal plain towards Samanda . We go on to a restaurant at Harbiye, by the Temple of Daphne (described by Gibbon who never came here) and meet Clive Gobby, British Council Director, Turkey. John relates to him in a way that is quite different from the way he relates to me. They talk of people as if they were pieces being moved around on a chess board. We part. Clive and John go on to Adana. We return to Damascus.

Tuesday, 1 July

We go to the citadel for the premiere of one of Sa'dallah's last plays, *al-Munamnamat al-Tarikhiya*. It starts after the final call to prayer and is about Timur besieging Damascus in 1402 and the historian, Ibn Khaldun, meeting him. There are dialogues about how to deal with the invader. I have read the play in Arabic and in French – which has been a help. Jamal Sulaiman plays the part of Ibn Khaldun and is superb, physically dominating the stage. Scenes take place on the walls of the citadel, enacting scenes that took place on the same walls, nearly six hundred years earlier. The play ends at about 1.30 am.

Wednesday, 2 July

I go to Ulfat's flat to say good bye. She receives me in the smaller lounge – the air conditioning is not working in the larger. There are portraits on the wall: her father-in-law, a Pasha-like figure with a hat as worn by Greek priests; a charcoal drawing of her mother-in-law at the age Ulfat is now; a lovely portrait of the young Ulfat aged 25, 60 years ago. Ulfat is animated and talks of her writing. "I do not try to write in a poetic style; I try to create situations that are poetic." I discuss her style, noting how it has changed since the 1940s. She gives me a present, a tray, coffee pot and cups. And as I leave she gives me a big kiss. Her Dongolawi servant, Abdul Rahman, drives me back.

I then take Theresa to the airport for her final departure.

Thursday, 3 July

I say my farewells to the Embassy staff and then my own British Council colleagues. Then lunch with Azza and Riad Ismat and Warqa Barmada.

I see Azza and Ismat again that evening at Mamduh Udwan's flat. Other guests include Intisar, a journalist, the wife of the film director, Muhammad Malas and Sadiq al-Azm. We discuss Sa'dallah's play. Mamduh thinks he had the siege of Beirut in mind. Sadiq liked the dialogue, the intellectual positions stated.

Friday, 4 July

Murshid, the driver of General Ahmad Yusuf, collects me in an army Mercedes and takes me to Zabadani. We pick up the General on the way and go up to the magnificent Andalusian villa of Hayan Atassi. I am shown round it all. The master bedroom has two massive triple beds and it takes me a minute to work out what refined orgies take place here. We then walk up the hill and identify plants – the slave's stick, the gazelle's blood, five fingers.

Murshid drives me back. We stop at Maylasun where Syrian forces finally fell to the French in 1920, leading to the Mandate. The Syrian commander, Yusuf al-Azma, has his grave, his *maqam*, where he fell, in a grove of pine trees.

In the evening I drive to the flat of Ahmed and Bouchra where I want to spend my last Damascus evening. I am beginning to be overwhelmed with sadness. All the family are present, including Ala, bespectacled, already addressed as *duktur*; Husam and Ghalia; Ghalia's mum; and others. I spend three hours with them, quietly, feeling at home, cherishing these dear friends.

Saturday, 5 July

I am up early. My son, Paul, phones from England to wish me luck, and Bouchra phones to say Goodbye.

The British Council driver, Zahir, is taking me to Izmir. We are on the road soon after 8. I feel sad, but not too sentimental. This is the end of a way of life I have lived and loved for over a quarter of a century.

We drive north by Homs and Tartus and up to the village of Husain al-Bahr, and to the cemetery. Sa'dallah's tomb is in the middle of a cleared area, enclosed by a two-foot-high breeze block wall. I leave my visiting card and some withering flowers. I take some photographs, one to include the background of an Alawite *maqam* and the cement factory.

We move on – to Lattakia, and have lunch with Nuhad Abdullah, Munzer Muhammad and their wives, and Majida Bouzo and Ahmad al-Sufi. Then north through the lush woodlands to the frontier, where I have, unexpectedly, to pay US$150 to take the car out of the country.

Julie Christie.

INDEX